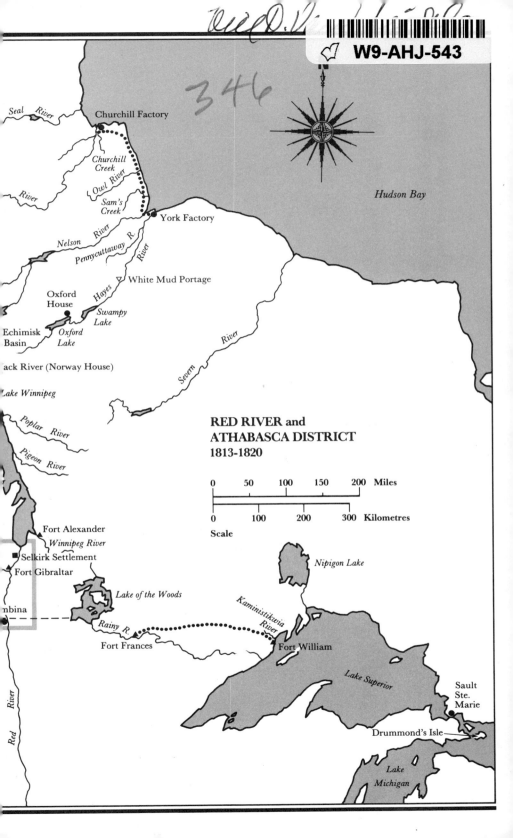

346

Seal River

Churchill Factory

Churchill Creek

Owl River

Sam's Creek

River

York Factory

Nelson River

Pennycuttaway R.

Hudson Bay

White Mud Portage

Hayes River

Oxford House

Swampy Lake

Echimisk Basin

Oxford Lake

River

ack River (Norway House)

Severn River

Lake Winnipeg

Poplar River

Pigeon River

**RED RIVER and
ATHABASCA DISTRICT
1813-1820**

| 0 | 50 | 100 | 150 | 200 | Miles |

| 0 | 100 | 200 | 300 | Kilometres |

Scale

Fort Alexander

Winnipeg River

Selkirk Settlement

Fort Gibraltar

Nipigon Lake

Lake of the Woods

Kaministikwia River

nbina

Rainy R.

Fort Frances

Fort William

Red River

Lake Superior

Sault Ste. Marie

Drummond's Isle

Lake Michigan

EXILE IN THE WILDERNESS

EXILE IN THE WILDERNESS

THE BIOGRAPHY OF
CHIEF FACTOR
ARCHIBALD McDONALD

1790–1853

Jean Murray Cole

University of Washington Press
Seattle and London

Library of Congress Catalog Card Number 79-5361

ISBN 0-295-95704-2

List of Illustrations

(between pages 108 and 109)
1. Archibald McDonald descending the Fraser River in 1828
2. Thomas Douglas, fifth Earl of Selkirk
3. Sir George Simpson
4. Edward Ermatinger
5. "King Comcomly's Burial Canoe" by Paul Kane
6. "Indians Playing at Alcoloh" by Paul Kane
7. Chief Factor Archibald McDonald
8. Sketch map of the Thompson's River District drawn by Archibald McDonald
9. Jasper House, a key post for the Hudson's Bay Company
10. Return of a Pacific Coast war party
11. The Tshimakain Mission near Fort Colvile
12. Fort Edmonton
13. Jane Klyne McDonald
14. John McLoughlin
15. Dr. William Fraser Tolmie

From the lone shieling of the misty island
Mountains divide us, and the waste of seas —
Yet still the blood is strong, the heart is Highland,
And we in dreams behold the Hebrides.
Fair these broad meads, these hoary woods are grand,
But we are exiles from our fathers' land.

Blackwood's Magazine,
September 1829.

ARCHIBALD MCDONALD
dit Gillespie
Moach Aonish
Ic Iain
Ic Alan Dhu
Glenocoan

Fort Langley, N.W. Coast
of America — 15th Decr.1830 —

Contents

Foreword   xiii
Foreword xiii
Introduction xvii
Prologue: 1813 1

Part One
Settlement at Red River

1   A Gentleman of Respectable Character (*1811–1814*) 5
2   The Long Walk: They Found It Somewhat Laborious (*1814*) 22
3   He Must Be Driven to Abandon the Project (*1814–1815*) 34
4   The Outrages Have All Been on One Side (*1815–1816*) 58
5   They Cannot Take From Us Our Good Conscience (*1817–1819*) 75

Part Two
The Waiting Wilderness

6   Two Novices in the Fur Trade (*1820–1821*) 91
7   A Sense of Separation (*1821–1825*) 100

Part Three
West of the Rockies

8   Along the Skirts of the Mountains (*1826–1828*) 113
9   Certain Death in Nine Attempts out of Ten (*1828*) 130
10   New Harvests in a Mild, Lush Land (*1828–1833*) 144
11   I Do Not Contemplate Remaining Much Longer in This Wilderness (*1833–1835*) 165
12   A Considerable Sort of Canadian Farmer (*1835–1841*) 179
13   Various Characters from All Nations Strolling to the Far West (*1841–1844*) 194
14   His Life Was One of Much Usefulness (*1844–1853*) 217
Postscript 228
Appendix 233
Acknowledgments 235
Manuscript Sources 236
Bibliography 238
Notes 245
Index 257

Foreword

This book is a notable addition to the literature of the fur trade. That literature is, of course, surprisingly extensive, but it is short on biography and autobiography. *Exile in the Wilderness* thus stands with Margaret Arnett MacLeod's *Letters of Letitia Hargrave* and W. Kaye Lamb's *Letters of John McLoughlin.*

Archibald McDonald came into the fur trade through service to Lord Selkirk and his Red River colony, and his career throws new light on the struggle to establish and maintain the colony. For the first time, for example, the full story is told of the winter in Churchill and the long walk to York Factory of the 1813 party who were put down, ill and unhappy, at Churchill instead of York. McDonald went through the troubles of 1815 and 1816 in the settlement, and served the colony until 1820. Then he joined the Hudson's Bay Company, just before the merger of the two great companies, the North West and the Hudson's Bay.

Launched in the fur trade, he left for the Athabasca District with George Simpson, soon to be the new governor of the Hudson's Bay Company, as new to the fur trade as McDonald, and a year later made the move west of the mountains to the Columbia. This began the next important part of his career, that on the Pacific slope.

The theme of Jean Cole's book is exile, and McDonald especially exemplifies the fate of most officers of the Hudson's Bay Company at that time. To be commissioned officers they needed some education. They were, moreover, the "gentlemen" of the Company and had a certain state to maintain. But they were put in charge of isolated posts, often with no company other than that of servants. What wonder that, besides their duty of keeping journals, many of them wrote numerous and usually lengthy letters.

And what wonder that the more gifted of them, like McDonald, took up scientific pursuits, as McDonald did, in forming a friendship with the botanist David Douglas, and corresponding with Sir William Hooker of the Royal Horticultural Society and Kew Gardens. Like Donald A. Smith in Labrador, they kept their minds alive amid the slow routine of a trading post by writing and by reading. Above all, they welcomed visitors, Company officials and travellers.

McDonald thoroughly identified himself with the exciting new country of the Pacific slope. Serving at Fort George, Kamloops, Fort Langley, Nisqually, and Colvile, he saw most travellers and came to know the personalities and life of the Oregon country. His letters are an addition to the historiography of the region.

He also softened the rigors of life in the wilderness by marrying Jane Klyne west of the mountains and raising a large family. Jane had country blood, and the marriage was a further, perhaps the final, tie with the new land. Certainly it was one in which he rejoiced. The family ties were close and enduring, and the marriage an exemplar of fur trade marriages.

The connection with Red River was maintained, largely perhaps because of the family, for there were the nearest schools, and there in time the older boys were to go to school. And his friendship with Edward Ermatinger was kept up by letter when Ermatinger went to Canada. It was a tie which was to take McDonald and his family to Lower Canada when he left the fur trade in 1845. Thus Canada too came into the circle of correspondence, and his letters to Ermatinger have some interesting comment on Canadian affairs.

The exile was thus in many ways a fruitful one. Neither McDonald nor his family became backward people. After the manner of the educated Scot, McDonald kept his family life a model of decorum and saw to it that his children were educated, above all in personal dignity and independence. So the wilderness was, when all was said and done, a home as well as an exile. This is a model biography of a model commissioned officer in the fur trade, Chief Factor Archibald McDonald of the Honourable Hudson's Bay Company. The great Company and its officers had learned to live with the wilderness without yielding to it.

W. L. MORTON
Winnipeg, Manitoba

Introduction

This is the story of one man's experience with the wilderness. Not today's wilderness of aluminum canoes, motorized rubber rafts, freeze-dried steaks and prepackaged survival kits, but the early nineteenth-century wilderness — untouched and untamed.

Archibald McDonald was not an explorer, although he explored lands and waterways unknown to any but the Indians among his contemporaries. His name is unfamiliar to most North Americans today, but he was an extraordinary man living out his quite extraordinary life in the only way he knew how — meeting the challenges, accepting the disappointments, rejoicing in the triumphs, mourning the tragedies. He was a gregarious, fun-loving bon vivant destined to spend most of his days in isolation. He was a devoted family man whose children were deprived in their formative years of the benefits of the civilization he admired.

As a young man — like all young men — he was ambitious. He had his hopes and dreams. But the reality was not a fulfilment. "How little does man dream of the career he is deemed to run in this earth," he once wrote to a friend. "Lucky he does not!" It had not been in McDonald's plans to spend a lifetime in the wilderness: fate and the death of his patron, Lord Selkirk, intervened. But accepting that fate, he turned misfortune to his advantage. Though in total isolation west of the mountains, it was awesomely beautiful isolation. If there was no school for his children, he would conduct one; no church of his own denomination, he would read the services; no convivial society, he would make his home a welcoming haven for all who passed his way. No doubt others would have seen the potential (and later did) in all those untapped natural resources on the northern Pacific slope: the silver salmon, the rich minerals, the tall trees, the fertile prairies. He was the first to urge its development, and he persevered against all odds — lack of manpower, proper equipment, experience — to make a beginning.

"In no other circumstance does so much depend on the personal qualities of the man," Professor George Bryce wrote in one of his early examinations of the fur trader's life. In McDonald's case it was not just going on in strength. His life was a positive joyous act. "The buoyant spirit is still in the old place," he wrote in a letter late in his life, at a time when, crippled and ill, he was facing a *walk* through the Rocky Mountains and across the continent to retirement in the East.

Remarkable, there can be no doubt. If some readers find this account understated, it is because I have attempted as much as possible to let McDonald tell the tale. Hundreds of his letters survive and many daily journals record his views and reactions to people and events throughout his life. His own words say it best, and in putting together his story I have quoted extensively, avoiding too much paraphrasing in order to convey the real flavor of the man — his warmth, his insight, his humor, his bite. It is for us to read between the lines and recognize a most singular man.

J.M.C.

EXILE IN THE WILDERNESS

Prologue 1813

He was leaving Glencoe — its little river shining in the May sun, its brooding mountains still brown with the heather that would just be turning purple in the late days of summer when his ship put into the remote harbor on Hudson Bay.

Young Archibald McDonald strode along the familiar road from Inverrigan, past Carnoch House, site of the murder of the Glencoe chief in 1692, by the old slate quarry near the village school, and on to the ferry at Ballachulish.

From the shores of Loch Leven he turned back momentarily, his eyes taking in the sweep of the glen, his mind full of memories. And then he went on, following the spectacular route up the Great Glen by way of Fort William and Fort Augustus to Inverness. He was bound for Stromness to meet his patron, Lord Selkirk, who was waiting to see McDonald off with the most promising group of settlers yet to assemble for his colony at Red River.

PART I

Settlement at Red River

CHAPTER ONE

A Gentleman of Respectable Character

1811 – 1814

"Can you recommend a gentleman of respectable character, and at the same time of talent, activity, and established popularity . . . to go out along with the men?" Thomas Douglas, fifth Earl of Selkirk, signed his letter to his old friend Alexander McDonald of Dalilia and affixed his seal.

The earl was obsessed with his ideas of colonizing in America. His earlier attempts in Canada (on Prince Edward Island, and at Baldoon, near Lake St. Clair) had not succeeded as he had hoped. His latest venture at Red River, in the wilderness west of the Great Lakes, he was confident would fare better.

Hundreds of sturdy Scots, recently driven from their crofts in the Highlands, victims of the infamous clearances and unafraid of hardship and self-denial, were anxious to take up a new life with a promise of a share in Lord Selkirk's 116,000 square-mile tract of land in Rupert's Land.* All he needed was suitable

* Under an agreement with the Hudson's Bay Company, who held rights to all lands draining into Hudson Bay, Selkirk received this enormous grant of land, called Assiniboia, in return for developing an agricultural colony at Red River to provision the fur trade posts, and supplying two hundred servants for the Company each year.

leaders — strong young men who held the respect of the settlers, who spoke their Gaelic language and understood their ways, and at the same time could guide them and care for their needs during the difficult journey and the early days of settling on the new lands. Had Dalilia any suggestions?

In a short time came the reply from Callander, recommending young Archibald McDonald of Glencoe. At twenty-one, Archy was perhaps still a little green for the responsibility that lay in store for him, but Dalilia had long known his family and knew him to be the kind of reliable, resourceful young man that Lord Selkirk was looking for. He knew too that McDonald possessed the confidence and independence that are often nurtured in the last of a large family and that all these things combined should stand him in good stead in the New World.

Archibald McDonald was born February 3, 1790, at Leacantuim, the old house where his aging parents still lived, near the south shore of Loch Leven in Argyllshire. He was the thirteenth and youngest child of Angus and Mary Rankin McDonald of Glencoe, and the blood of generations of Highland warriors flowed in his veins.

Angus, although one of the Episcopalian McDonalds, had joined his Roman Catholic kinsmen in support of the Jacobite cause and fought at Culloden in 1745, when but a lad of fifteen. Angus's father, John, as a child had escaped to the hills with his mother on that fearful morning in February 1692 when Robert Campbell of Glenlyon set his men to massacre the McDonalds of Glencoe, and one of the Rankins was the first to die that day. Archibald McDonald's great-grandfather, Alan Dhu, had served with Montrose in his battles against the Covenanters at Inverlochy, Aldearn and Alford in 1645.

When Archy was a boy in the glen his father was tacksman of Inverrigan,* the very tract of land that had been the site of Glenlyon's camp in 1692. The rocky hills which harbored the fleeing women and children a century before were peaceable and friendly. There were days then, as now, when the mist hung low over the towering hills and the valley brooded over its past, but the McDonald boys — brothers and cousins — fished in its quiet

---

* In the Highlands, a tacksman was one who held a large "tack," or lease of land, which he sublet in small farms to his neighbors.

streams and roamed the slopes. The only shooting done was of grouse and pheasant and deer.

Within weeks of Dalilia's recommendation Archibald Mc-Donald was appointed "clerk and agent" by Selkirk, and the twenty-one-year-old Highlander was travelling through the towns and villages of Argyll and Inverness signing up suitable young men for the service of the Hudson's Bay Company, talking to their families about following their sons to the recently founded colony at Red River. He had read the attacks on his patron's project in the *Inverness Journal* the preceding summer, but decided to ignore the admonitions of the anonymous writer who signed himself "Highlander,"* about the "dangers and distresses" to the prospective settlers. That winter of 1811–12 in the Highlands had brought more immediate dangers and distresses to the small crofters. The Highland clearances were at their height — particularly in Sutherland where the remorseless duchess and her factor went on with their program of evictions and croft-burnings, and those who had not already lost their homes to the invading sheep farmers had faint hope of retaining them for long. Small wonder Selkirk's agents had no trouble gathering together a promising group of prospective settlers for the new colony in America.

In April, with his eighty-two-year-old father, McDonald journeyed down to Stirling, stopping at Callander en route to visit McDonald of Dalilia and receive further instructions from Selkirk. Plans had been made for some of the Scottish emigrants to gather at Tobermory and to sail from there to Sligo, where Lord Selkirk and a group of Irish who were to join the colony would await them. Archibald McDonald was to continue his recruiting in the North, and prepare to depart with his charges at the end of May. Things were moving very quickly. He did some necessary shopping in Stirling, anticipating an imminent departure and a long absence from civilization, and then made his way back to Glencoe to say good-bye to his family.

By mid-June Selkirk was in Ireland waiting to see his first party of settlers on their way. The previous year he had named Miles Macdonell governor and sent him with a group of men to select a site and establish the beginnings of the settlement. He

* Simon McGillivray, partner in the North West Company.

could have wished for a more auspicious group than the ill-assorted collection of Scots and Irish assembling before his eyes at the port but he had great hopes for the Highland families who wanted to go the following year, and meanwhile this party would plant some crops and create a nucleus around which to build. The sloop *Staffa* had been delayed and he waited impatiently for the last group to arrive from Tobermory. While the Irish settlers quarrelled amiably amongst themselves and jostled for bargaining positions, the distracted earl decided to appoint one of their kinsmen, Owen Keveny, to take charge of the party.

By the time Archibald McDonald and his group arrived on the *Staffa*, about eighty settlers were assembled, including a number of families with small children, some of them still wondering whether they had made the right decision in embarking for the new colony. With the arrival of McDonald, Selkirk was cheered. It was their first meeting, and all the good things he had heard about the young Scot were confirmed. On June 24 with its cargo of emigrants the *Robert Taylor* sailed, in convoy with the Hudson's Bay Company ships *Eddystone* and *King George*. At the last minute Selkirk decided to hold back Archibald McDonald "that I may become better acquainted with him, and that I may give him an opportunity of acquiring some branches of knowledge that will be useful."

After a last dinner aboard the ship with the departing colonists, Selkirk and his protégé took their leave and made their way down to London. "I am greatly pleased with young Archibald," wrote Selkirk to Dalilia a few weeks later. "He seems indeed a very fine young man and of the best dispositions. His heart is certainly uncorrupted, and I only wish (before putting him into the situation which I have in view for him) to ascertain that his principles are sufficiently rooted, to bear up against every temptation, a point of which is not so easily judged of, as it depends more on early habit & education than natural disposition."

That summer of 1812 in London opened a whole new world to the young Highlander. The stern old schoolmaster at Glencoe had already provided him with a good background in traditional subjects, including mathematics and Latin, English and Gaelic literature, and other branches of "common instruction." He was ready to be introduced to a broader range of scientific lore, and it was Selkirk's intention to set his young friend on a course of medical studies and later to apprentice him to a doctor, thus increasing his usefulness at the colony. His role was to be an unusual one. He was to serve as the earl's personal representative at Red River, unattached to the Hudson's Bay Company and with no thought that he should eventually settle there himself. Selkirk was anxious that he should be equipped to function in a wide variety of capacities, from overseer to intermediary, from accountant to physician, wherever his talents were needed.

"Tho' he has not time to attain a complete knowledge of the subject he may become acquainted with the fundamental principles, & with those applications of them to practice which most frequently occur," wrote Selkirk to Dalilia. "At all events, these studies are calculated to open his mind to a taste for the pursuit of liberal knowledge."

Lord Selkirk had found a fit subject for such a program. Archy McDonald seized the opportunity with characteristic enthusiasm. His friendly, gregarious nature, his spontaneous expressions of delight at the wonders of his new surroundings, the sense of humor which was so often to be the saving grace in the difficult years to come, all endeared him to his new companions. Selkirk found his earlier good impressions confirmed. "I have introduced him to some individuals of equal worth & attainments, who promise to give him proper directions for the prosecution of his studies, & who already seem to take an interest in his welfare. . . ." He wrote to Miles Macdonell expressing his confidence in his protégé. "His abilities are very good, his manners popular, & I have reason to entertain the highest confidence in his candour & fidelity. I believe you may safely trust to him anything that zeal & assiduity can accomplish."

"I trust that with the benefit of full occupation, he will be kept aloof from the temptations of a large town, which are chiefly dangerous to those who are idle," he told Dalilia, who had expressed concern over "a danger, which is incident at his time of life to most men who are in any degree superior in mind to the generality of their companions — that of forming too high an idea of his own importance." To counteract such a possibility, Selkirk assured his old friend, "I have given him a few lessons in mathematics, which I believe have also been lessons in humility."

But all was not work and study. Archy was welcomed into

the Selkirk household with great warmth and affection, not only by the earl and his wife Jean Wedderburn — herself only a few years older than McDonald — but also by the Selkirk children, three-year-old Lord Daer and the baby Isabella. To the young man recently removed from the centre of a large laughter-loving family, the countess and her children were a source of great delight, and those summer weeks in London began a long friendship.

By September the Selkirks had returned to their family home on St. Mary's Isle, Kirkcudbright, and McDonald remained in London to continue his studies. In November Selkirk was in Edinburgh to attend the ceremonies surrounding his re-election as one of Scotland's representative peers, but he returned to London before Christmas to a mountain of mail from Hudson Bay and disheartening news of the party of settlers he had seen off in such high spirits from Sligo.

Keveny's harsh treatment of his charges had brought a near-mutiny on board ship, and rivalry amongst the Scots and Irish in the party had led to further difficulties. Criticism of Miles Macdonell, governor of the colony, particularly from William Auld, superintendent at York Factory, and other Hudson's Bay officers on the scene, aroused serious concern, but Selkirk stood firm in his conviction that the settlement would succeed.

He believed that much of its success depended on the quality of the people he sent to the colony, and he proceeded energetically to step up recruiting in the Highlands to provide the right kind of solid, hard-working families to carry out his aims. Approaches from representatives of the large numbers of families recently turned from their crofts in Sutherlandshire soon brought more volunteers than he could cope with — more than 1,300 men, women and children indicated their willingness to emigrate, their hope to escape from the tyranny and the despair of their situation. It was decided that Archibald McDonald, when he completed his series of lectures in the spring, would go north to help interview the prospective settlers.

Selkirk was delighted with his educational experiment. "Archibald McDonald is going on with assiduity," he reported to Dalilia that winter. "He has gained a great deal of information for the time, & his desire of improving himself seems to suffer no abatement." The classes ended in mid-March and McDonald promptly sailed from London to continue his recruiting efforts in the north of Scotland, principally in Kildonan where the merciless burning of the Sutherland crofts had blackened the land for miles and the spring green had not yet appeared to mask the horror.

Pitiful but proud, the Highland folk gathered around Selkirk's emissary, comforted by the soft cadence of his Gaelic speech, hopeful that they could transplant their Scottish ways to the new colony. Sutherlands, Bannermans, Mathesons, McBeaths and Gunns, parents with babes in arms, children, aunts, uncles, teenagers — all sought to set off for a new life in the New World. From amongst the throng ninety of the fittest were selected. Young men and women, most of them in their teens and twenties, were to prepare the way for their parents and younger brothers and sisters to come out in the following year. Included in the group were only eight couples with their families, among them one not from Kildonan, Donald Stewart of Appin, a relative of Archibald McDonald.

At that, there were more families than Selkirk had intended to send out in the early stages. He knew well the hardships they would encounter and would have preferred to send strong single men to break the ground and provide the shelter of a more orderly community before allowing women and children to join them. Compassion for the homeless Sutherlanders overruled his good judgment, however, and he optimistically accepted these few, knowing they had nowhere else to go and that they would send back reports to their families in Scotland that might encourage the kind of development he envisioned for his settlement in the future. He had high hopes for this "fine race of men."

In his belief that "those who pay for what they receive, feel the value of their independence," Selkirk stipulated that the emigrants pay the passage at the current rate of ten guineas per person, young or old, but willingly accepted their promissory notes, and in a number of instances sons who were suitable for the Hudson's Bay Company service were allowed to pledge their future wages as security for their parents' debts. He had already in the preceding year provided a township of ten thousand acres as "encouragement" to induce one Alexander McLean to go to the settlement "for the sake of having one settler of the rank of a gentleman," and his plans included providing doctors and clergymen for the colony as well. He was concerned about preserving law and order and had some discussions with the colonial secretary, Lord Bathurst, and others about sending out a military force. These came to nothing and in the end twenty-five muskets and bayonets and some small artillery were provided by the government in a token gesture.

Early in June, Selkirk went north to Orkney where the Hudson's Bay ships were waiting at Stromness to board their passengers. By the tenth of the month Archy McDonald had gathered all the prospective settlers at the port, and Selkirk watched anxiously for favorable weather conditions to allow their departure. He introduced McDonald to Peter Laserre, a young doctor from Guernsey whom he had appointed to be surgeon for the settlement and to take charge of the party with Archibald as his "coadjutor" and was pleased to observe that "they seem to like each other very well." McDonald on his part wrote in high spirits to Dalilia that Lord Selkirk had introduced him to the doctor as his only pupil. "Lucky for me he being the surgeon and super cargo, that I never could expect a better opportunity of attending to every case that comes in his way."

Prospects appeared bright as Selkirk looked over the men, women and children bound for his settlement. There were the eight families — "rather more *entire families* of the Kildonan people than I could have wished" — and representatives of twenty more, he reported to Dalilia. Of the total of ninety-four persons, thirty-one were children and teenagers and thirty-seven were in their early twenties. There were twenty-one Sutherlands, fourteen Gunns and thirteen Bannermans, and the five McBeaths, six McKays and six McDonalds represented larger numbers of these families who were to go out to Red River the following season. A number of tradesmen — weavers, tailors, shoemakers, a carpenter, a millwright, and of course a piper — were included in their numbers to provide necessary services at the colony.

After a week of waiting, an attempt was made to sail but the weather was so calm that the *Prince of Wales* was driven back by the current of the tide, and all the passengers had to disembark and await the stiff breeze that was needed to carry them westward past the Outer Hebrides and into the North Atlantic. Finally on June 28 the ships got off, but the anxiety and uneasiness that Selkirk felt at the long delay were to prove well founded.

Within days of the *Prince of Wales*'s departure from Orkney it was discovered that one of the passengers had contracted typhus fever, an event that might well have been avoided had there not been such a long stay in the port. Laserre and McDonald set in motion all possible precautionary measures. Beds and bedding were brought up to air and the decks were scrubbed and disinfected. Lime juice was administered in large doses to all the passengers. In spite of their efforts and those of the ship's surgeon, it was impossible to check the spread of the disease. One by one, passengers and crew fell victim until more than sixty of the settlers and a proportionate number of the crew were stricken. By mid-July the *Prince of Wales*'s log was one long tally of the sick, and it continued on into August as the convoy approached Hudson Strait: "Sunday 15th August, 1813. This day have 19 passengers & 8 seamen ill . . . the groans and cries of the sick on one side and the delirious on the other, is dreadful beyond description."

By this time Dr. Laserre himself was totally disabled by the disease, and at half past noon on Monday, August 16, the young surgeon to whom Selkirk had entrusted the protection of his ninety-four settlers died. A saddened McDonald, who had looked forward to a congenial apprenticeship with his new friend, was stunned to find himself in charge.

Lord Selkirk would have reason to be grateful for the forethought that led him to take such pains over preparing his protégé for his responsibilities. To Archy McDonald, by now only twenty-three years old, was left the sole care of ninety-four simple, inexperienced Highland folk, many of them ill and bereaved, and all about to be landed on the shores of a harsh northern land that neither he nor they had ever laid eyes on before. That he was possessed of the strength of character and the resourcefulness and determination that enabled him to measure up in this time of crisis, to accept the challenge thrown at him and grasp his charge with decision and dependability, was sheer good fortune.

Captain John Turner, master of the *Prince of Wales*, was distraught. He was ailing himself with a recurring case of rheumatic gout and an epidemic of the dreaded ship's fever was more than he could contend with. When Dr. Laserre died, Turner contacted Captain Sterling on the convoy's senior ship and stated his intention to put in at Churchill, the nearest port, rather than continue down to York Factory. There Governor Miles Macdonell was even then waiting to welcome them and provision had been made to receive the new settlers and transport them to the settlement before winter set in. There was nothing McDonald could do but accept his decision.

On August 18 they landed at Churchill. Fortunately fair weather prevailed and McDonald was able to go ashore and have tents erected to house his sick passengers, and to have fresh provisions brought on board for those who were recovering. Four days later, a Sunday, Donald Stewart, McDonald's one kinsman in the party, died without ever having set foot on shore. The same day the ship's quartermaster was another victim, further affirming Captain Turner's determination to rid his ship of its frail human cargo. The gloom was all-pervading.

Within six days of their arrival at Churchill, all the sick were housed in hospital tents on shore, but only nine of the ship's company of twenty-nine were well enough to be on duty and, of these, two were helping to attend the patients. Captain Turner was unsure that he would even be able to get his ship back to England, and he sent to York Factory for the schooner to come to assist in discharging the *Prince of Wales*'s cargo and to bring another surgeon to assist in the emergency. Four men had died since their landing, including three seamen. Within days two more of the settlers were to succumb.

When the distressing news reached William Auld, the Hudson's Bay Company's chief at York Factory, he set out immediately for Churchill, already convinced that his direst predictions about the folly of bringing colonists to the hostile northland were coming true. After twenty-three years in the service of the Hudson's Bay Company, Auld was all fur trader, and his irascibility, which had grown with the years, showed itself in open opposition to the proposed settlement at Red River. He had been Superintendent of the Northern Factories since 1810. Although he had already tendered his resignation, it was still his duty to cooperate with Selkirk's agents, however much it went against the grain.

In later years Colin Robertson was to reflect that William Auld was "one of the greatest enemies [Selkirk] . . . ever had." Certainly the superintendent had made no secret of his animosity toward Miles Macdonell, governor of the colony, and this attitude he automatically extended to all of the colony's friends.

Macdonell himself wrote to Selkirk in July 1814 that Auld "never loses an opportunity of raising objections to the utility of a settlement on R.R., sneering & ridiculing many of your Lordship's projects & plans . . . in a most unreserved manner. . . ."

One glimpse of Archibald McDonald was enough for Auld to form an opinion of him. Within days he sat down to report to Andrew Wedderburn (Colvile),* brother of Lady Selkirk, on the emigrants: "wretches whose filthy & indolent habits fostered & cherished by the shameful & familiar mismanagement of the young man Ad. McDonald . . . in all likelihood would occasion fresh misfortunes." Instead of the help and support both needed and expected, Auld provided only opposition and criticism. Trouble from the North West Company was to be expected. From the officers of the Hudson's Bay Company it was a cruel blow.

Fortunately, also from York Factory came Abel Edwards, surgeon for the settlement during the preceding season, who had intended to return to England by the fall boats. While Auld was writing to Wedderburn: "What will become of these miserable people & ourselves the God in Heaven alone can know. I look forward with horror to the long dreadful winter," Edwards took immediate action to assist McDonald with his charges. Archy welcomed the older man's advice and help and was happy to turn over his most seriously ill patients to Edwards's care. He turned his attention to the convalescents and those who were well enough to lend a hand with unloading their possessions from the ship and setting up some kind of temporary camp.

It was evident to all concerned that the settlers would not be able to get to Red River before next summer, and a site for their winter camp was selected at Churchill Creek, some fifteen miles upriver from the fort. Abel Edwards installed the acutely ill, about fifteen in all, in a small house three miles above Churchill Factory which he fitted up as a hospital, with a small tent for himself nearby. William Linklater, a Hudson's Bay Company officer who had been a passenger on the *Prince of Wales*, set off for Churchill Creek with a party of men to supervise the building of quarters to house the eighty people who remained of the original party. A few days later, on September 23, McDonald moved off

* Lady Selkirk's brother, Andrew Wedderburn, changed his name to Colvile in 1814.

from the fort with his feeble procession of convalescents to stagger along the rock-strewn banks of the Churchill River to the campsite fifteen miles distant.

Linklater and his men had already made a good start on the four buildings that were intended to house the people, and those of McDonald's party who were well enough to assist with the construction and carpentry were put to work immediately. The women and children went into the nearby bog to gather cranberries in great quantities, to be set by for winter as a remedy against scurvy. Edwards had provided McDonald with a long sheet of written directions designed to preserve the health of the people — diet, cleanliness, exercise (Sundays *not* excepted) came in for their fair share of attention — and suggestions were made for the apportioning of supplies, including the staple oatmeal, and the small amounts of free liquor which Edwards said should be diluted with lime juice, another precaution against the dreaded scurvy.

By October 8, when the first snow fell, three of the houses were completed except for "doors & windows & beds" and McDonald's own house, though roofless, was to be finished within a few days. The "refractory spirit . . . amongst some of the people" which had worried Edwards back at the fort was temporarily submerged in the activity of settling into their new homes. On October 17, when Edwards moved from his small hospital to Churchill Creek with the four remaining convalescents on sleds, he found the little community established and all but one of the inhabitants, who showed some symptoms of typhus, in good health. The situation was far from ideal but it could be endured.

There was still some hope that York Factory would harbor some of the settlers for the winter, as supplies were getting low at Churchill and with so many mouths to feed it was already, so early in the season, necessary to curtail rations of meat at the fort as well as at the Churchill Creek settlement. By early November with the settlers getting meat only twice a week to augment their regular ration of oatmeal and molasses, Auld returned to York Factory, having deemed it inadvisable to take any of the party there.

It was not the reception young McDonald had expected or the treatment his patron confidently believed his settlers would receive at the hands of the Hudson's Bay people. Auld's rejection of any responsibility for the newcomers' welfare threw an even greater load on McDonald and his new doctor friend. Abel Edwards never questioned the need to remain, to forgo his passage home that year and lend aid to the unfortunate band of colonists crowded together in their makeshift quarters, isolated even from the few more experienced countrymen who were living at the fort fifteen miles away. Where the food would come from to sustain them through the winter neither McDonald nor Edwards knew. Their rations of oatmeal and other staples would have to be sharply curtailed, and they would pray that providence would send game to nurture them.

As the days grew colder nature did prove benevolent and the fort hunters began to bring in quantities of ptarmigan such as have seldom been seen around Hudson Bay. Four hunters netting their prey could bring back as many as 350 birds from a foray to the Bushy Islands, the Woody Islands or the "Neverfails," and all winter long the supply continued. Twice a week in November and, as the winter progressed, four times a week the entire camp of more than ninety people was sustained by this Arctic grouse. It was a bleak, cheerless land, but that winter the barren rocky plains of the Churchill Basin were by some miracle fruitful.

With the problem of food under control, the difficulty of providing active employment became more acute. Much of the party was made up of restless young men and teenaged boys who needed constant direction to keep them employed at wood-cutting, hunting, even making mittens which seemed to be worn out with astonishing rapidity by the settlers. One young Irish boy, "whose uniform conduct . . . during the passage from Europe & since his arrival [at Churchill] has been turbulent and refractory," was, after repeated warnings, flogged "18 lashes with a small willow," and finally Edwards sent to the fort for handcuffs, feeling that Edward Shields would provide "much occasion for their use."

"The greater part of them seem to be much like children," Edwards wrote in November, "not capable of being trusted a moment out of sight." Unaccustomed to the harshness and severity of the climate around the Bay, they repeatedly, in spite of constant warnings, went off on walks without blankets, mittens, even socks, and Auld's edict that the settlers must obey every order issued by the officers of the Hudson's Bay Company was impossible to enforce as they were not indentured to the Company and in no way responsible to its employees. Finally as the winter wore on and the thermometer at the fort registered forty-eight below zero, Edwards issued a circular addressed to "The Emigrants at Churchill Creek":

In consequence of the little attention that has been paid to the repeated, urgent and *pressing* entreaties, frequently made to all the settlers, by the medical officer in charge here, respecting the absolute necessity of their wearing sufficient cloathing, to guard against the inclemencies of the season — he takes this method of acquainting them, that unless they comply with the undermentioned directions, for the better preservation of their health, each settler so neglecting him or herself, will, if taken ill from this neglect, be attended as usual, but a charge will be made of all the medicines used for the recovery of such settler & placed to his account. —

Every man & boy on leaving his residence to go to the woods or elsewhere to have his waistcoat & jacket buttoned closely about his neck & breast, over which he is to wear his toggy or great coat — He is likewise to have his handkerchief or stock about his neck — his chin-cloth & mittens (of course his cap) and *never* less than two pair of good socks — a piece of string to be tied round the wrist, so as to keep the cuff of the coat close, in the way which Mr. Edwards has often shewn them, whereby the hand will slip more effectually into the mitten, & the wind prevented from passing up the arm. —

Every woman to wear *constantly* three petticoats, one of which must be of cloth or thick flannel, also thick leggins, and they are never to go out of doors without the Hood, mittens, & pelisse — the latter of which may be thrown over the shoulders, when going to the river for water and this must be *most religiously* observed as the number of coughs & colds now prevailing owe their origin entirely to negligence in this respect. —

Another complication had arisen early in the fall. Auld had returned to York Factory leaving Edwards with the impression that he had been put in charge of the group at Churchill Creek, without consultation with McDonald, whose orders came from Selkirk and not the Company. The resulting confusion caused a temporary lapse in the good relations between the two, but it was quickly settled and within a few days Edwards wrote to Auld, "I shall not again have occasion to touch upon the subject."

All the settlers had become accustomed to applying to McDonald for their needs. The "familiar" manner Auld complained about was exactly what Selkirk had understood the people would require through the hardships of the early days at the settlement. That the young Highlander could speak to them — homesick and disheartened as they were — in the familiar Gaelic tongue, that he was firm and carried out his duties without resorting to harshness and arbitrary commands, no doubt prevented more serious outbreaks of the unrest and disobedience which were already causing difficulties at the camp.

Edwards agreed to leave these responsibilities with McDonald while he supervised medical matters, and together they shared the morning inspection tours, visiting each house to check on the condition of its inhabitants and their surroundings. "It is now an established rule for Mr. McDonald and myself to visit all the houses before breakfast every morning to *see* each individual wash himself and to see also that he takes a full pint of the decoction of spruce [to prevent scurvy]," the doctor noted in his journal. Constant surveillance was absolutely necessary to encourage the people, unaccustomed to the bitter cold and primitive conditions they found themselves in, to maintain healthy standards of cleanliness. On one occasion, early in the winter, the ration of molasses was cut off as punishment for the "filthy condition" outside the houses "notwithstanding they have two necessaries erected."

It was a hard, uphill fight against cold, dirt and disease, and a tribute to Edwards and his youthful coadjutor that there were no further outbreaks of fever, although in October one young woman, Betty Sutherland, died of consumption. In January a sister and brother, Christian and John Bannerman, followed her. An old man who had "scarcely moved from the fireside since his arrival" fell victim to scurvy in February and an immediate program of "liberal decoctions of spruce" twice daily to all was introduced. With the help of cabbages sent from the fort, regular portions of cranberries and rich soup, the patient was quickly brought back to health and the ailment confined.

Throughout the winter there was constant traffic between the settlers' camp and the fort fifteen miles away, particularly after the fort hunters returned to Churchill and left the newcomers to form their own hunting parties. It was on one of these occasions late in November when four of the hunters from Churchill Creek were sleeping overnight at the fort that a disastrous fire broke out and left the building in ruins. All the personal possessions of the Hudson's Bay officers at the post and much of the Company's provisions were destroyed.

Auld was quick to blame the settlers, whom he accused not only of causing the fire, but also of failing to give the alarm so that it could be checked. He rushed to Churchill from York Factory and proceeded to take depositions on all sides. It quickly became apparent to everyone but Auld that the hunters were innocent of his charges and that they had, in fact, done all they could to assist in saving what they could from the building and preventing the spread of the flames.

In his correspondence, Auld continued to rail about their iniquity, but sympathetic and amiable relations continued between the settlers' camp and John Charles, the Hudson's Bay Company officer in charge at Fort Churchill. Charles wrote to Edwards asking for a few candles from "your small stock" and as many moose skins as could be spared, and to help out further Edwards and McDonald immediately surveyed their meagre libraries and sent their homeless neighbor some of their own books "to cheer you in your present melancholy situation. Mr. McDonald's library is much of the same stamp as mine. He will send Franklin's life, 1st. vol., the 2nd not being at hand at the present, but will get it another time. He has likewise McKenzie's Voyage which I suppose you have read. A few old newspapers will make up the budget," wrote Edwards.

By mid-January, when Auld conducted a full-scale, official inquiry into the fire attempting to fix the blame on the settlers' party, Edwards and McDonald had apparently agreed to overlook his fury. Edwards accompanied three of the four hunters involved from Churchill Creek to the fort where they gave their testimony, along with other witnesses. Auld's design was to call "every person present at this place on that night to give his testimony on oath." Much to his chagrin, even John Charles refused to fault the party from Churchill Creek, and suggested the fire had been smouldering in the roof for two days before the hunters' arrival, left there when a band of Indians visiting the fort had an "uncommonly large" fire.

The winter dragged on, the environment as hostile as the old fur trader Auld had predicted it would be. It was not uncommon for the temperature to drop to fifty below zero, and the wind gusted furiously from the broad, endless flatlands lashing the snow in swirls and drifts in a tireless assault against the impermanence of the flimsy walls of their huts. McDonald and Edwards maintained their vigilance, ever wary of the dangerous symptoms of scurvy or fever that could reappear at any moment, threatening to render their charges incapable of attempting the 750-mile journey to Red River as soon as the weather broke.

It was agreed that fifty of the ablest would get a head start and set off for York Factory even before the winter storms ceased, to make their way on snowshoes to the mouth of the Churchill River and then follow the shoreline of Hudson Bay to the Nelson and the Hayes. There was a rough road of sorts there, in reality merely a track used by the fort hunters and messengers, but Auld would send an Indian guide from York Factory to show them the way; "home guard" hunters would go ahead to lay up caches of ptarmigan at their appointed encampments each night; and Archy McDonald would lead them and cheer them and doctor their ills on the long trek, one hundred and fifty miles to the river that would then carry them to Lake Winnipeg and south to the settlement.

CHAPTER TWO

The Long Walk: They Found It Somewhat Laborious

1814

At the camp preparations had begun for the first move toward the settlement. Spring comes late at Churchill. Even in July the Arctic ice still clogs its harbor, and in early April, the target date for the settlers' departure, winter still holds fast, the rugged ice floes piled crazily in enormous hummocks along the flat shore-line.

Inland, just a mile or two, the primitive path stretched over the plains, the pauses marked by the little rivers that flow into Hudson Bay, their edges lined with meagre bluffs of scrubby trees, barely enough to afford shelter for the settlers' simple skin tents and wood for their evening campfires. Most of the way the snow would be deep and soft, and added to the discomfort of the cold and the wind and the laborious nature of the long walk itself would be the unaccustomed exercise of making their way on snowshoes, those strange utilities peculiar to this northern region that none of the Highlanders had ever encountered before.

There was much to be done to make ready for the trip. Of the fifty chosen to go, about half would be required to draw sleds each carrying his own belongings and provisions and bedding and those of one of the girls or younger boys. Samuel Lamont, the millwright, supervised the building of the sleds, and the women and boys were put to work making snowshoes, moccasins and extra mittens. All was to be in readiness when the guide arrived from York Factory, so that the party could move quickly on to the fort in time to proceed up the Hayes River as soon as the ice was out and thus ensure an early arrival at Red River.

With provision made for feeding and clothing the party, Edwards put his mind to instructing his young apprentice in treatments for the various ailments of the winter in the wilds that he might be called upon to doctor. Little had Archy realized, in his enthusiasm for "attending to every case" on this new adventure, that he would be flung so quickly into tending, alone, on the trail such unfamiliar ills as snow blindness and snowshoe cramp, along with any other emergency that might crop up. William Auld was free with advice, writing from York Factory: "I hope that young fellow McDonald will enter into the true spirit of the thing . . . he is fond of responsibility & God help him if he does not acquit himself properly."

Snow blindness was the greatest concern, and Auld admonished Edwards to "be sure to let McD. have with him Jalops to purge them on the way who shall appear most affected with snow blindness. But if he could bleed that is the grand preventive as well as the cure. For God's sake tell him or shew him the danger of operating near the artery." So followed lessons in blood-letting and when McDonald set off from Churchill Creek with his charges he carried with him Edwards's written instructions — a follow-up to the actual demonstrations on bleeding. Many occasions were to arise when he was grateful for the knowledge.

A vein ought to be opened, & from 10 to 16 ounces of blood drawn, according to the severity of the attack, degree of *plethora* or *inanition* most apparent in the patient. In every case it will be advisable to make rather a large orifice, which will allow the necessary quantum of blood to flow in a shorter time, and will prove much more effectual, in preventing and removing the complaint. *Great care* should be taken in performing this (easy & safe) operation (as most people generally consider it) and *that* vein which does not run contiguous to the artery, ought to be selected. In general, either the great cephalic or basilic may be opened with safety, but as the distribution of the blood vessels varies much in different subjects, the safest method will be to ascertain by the fingers if there is any pulsation, which will always be felt when the vein runs over an artery. If the attack is severe, the bleeding should be followed up with a smart purge.

Another of the dangers frequently encountered was the temptation to eat snow: "The pernicious practice . . . must not on any account be permitted," Edwards directed, "the inevitable consequence will be the utter incapacity of the person's proceeding."

Together McDonald and Edwards selected the settlers they considered best able to undertake the arduous journey. Twenty-one of those they chose were teenagers. Most of the other thirty were in their early twenties, about the same age as McDonald himself, but one "elderly man" of forty-nine was allowed to accompany his son. Alexander Gunn was so anxious to go along on the journey that he went in training to prove he was able and Edwards wrote in his journal a few days before the departure that the "noted pedestrian" had walked the thirty miles to the hospital and back the same day "without much fatigue." At journey's end McDonald wrote to the doctor at Churchill Creek that old Sandy Gunn had done "uncommonly well."

By the last week in March all was in readiness and the party waited impatiently for the Indian guide to arrive from York Factory. Delayed by bad weather, he finally arrived on April 5 bringing with him the dog-sled that was to bear McDonald's own possessions. The guide himself carried a pack containing eighty pounds of oatmeal and twenty-five spare pairs of "Indian shoes," and each one of the settlers was issued with a ration of ten pounds of oatmeal and a brace of partridge as provision for the first leg of the journey.

And so they set off on this improbable journey, the vast, rugged wastes of the Churchill plains stretching before them as far as the eye could see. It was a fine, clear morning — Wednesday, April 6, 1814. Spirits were high and the young piper, Robert Gunn, who had accompanied the group from Kildonan, strode along in the middle of the line providing an incongruous pace for the figures on snowshoes winding through the deep soft snow.

"They took their departure by single files," McDonald

wrote in his report to Selkirk some weeks later, "the Guide . . . took the lead followed by the men & sleds, & they succeeded by the women, the rear was taken up by one of the sturdiest young men. . . . Single files . . . would tend to make the track more firm & smooth that the women were enabled to walk in the snow shoes with greater facility, as they were by no means calculated for that arduous task . . . as well as the Natives of this country. Nevertheless, I must do them justice in the great reformation they made in the science before they came to their journey's end." McDonald himself varied his position in the line, sometimes taking the lead, then pacing the girls in the middle, at other times following along behind with one of his overseers or lending a hand to one of the boys who was tiring of hauling his sled.

The first symptoms of distress did not take long to show themselves. Even on the first day out from Churchill Creek three of the party began to complain of "a cursed distemper which we call the *cramp*" and on the second day one of the victims, nineteen-year-old Andrew McBeath, was completely disabled by the agonizing muscle spasms in his legs. "We struct fire," McDonald reported, "and got boiling hot decoctions of spruce immediately made ready with which he was all over smartly washed after extracting from his arm from 12 to 14 oz . . . blood, so was now with the assistance of his wife able to keep up with the party; the strongest of the females & myself hauling his sled in turn until we arrived at the Tent at 5 p.m."

Andrew's younger brother, Charles, also began to complain of cramps, along with seventeen-year-old George Sutherland and his sister, Jannet, thirteen. Even Robert Gunn was afflicted, silencing the comforting skirl of the pipes, and his sister Mary Gunn, twenty, was a victim too. When some of the women began to lag behind, the order of march was altered and they were sandwiched in between groups of the men, and when there were plains to cross, the lines spread out six abreast to break the force of the winds sweeping down on them.

In spite of cold and sickness, on the second day the party pressed on to the "Eastward Tent," Churchill Factory's hunting camp twenty-two miles beyond the little wooded bluff opposite the fort where the travellers had stopped their first night out. Here they were provisioned by the Churchill hunters, helping themselves to the large cache of partridges they found awaiting them. McDonald's journal records that he got one hundred and sixty birds from the Hudson's Bay Company hunters that night and next morning, in addition, he "issued 457 partridges plus 120 for today."

In the evenings when supper was over and the fires banked low "to get the cakes baked, and the partridges cooked overnight," Archy McDonald made his rounds, visiting each of the five tents in turn to check on their inhabitants. On arrival at the Eastward camp, he found Jannet Sutherland and Mary Gunn both "very poorly with the eyes" and had to resort to bleeding, and the next day Mary needed the treatment again, along with Alexander Matheson who had a "very bad" case. Many were complaining of cramps and soreness caused by the unaccustomed exertion of walking on snowshoes and McDonald decided to lay over for the day to rest, in the hope of reviving them to continue the long walk.

Early starts were the order of the day, and the morning gun was usually fired around 2 A.M. to signal the time to rise, in order to get on the trail and cover as much distance as possible before the sun's penetrating rays could take their toll. On the 9th they set out at a quarter to three, refreshed from their day of rest at the Eastward Tent, maintaining a "steady step" for twenty miles before they put up at a small bluff of wood at 10 A.M. "Notwithstanding pitching our camp so early in the day," the fierce glare of the sun brought on seven attacks of snow blindness, in two victims, George Bannerman* and Hector MacLeod, "more violent than the others." All were bled and dosed with jalop, and the only consolation as the young physician made his evening rounds that night was that "the cramp subjects [were] not so bad during this day."

And so they journeyed on. On the fourth and fifth days they covered twenty miles each day, stumbling wearily over the uneven furrows of the hard, crusted snow. "They found it somewhat laborious . . . in consequence of falls & tumbles they met with in ascending & descending the banks and ridges of hard snow formed on the plains," McDonald wrote.

One of them found it more difficult than most. After seven

* Great-grandfather of former Prime Minister John Diefenbaker.

days of steady walking, Jean McKay, shivering and faint, slipped on a patch of ice and collapsed on the ground. Two of the other women carried the sick and feverish girl to the encampment, and McDonald, aware she had been suffering from the snow blindness that had afflicted other members of the party, prepared to minister to her. "On enquiring her the state of her health I found she was 4 months on in her pregnancy," he wrote later to Edwards. "I was now alarmed that the symptoms might threaten abortion.

"I extracted a few oz. of blood from her arm immediately & applied tepid fomentation & gave her 20 grs. of Jalap." Jean's husband, Angus, was instructed to keep her quiet and warm and by evening her condition was considerably improved.

With so many of the party struggling to keep the pace, McDonald decided to lay by another day. Jean McKay would require further treatment. The two Sutherlands were still flagging. And fifteen-year-old Charles McBeath, a burden since the first day on the trail, had irritated everyone by complicating his condition, "the lazy, ignorant, stubborn youth . . . eating the snow in defiance of all who witnessed him." Poor Archy McDonald, his patience sorely tried, his sense of humor failing him momentarily, remarked testily in his journal that McBeath was also "complaining of his eyes as well as every other defect he is subject to." McDonald found it difficult to comprehend the obtuseness of some of his youthful charges, but there was nothing to do but summon what sympathy he could muster and try to make the boy as comfortable as possible and get him on his feet to continue the journey. Both McBeath and Robert Gunn had been forced to leave their sleds behind. McBeath himself was unable to walk and had to be pulled by sled, and McDonald's dogs had taken on the extra loads. Difficulty piled on difficulty but there was no choice but to go on.

Next morning Jean McKay was "easier in every respect" and after bleeding her again and treating all the others on the sick list McDonald decreed a day of rest, there near the banks of the Owl River. Six days late in departure, two of the first nine days spent resting: McDonald knew there was no hope that they would get to the York Factory by mid-April. More important was to get there with all his people in good health.

Angus and Jean McKay wanted to move on with the rest of

the party when they set off from the rest camp at seven on the morning of the 15th. Snow was falling heavily and the wind piled huge drifts around their makeshift shelters. George and Jannet Sutherland were still weak and unlikely to be able to keep up, and of course the McBeath boy would be unable to manage on his own. McDonald assigned one of the Indian hunters who knew the route to remain with the laggards and told Angus to stay behind with Jean and the others and to catch up with the main party when their condition improved. They were still three days from York Factory, but with sufficient provisions to see them through they would be better off to stay back and McDonald would return to meet them after conducting the rest of the settlers on to the fort.

That day even the guide was in difficulties. The route stretched twelve miles across a flat plain and the whirling snow made it impossible to see more than twenty or thirty yards in any direction. "The Guide expressed himself incapable of making out the way across the Plain," wrote McDonald. "Nevertheless the Hero came within 2 gun shots of the right track — put up in the first wood when we came to a stachakan of 41 partridges which was served to the people."

It was not the first time in Archy McDonald's experience in the wilderness that his faith in an Indian companion was so soundly justified. From the day of his arrival at Churchill he had observed the fur traders' dependence on their Indian neighbors, and the days and weeks of this first of his many long journeys in the northwest merely verified his realization of the newcomer's need for their good will and help. These days forged the foundation of his lifelong regard for the native people and established the pattern of friendship and trust that overlay all his relationships with them throughout his life.

They were by now nearing Sam's (Salmis) Creek, a little stream that runs into the mouth of the Nelson River at its widest point near Hudson Bay, and the guide assured them that York Factory was but two good days off. "The whole of the people was rather improving than otherwise for the journey," McDonald noted, grateful that the cases of snow blindness had subsided and the painful cramps were no longer hampering their progress.

The worst was over, they thought, and the party moved on in good spirits. Soon they would reach York Factory and there would be plenty of good food and time to rest. They knew there was still a long journey ahead — six hundred miles to the colony — but through most of that they hoped to travel comfortably in boats along the sparkling waterways. The long walk over the rugged, snow-encrusted track was nearly at an end.

They had already met several "half Indians" from the fort, hunters sent out to lay by partridge for the settlers' use as they approached their destination, and to bring pork and a fresh stock of oatmeal to replenish the small store they had brought from Churchill Creek. One of them was sent back to Angus McKay and his party to take them a share of the new provisions and return with word of their welfare. Another hurried on to the fort to warn the Hudson's Bay men of the imminent arrival of their fifty-two guests.

On the 18th, the wide, deep mouth of the Nelson River formed the last barrier, clogged with rugged ridges of ice thrown up by the tide. The party moved four miles up the north bank "and then crossed by making a kind of semicircle to the other side . . . by no means an easy matter from the large hills of ice collected on the surface." Another few miles across the peninsula that separates the two rivers and the Hayes River appeared in sight.

Late that afternoon, after thirteen days on the trail, the party approached York Factory. A few miles above the stockade, on the banks of the Hayes, two men from the fort working along with several Indian women to erect tents to shelter the newcomers were startled to hear the distant strain of the bagpipes. And as they looked out the newly cut path through the woods they saw the young piper at the head of a long column, men and women alike singing a familiar Scottish air, plaids thrown over their shoulders to brave the wind and cold of the harsh northern air.

McDonald went on to the fort to announce their arrival, leaving the party to settle into their temporary camp. There was no word from Miles Macdonell, no letter awaiting him expressing the governor's wishes about how the settlers were to proceed. He was welcomed by W. H. Cook, chief officer for the Hudson's Bay Company at the factory, but was shocked to learn that provisions were so scarce that he would be forced to cut the daily rations of his people rather than increase them. Even his hope of rewarding each of the settlers with a "dram" to celebrate the end of the difficult journey was dashed. Auld had left specific instructions that Cook was to give no rum to the settlers.

McDonald was forced to make the best of it. Instead of the festive occasion he had hoped their arrival would be, he resigned himself to explaining to his people as best he could that they must continue to make do. He saw them established in tents and distributed rations to get them through until a party returned next day with provisions from the fort.

More tents were needed, even with ten persons housed in each. Cook sent back leather sails as substitutes and moose skins to serve as doors, along with a supply of oatmeal (one pound per person per day), molasses, rice, tea, sugar, butter, flour and, in the end, a little rum. But there was no gaiety, no festivity, to mark the end of their heroic march. York Factory seemed a singularly joyless place, and the people settled in to wait resignedly for the river's ice to begin to move. It was to be more than a month before they could continue their journey.

At the fort there was much interest in the new arrivals camped outside the gates. So few white women had ever made their way to the remote outpost that servants and Indians alike were anxious to get a look at the newcomers. Most curious of all were the "country" wives of the officers of the fort, and on the Sunday morning after the settlers' arrival, the "Gentlemen from the Factory" walked out with their ladies to pay a formal call at the encampment.*

The weeks at the factory passed slowly, the settlers bored, rebellious and dissatisfied with the inadequate provisions. In vain McDonald applied to Cook for extra supplies — even for cloth to make trousers for some of the men who wished to replace their

* In the hierarchy of the Hudson's Bay Company, the "gentlemen" — the officers and clerks — were privileged, men of some education, most of whom joined the Company in England or Scotland as apprentice clerks and came out in their youth to learn their way in the fur trade. The "servants" — voyageurs, laborers, tradesmen and others — were well down on the social scale with no opportunity to move into the upper stream. Many of the gentlemen established alliances with Indian women, who not only provided companionship and "domestic comforts" but also acted as interpreters and shared their husbands' special status. The coming of the European women as settlers disrupted these comfortable old ways, and "custom of the country" marriages (marriages à la façon du pays) no longer sufficed. Within the quarter-century after the beginning of settlement in the West there was an almost universal move on the part of the fur traders to legalize their liaisons, particularly when missionaries appeared at the remote outposts to perform the religious ceremonies. See Sylvia Van Kirk, "Women and the Fur Trade," *The Beaver* , Winter 1972, pp. 4–21.

leather ones for the journey down to the settlement. Repeatedly Cook refused, explaining that he could not give them any "in consequence of the strict order he had from Mr. Auld." It was disheartening. On May 3 the arrival of a single goose heralded the first sign of spring and Archy McDonald rejoiced to think that they could soon be on the move.

Only two boats were available to transport the settlers up-river, which meant that they would have to leave behind all but the most essential of their personal belongings until later. Lamont, the millwright, along with several carpenters from the fort set to work to put the craft in shape for the journey. Six Company servants were to go with the group and McDonald selected eighteen of his own "most effective" settlers to help man the boats, whose thirty-five-foot keel and three- to four-ton capacity demanded both strength and skill. The settlers were to provide the former; Charles Flett and Jonathan Wishart, the two old hands who were appointed steersmen, and four other experienced Hudson's Bay men, the latter.

At 7 A.M. on May 23 the party got under way. McDonald had purchased a supply of tobacco on his own account in an attempt to make up for the many other deficiencies and, as he distributed it, he assured his people that the only way to improve their condition was to make the quickest possible passage up Hayes River and along Lake Winnipeg to the settlement.

Once again their natural optimism provided momentum. A fair wind filled the sails and carried their boats along through the rain of the first day out from York Factory. Next day two of the hunters shot five geese and provided a welcome change of diet. There was some grumbling but they all were so happy to be on the final leg of their journey that it was several days before their dissatisfaction became acute. The river was rough and on the shady side still ice-covered, but during the first day, at least, the boats moved smoothly, sailing against the current without difficulty along the wide, winding waters as far as the Pennycutt-away tributary. Next day the scene changed and the Hayes River began its climb. From the Bay to the forks of the Red River the Hayes rises about seven hundred feet above sea level, and all of that had to be contended with in a series of falls and cascades and rapids along the meandering path of the river. That day the ascent was gradual and the boats could be tracked: the six Hudson's Bay hands and the eighteen "most effective" men of the settlers walking along the banks with towing lines, hauling the heavy craft up the waterway by brute strength. Where the shores were flat, "old" Sandy Gunn, along with the twenty women and twelve young boys of the party, followed on foot along the river's edge. But as the days passed and the river left the flat tundra and formed a deeper gorge in the land, its banks rising straight up from the water, the trackers struggled from their path along the rugged cliff tops to keep control of the heavy boats, and the others scrambled along as best they could seeking footholds in the rocky terrain.

An occasional dram of rum encouraged the tracking men in their efforts, but nothing had prepared these simple, inexperienced Highland folk for the rigors of getting about in the rough northern waterways. In his diary McDonald remarked: "The whole party, I'm sorry to say, often expressed a dissatisfied tone all the way from Y.F., seeing the rough state of the River & unexpected obstacles that every now & then presented before them."

There was worse to come — the long stretch of high falls and cascades that could only be portaged. On the 29th they were able to bring the boats across Borrox's Falls with a hand line without moving the cargo "except that part of it which is alive," McDonald noted, but to get over the White Mud and Rocky Landing carrying places the boats had to be emptied and all the women were called upon to make themselves useful carrying their share of bundles across the portage. Next day it was Brasse's Falls, and the men were grumbling, demanding more food to give them strength for the unexpected exertion. Even the experienced steersmen complained about their rations, saying they thought they "deserve nearly their belly full." In spite of it all, bright and early next morning, May 31, they hauled their two awkward craft over the Upper Burnt Wood carrying place and made the Rocky and Swampy portages before breakfast.

Up the Hayes River they continued, into Swampy Lake, and finally on a lovely day in early June they reached one of the traditional fur trade landmarks — the "Dram Stone" in the last rapid at Hill River — and "all hands, including the women & Coy's servants got a glass of rum." Next morning, June 3, the boatmen had to break through the river ice with axes and poles before proceeding, but the brief relaxation of the preceding day had given the people fresh heart.

When McDonald realized they were making such good time that they would reach the Jack River post (near what is now Norway House) and fresh provisions sooner than expected, he decided to increase the food allowance. To add to this there were plenty of fresh fish to break the monotonous diet and an occasional stimulant to help forget the difficulties and make the outlook brighter. "I find that giving them a dram now & then unexpected makes them enjoy it & more contented than if they had it daily which of course they would claim as a right if this was the case."

At Oxford House, at the east end of Oxford Lake, they arrived in time to share the eighty pounds of fish brought in that day, June 6, by two of the Company's men. And two curious Indians paid a friendly visit to their camp for their first glimpse of European women.

Five days later, after hauling through the marshlands of the Echimamish basin to the North River (the Nelson), the party arrived at the Jack River post, bagpipes skirling, colorful neckerchiefs and tartans rippling in the breeze as the two boats pulled into the camp. Much to their delight, in the crowd of Hudson's Bay Company officers and servants who gathered to greet them the settlers saw the familiar faces of relatives and friends from Sutherland. One of the girls was welcomed by her brother who presented her with a large cake of maple sugar "as a positive proof of the goodness of the country," and all around them they heard tales of the bounty and abundance of the settlement lands. There was still the long, boisterous passage of Lake Winnipeg and the last slow stretch of the Red River to the Assiniboine, but even knowing that, they felt, at Jack River, that they had reached their destination.

It was an emotional moment, a mingling of relief, of hope and of joy, and the officers of the fort knew well that some festivities should mark such a memorable event. It was time for a dance — a gala occasion. The men of the post gathered in the hall with the new arrivals to celebrate with reels and country dances — and two gallons of spirits supplied by the "gentlemen" of Jack River.

CHAPTER THREE

He Must Be Driven to Abandon the Project

1814 - 1815

What seems most remarkable is the strength and endurance of these otherwise quite unremarkable young men and women. They could have been forgiven had they weakened. The whole story of their emigration thus far had been one of disappointment and hardship: sickness and loss of loved ones; bitter cold and privation and hunger; and added to these ordeals the unimagined difficulties and discomforts of their journey. It would be easy to understand if they had looked about this bleak headland at Jack River and wondered if it had been worth it all.

They had already shown that it was not their way, though, to be discouraged and despairing. One happy evening of music and dancing and conversation with old friends was enough to convince them that this new land did indeed promise peace and plenty. "No country in the world is better," they were told, and they believed it. They came next morning to their young leader "expressing their gratitude," telling McDonald that they wished "to write from here, home to their friends to come out next year."

They knew a party of Hudson's Bay men was setting out for

the Bay immediately and that their letters could go on the first ships back to Britain. McDonald demurred. He suggested that they wait until they reached the colony and had first-hand knowledge and "occular proof" to relay to their friends and relations back home. His instinctive caution was well-founded, although even he could have no idea of the difficulties and dangers that awaited them at the settlement.

He had, however, by now, as he passed from post to post, heard enough about the colony's governor to realize that there were serious problems. Even his own youthful enthusiasm could not blind him to the disturbing situation that unfolded before him. Miles Macdonell, Selkirk's choice to establish his colony, had arrived with the first small group of settlers at the Forks of the Red and Assiniboine rivers in the summer of 1812, inexperienced in the ways of the West and the fur trade. He had been a captain in the Royal Canadian Volunteers until they were disbanded in 1802, but had retired to farming near Cornwall when Selkirk first met him in 1804. Selkirk judged him to be a leader of men. Whether his faith was unfounded, and another might have overcome the many obstacles that confronted the settlement, is questionable. Perhaps it was simply that the time was not yet ripe. It is certain that the fur traders of both companies were not ready to relinquish their claims on the land.

From the beginning, McDonald knew, Selkirk had been opposed in his scheme by the North West Company, who were convinced that settlement in the fur country would interfere with their trade. They had never acknowledged the charter which gave the Hudson's Bay Company rights over all lands draining into Hudson Bay and they believed that Selkirk's grant was meaningless. At first they were prepared to watch and wait, convinced that the natural difficulties would be such that the settlement could never prosper, and that any colonists who did come would soon move on to a more settled part of America.

The Hudson's Bay men, on the other hand, were grudgingly willing to give what assistance they could to their unfortunate countrymen who were unwise enough to attempt to establish a colony in the wilderness. The Company had pledged support to the settlement, but some of the most influential of the Company's officers, William Auld among them, actively opposed the whole idea, and in Miles Macdonell they found much to criticize. Macdonell's arrival at the site of the colony that first summer had been so delayed that he was unable to get crops planted and was, as a result, dependent on the help of the neighboring posts of both fur trade companies to provision his people during their first winter in residence. He had certainly been dealt more than his share of problems, and the fractious Irishmen of the second contingent did not make his task any easier, but there seem to be some grounds for the charges of mismanagement laid against him by the Hudson's Bay men.

During the summer of 1813 some semblance of a village was beginning to take shape near the Forks, and the large body of Kildonan settlers expected that autumn were to fill out and consolidate the little community. Perhaps it was just as well that in the end they did not arrive at the settlement before winter, because again that year provisions were scarce, and when Macdonell moved his people down to Pembina to winter near the buffalo hunting grounds, the source of their staple meat, he found that the animals had moved too far away from the camp for his men to pursue them on foot. He had about a hundred people in his care and they were seriously short of food. He convinced himself, in spite of Selkirk's written admonition to be cautious and to "remember that any violent overstretch of authority would be extremely pernicious to our cause," that he must take drastic action.

On January 8, 1814, Governor Miles Macdonell issued his ill-advised "Pemmican Proclamation."* He decreed that no provisions could be taken out of Assiniboia, Selkirk's territory, for a twelve-month period. In effect, in enforcing the embargo, he cut off the regular food supply of the North West Company posts in the interior, and he could have had no doubt that his action would provoke the Nor'Westers to retaliate.

When he sent his sheriff, John Spencer, to the North West post at La Souris, near Brandon House, with orders to seize the store of pemmican there (although his proclamation gave assur-

---

* In one of his published letters to the Reverend John Strachan in June 1816, Archibald McDonald describes this staple food of the Northwest. "For the sake of those who had never been in the Indian country, it may be necessary here to explain, that Pemican is a preparation of meat, very ingeniously contrived by the Indians for preserving it without salt. The lean of the Buffaloe beef, or of venison, is dried by the heat of the fire, and is then pounded small, mixed in a large trough, with melted fat, crammed, while still warm, into bags made of Buffaloe hide."

ance that any provisions taken for the use of the colony would be paid for in British money), it was tantamount to a declaration of hostilities. The Nor'Westers were no longer willing to wait and watch. They were ready to engage in open opposition to the colony. As Simon McGillivray, partner with his brother William in the Montreal company, wrote: "It will require some time, and I fear cause much expense to us all as well as to himself, before he [Selkirk] is driven to abandon the project, and yet he must be driven to abandon it, for his success would strike at the very existence of our trade."

The first movement of the North West brigade taking supplies out would not begin until the northern rivers opened in the late spring, but Macdonell's seizures of their stores of pemmican during the winter months only served to ensure that the old fur traders would resist. To back them in their fight they had the support of their half-Indian sons, not only those in the employ of the company, but also the independent bands who roamed the plains on horseback, always ready for action and adventure. It was a dangerous situation and Macdonell finally realized that he would have to back down and return a large part of the provisions he had taken. In return, the Nor'Westers agreed to supply a quantity of pemmican for the settlement the following winter, and to provide transport for some of their provisions from Hudson Bay that autumn.

It was into this atmosphere that Archy McDonald and his fifty-one new settlers unwittingly came as they sailed south from Jack River, into Playgreen Lake and on to Lake Winnipeg. The Playgreen waters were rough and boisterous, and in the violent buffeting of Lake Winnipeg as they hugged its east shoreline past the Poplar and Pigeon rivers to the calmer narrows past Fisher Bay was a foreboding of the stormy days to come.

For the moment, though, they were calm. Having endured the hardships of the preceding weeks, the settlers were able to be optimistic about the future, and as they moved farther south and drew near the settlement, the land grew softer, the waters calmer. They gazed about them at the lush countryside. It was mid-June and the marshes were full of nesting water birds, the waters abounding with fresh fish so easily caught and set to sizzle over their campfires. They could not suspect that the serious struggle for possession of the Red River country was just beginning.

On June 20, as they reached the mouth of the Red River, they met three North West batteaux, their first encounter with the hitherto unknown "enemy." Next day, within a few miles of the Forks, more canoe-loads of Nor'Westers from Fort Gibraltar passed them on the river, and the new settlers cheerily saluted them with a round of the bagpipes. Excitement was running high and that night they made camp a short distance above the settlement to freshen up and dig into their packs for their most colorful raiment to prepare for a ceremonial arrival at Point Douglas. Bagpipe answered bagpipe as they put in to shore next morning, three hundred yards below Miles Macdonell's government house, and the old settlers gathered along the banks to greet the new. It was Wednesday, June 22, 1814, a day of hope and cheer and good will at Red River. Troubles were forgotten and the governor's welcome was warm and happy. Congratulations were in order, too, for Archy McDonald, whom Miles Macdonell was meeting for the first time. There was no doubt Lord Selkirk's youthful protégé had acquitted himself well and the settlement councillors were generous with their compliments.

There was little time to waste on frivolity, though. The planting season was well on and every precious day of labor in the fields meant more food for the coming winter. With fifty more mouths to feed and another thirty expected from Churchill Creek before the summer's end, the governor knew he must get the new arrivals to work immediately. He issued tents and other supplies and saw them comfortably settled that first day, and next morning they were divided into small parties and assigned plots for potato planting.

There was no clearing to be done. The beauty of these lands along the Red River, and one of Selkirk's main reasons for choosing them as the site for his settlement, was that although the banks were lined with trees to provide enough wood for building and for firewood, the plains stretched out behind, the rich black soil ready for the plough. In the Canadas, new settlers spent years cutting and burning and clearing their acres before ever planting a crop of any size. At Red River, on the day after their arrival, colonists were out with their hoes in the flat, fertile fields, and within weeks green shoots gave promise of the bounty to come.

While men, women and children worked contentedly side by side in the sun-warmed fields of the "colony gardens," Archy

McDonald joined the governor and the old Hudson's Bay Company surveyor Peter Fidler downriver, selecting the sites for the new farms. Macdonell had established his first settlers with long, narrow strip lots along the river above Point Douglas, and he proposed to continue the plan northward. Already a small truculent element amongst the newcomers, led by Sandy Gunn, was muttering in protest against the governor's plans. They thought they would prefer the lands to the south, toward the forks of the rivers and the headquarters of the North West Company, and had already made representations to their young leader.

To Archy McDonald fell the task of appeasing the rebels. As soon as he had arrived at the settlement the governor had given him charge of the accounts, and in particular assigned to him the continued care of the settlers. Selkirk, who had named him to the five-man Council of Assiniboia, had written Macdonell about his protégé some months earlier, praising his abilities and expressing confidence in his "zeal and assiduity." Macdonell soon concurred in this judgment. For months he had been faced with criticism and outright antagonism, even amongst his own men. To have such a stalwart supporter — for the young Highlander quickly asserted himself "a true wellwisher to the colony" — was a great comfort and a relief to the hard-pressed governor. "I am highly pleased with Mr. Archd. McDonald. He is a fine, active young fellow . . . most attentive to the welfare of the people he brought with him, as well as to the interests of the concern in every respect. . . . a popular officer like him is much required here . . ." he wrote to Selkirk.

But it took more than popularity to handle the complaints of the settlers, some of them men more than twice his age. All day on the Sunday after their arrival at the settlement the people wandered around the lands proposed for them, and Sandy Gunn did his best to stir up dissatisfaction. The following week, when the men refused to join the women in the fields weeding and cleaning the crops that had been planted before their arrival, McDonald met with them to discuss their grievances, and told them of the experiences of some early emigrants to Cape Breton described by Lord Selkirk in his *Observations on . . . Emigration* published after his visit to Canada in 1803–4.

On their arrival these settlers were "delighted" with the situation shown to them. "An other place, however . . . was still more agreeable to them, but before they could make their determination . . . a still better place was further on, which in short induced them to go on so far that ultimately they came to an inferior situation to the first, and were so reduced with the great expences incurred as well as loss of time that they had no other means than settle there with diminished resources." The object lesson took some time to take effect, but one young man, John Matheson, was impressed enough to bring his influence to bear on the others, and by the end of the week a delegation appeared at McDonald's tent to apologize for their "obstinacy" and indicate their willingness to accept the lands that had been chosen for them.

It was obvious that it required both firmness and tact to deal with these independent Scotsmen. Although the women went quietly about their work in the fields, regularly being credited with their pay — "1/6 per day if they feed themselves or 1/ & be fed by us" — the men looked for any excuse to withhold their cooperation. When they finally did return to the fields, McDonald realized that he must devise some ingenious method to make them accept the final allotments of their individual farms.

Through the early days of July, McDonald and Fidler went together to the new village to mark out the hundred-acre lots, three acres wide, along the wooded river bank. On the 6th, in spite of rainy days, they had surveyed twenty parcels; by the 11th, fourteen more. By the 12th they were ready to assign the properties, and the governor gathered all the people together at the breast of the river where there were three lots slightly apart from the others. These he gave to George Campbell, John Smith and the Widow Stewart, all of whom had families with them. The twenty-four lots for the remaining families were divided into "four big lots of 6 lots 100 acres each — The people were then formed into 4 divisions & each division consisting of six families the nearest friends as they themselves choosed to sellect. Then every grand division had by tickets their chance of the four big lots — Afterwards every 6 families formed themselves into sub-divisions of two each, & they by ticket got two lots conjunctly, which they had at their own pleasure to settle for." This eminently fair method of distribution so satisfied the people that by evening "no one would change his lot for another's," and first thing next morning McDonald went down to the new village and helped them choose the best situation on each property to build their houses, making sure that "every two build their houses near one another for the sake of company, etc."

Within days all the new settlers were established in their own tents on their own lands, and immediately they set to work to build their first permanent homes at Red River. At last there were tangible signs of the developing community, and those of the young people who were not engaged in house-building spent the days in the fields harvesting the hay crop, and hoeing potatoes in the communal gardens, or erecting the necessary barns and outbuildings.

Things were going so smoothly that late in July Miles Macdonell decided to go to York Factory to meet the settlers arriving that year, leaving the settlement in charge of McDonald and Peter Fidler. He had reservations about the latter, who, he told Selkirk, was "far from a well-polished man & is not well-liked by the people," but he valued his long experience in the country and felt that McDonald could take care of any dealings with the people, while Fidler superintended the practical aspects of running the settlement. Macdonell himself was seriously depressed and exhausted from his cares and tribulations and no doubt realized that his capacity for sound judgment and management was much depleted. His last official act before moving off on July 25 was to issue yet another decree that was to prove troublesome to the colony. Hoping to prevent the buffalo herds from being driven away from Fort Daer, the hunting camp near Pembina, he posted a proclamation forbidding the Métis to continue their traditional method of running buffalo on horseback, thus incurring their wrath. It was another bad mistake, but when he sat down on the day of his departure to finish his report to Selkirk on the state of the settlement there was little to indicate that all was not well with the people. "Relatives & connections wishing to be near neighbors have got their different allotments adjoining each other," he said; "they are now most industriously & cheerfully building houses for themselves & their friends."

Archy McDonald, too, took time that day to write to his patron. He had much to report on events since his last letter written at York Factory in May, and it was time to send off any mail that was intended to go out on the fall ships returning to England. He had already seen letters written by the settlers for their friends and relatives at home, in fact had written some for them, and he knew that in spite of all the difficulties they were urging their parents and friends to make the journey out as soon as possible. He joined them in the plea directing his appeal to Selkirk. "It is with greatest pleasure I now can report to your Lordship that they never were happier & more contented in Kildonan than they are here already & take the liberty . . . to wish that the parents of these young people who came out with me from that parish should be sent after them as soon as your Lordship may find it convenient." More than that, he urged that Selkirk himself visit the colony, in the hope that he might be able, in person, to garner support for the project that the governor had failed to do. "It is surprising to see how well that Gentleman carry on the business here, with the very little support he has from the Gentlemen in the country . . . I was no time in the country when I heard much of such misunderstanding going on between them. . . . I clearly see though Capt. McD. has officers under him they don't consider him their superior officer at all," McDonald remarked, expressing his reservations about Macdonell's ability to "carry on your Lordship's concern in this country to the highest perfection" in the circumstances, and further saying that he felt he himself would have difficulty performing his duties in the face of the uncooperative spirit of the Hudson's Bay officers. He sensed that Macdonell was in a hopeless position, but perhaps did not realize that his mental state was so serious that he would break down completely on arrival at York Factory and have to be restrained by the officers at the fort from committing suicide.

While the governor was incapacitated at York Factory, McDonald and Fidler were having their differences at the settlement. Fidler was, of course, an officer of the Hudson's Bay Company; like his fellow fur traders, he had no high regard for the colonists. He was prepared to obey orders, to supervise the construction of outbuildings and supply necessary provisions, but he would not go out of his way to appease the newcomers and his brusque manner betrayed his impatience with them. McDonald's whole allegiance was to Lord Selkirk and his settlement. As a member of the Council of Assiniboia and having been appointed to take charge of the settlers in the governor's absence, he felt his first duty was to see to the progress and contentment of his people.

Fidler had decided to build a small house for himself at the settlement and trouble arose when construction of the new dwelling began to take precedence in Fidler's view over feeding the men who were working for the settlement. The messing arrangements varied. In the main the farmer-settlers purchased their provisions on credit from the colony stores. Those who were in the employ of Selkirk — the carpenters and other tradesmen — could elect to be fed in the communal dining room. When one day Fidler assigned the kitchen help — including the cook — to the building of his house, leaving them no time to prepare the fish for breakfast, McDonald was forced to step in and insist that they give up their carpentry and provide a proper dinner. Meanwhile the workmen chewed on pemmican for their morning meal.

The young Scotsman simmered with indignation at the callousness and lack of concern displayed by the old fur trader. The two had worked congenially in the fields for days on the survey of the village, but as the summer wore on their relations became strained and McDonald found himself increasingly taking the settlers' part in attempting to get Fidler to provide more and better provisions.

Except for these relatively minor aggravations, it was a summer of contentment at the settlement. As the days passed the log houses began to rise along the river bank, and the people brought in the harvest and prepared their new fields for next year's first crop. There were births and marriages. Jean McKay's son, John, made his appearance on August 23 and to celebrate the safe arrival of the baby who had almost been lost on the icy walk from Churchill Creek, McDonald gave the new father, Angus, "½ gal. rum ½ gal. rice 3 gal. oatmeal and a little loaf sugar of my own. . . ." William Sutherland's wife, Mary, had produced a daughter, Christy, two weeks earlier; both babies were baptized by McDonald, and the ceremonies were later (in 1823) recorded on the first page of the register of St. John's Church (now St. John's Anglican Cathedral, Winnipeg).

On August 25 there was further cause for rejoicing, when the thirty-three settlers who had remained at Churchill arrived at the settlement. In charge of the group was John Spencer, Miles Macdonell's sheriff, who had enforced the ill-advised pemmican seizures six months earlier.

There were only a few more days of calm before Duncan Cameron, the North West Company partner who was sent to take charge at Fort Gibraltar, arrived at the Forks with firm orders to do everything in his power to obliterate the settlement, and the knowledge that the Montrealers would tolerate no such thing as failure. With him came Alexander Macdonell, a cousin of Miles, but a clerk in the North West Company, who, on the way up, wrote to a friend that he and Cameron were "on our way to commence open hostilities against the enemy in Red River . . . something serious will undoubtedly take place — nothing but the complete downfall of the colony will satisfy some, by fair or foul means — a most desirable object if it can be accomplished — ." The Nor'Westers were determined that there would be no settlement to interfere with the fur trade.

Cameron appeared on the scene resplendent in a scarlet tunic borrowed from another Nor'Wester, Archibald Norman McLeod, claiming that he held a captain's commission in the Voyageurs Corps, a regiment which had disbanded some two years previously. To the settlers, and to the Métis as well, the sight of the uniform did just what was intended — it put doubt in their minds about the authority of their governor and his council, and gave some credence, however false, to Cameron's claim to authority. When he produced warrants signed by McLeod for the arrest of Miles Macdonell and John Spencer, they half believed in their validity, but when Spencer was actually taken into custody, they immediately rose up to protect their own and went in a body to Archy McDonald urging him to lead them to Fort Gibraltar to release the prisoner forcibly. Remembering Selkirk's order to avoid direct confrontation, McDonald refused to take such drastic action, and instead went himself to offer bail for the sheriff and plead for his release. His protests fell on deaf ears and Spencer was carried off in a North West canoe bound for Montreal before the bewildered and angry eyes of the settlers watching from the banks of the river.

It was the first firm step in the bitter, relentless campaign to destroy Selkirk's fledgling settlement. Cameron was to have a great measure of success in his cruel objective, but it took more than wining and dining and blandishments to lure these people from their lands. Before he achieved even temporary destruction of the settlement he had to commit violent crimes — leading his men to vandalism, arson and, in the end, mass murder.

During the early days of the autumn of 1814 Cameron was content to confine his campaign to one of friendship and offers of assistance. His smooth Gaelic tongue flattered the men of the settlement, confused as they were as to who was truly in authority over Assiniboia. "He began by prevailing upon several of the heads of families to visit him at the Forks," wrote Archibald McDonald, "where he treated them with the greatest attention; gave them dinners, balls, and large allowance of liquors and even of wine. . . ." In a later letter of McDonald's addressed to the Reverend John Strachan, he described Cameron's "pretensions of personal friendship towards them. He used to treat the men, on every occasion with rum, and the women with wine, shrub, tea, Buffaloe tongues; and in short, every luxury that his house could afford, entertaining them with sumptuous balls at least once a week. The common labourers were always made welcome, to sit down at his table, and partake of whatever he had."

Cameron played, too, on the feelings of the women, commiserating with them over the "dreadful situation" they found themselves in and striking terror in their hearts with vivid stories of the treachery and murderous instincts of the Indians, though, as McDonald asserted, "the Indians in the neighbourhood had always conducted themselves in a manner that proved their friendly intentions towards the Colony," and in fact had "resisted all his [Cameron's] solicitations to take up arms against us. One of their Chiefs [Peguis], even proposed to become a mediator, and to settle amicably whatever differences might have led to his hostility to the Colony," but he was "treated with contempt" by Cameron who "scoffingly called him the Peacemaker."

Although Cameron had no success in rousing the Indians against the colony, he fared better in his aims with the Métis. He had no trouble convincing them that the settlement was a threat to their way of life, and with the help of Cuthbert Grant and three other North West employees whom he appointed "captains of the Métis" he formed of them a force that would willingly perform any act of violence at his command, while he sat on the sidelines and denied responsibility.

Whatever might be said in retrospect about the events of that winter and spring at Red River, there is no doubt that Cameron's actions had the desired effect on many of the colonists, particularly on the young men and girls not long out of childhood, for whom the hardships and the challenges had come too soon. Robert Gunn, the piper, was the first to desert. George Campbell, a man of twenty-five, who with his wife and two-year-old daughter had arrived with the second party of Kildonan settlers in late August, had no time to establish any sense of loyalty to the settlement before he responded to the flattering attentions of "Captain" Cameron and set himself up as a leader amongst the youthful rebellious faction, and finally left the colony to join forces at the North West Company fort.

In the warmth and comfort of Cameron's house at Fort Gibraltar, lulled by the luxury of food and drink that was unavailable to them in the Spartan confines of their own rough log dwellings, many of Selkirk's people were gradually won over to the idea of abandoning the colony for the easier life that Cameron promised them in Upper Canada. "I have no interest whatever . . . but what humanity points out to me," he insisted, as he offered them transport in the North West canoes and the influence of the North West partners in procuring free lands for them in the East. Can one wonder that they fell under his spell?

Miles Macdonell had returned to the colony restored in health and spirit late in October, and Peter Fidler left soon after to spend the winter at Brandon House. Cameron had already made inroads on the loyalties of many of the settlers and it was a disgruntled collection of people who, encouraged by the "Captain," constantly made demands of the colony stores that could not be met. "It defies us to satisfy them," McDonald wrote in his journal. The few faithful were almost afraid to ally themselves with the governor. Macdonell had brought with him a few government muskets and organized some of the settlers into a company of volunteers "for their own defence and that of the colony," enrolling John Matheson, Junior, and a few of the strongest supporters as sergeants. Andrew McBeath refused the office of constable, and William Bannerman said he would accept it only if another settler would too "as he is already not well beloved by his countrymen merely for adhering to us so much. . . ." In mid-February the governor took a few men to the hunting camp at Fort Daer, near Pembina, leaving Archy McDonald to contend with the mettlesome crowd. Undeterred by temperatures of thirty and forty degrees below zero, men and women alike made frequent trips to Fort Gibraltar two miles up the river, never making a move without consulting Cameron and asking his advice. McDonald struggled to keep some of the men at wood-cutting to provide fuel for the winter fires, and as supplies grew short and word came from the governor that there was plenty of meat at Fort Daer, he assigned a group of the young single men to make the journey and bring back a supply of food for the rest of the settlers. His order brought on the first open revolt. Every excuse was called up in their refusal to undertake the trip, but in truth these unattached young people had already decided to abandon the settlement and go east. John Bruce, one of the senior settlers, shook his head and remarked to McDonald, "all the people that came with you are only children that do not know yet what is good for themselves." There was little to cheer the young councillor in the prospects, and when word came from Macdonell's camp that there was trouble with the Nor'Westers at Pembina too, McDonald wrote in his journal that it was "unpleasant to hear how happy are our settlers with this report."

As the winter of 1814–15 progressed the majority of the people responded to Cameron's overtures, but in spite of setbacks the settlement continued to make progress. There was a happy New Year's celebration in the old Scottish tradition, with the firing of guns, and a dram issued to the men, and several weddings provided excuse for feasting and dancing as the months passed. McDonald had a cariole built by Jean-Baptiste Lagimodière, then employed at the settlement as a buffalo hunter, for which he paid fifteen dollars, and took pleasure in driving it around the colony. John Matheson, who had been overseer on the long walk from Churchill to York Factory, was appointed schoolmaster and all the youngsters in the settlement were in regular attendance in the classroom until many of them were withdrawn by their parents when they moved to the North West house in the spring. In March the foundation was laid for the colony's first mill, and work on the project was still going on in May, a month after a large body of people had already left the settlement.

It was all in vain. So successfully had Cameron sown his seeds of discontent, he was bound to reap the harvest. Early in April "the greater part of the settlers removed with their families and all their effects to Mr. Cameron's house," taking with them tools, farming utensils and arms belonging to Selkirk, as well as the twenty-five muskets and bayonets furnished to the colony by the British government. It marked the end of the long winter siege, but the beginning of a more overt intimidation that eventually drove even the staunchest of the Red River settlers to abandon their homes.

The day of the final desertion, April 3, George Campbell led a party of the most aggressive young settlers in an assault on the colony's government house, "arresting" McDonald and James White, the colony's new surgeon, along with James Bourke, a clerk and assistant storekeeper. Bearing a letter from Cameron to McDonald in which the Nor'Wester "authorized the settlers" to take possession of the settlement's field pieces, Campbell told his former leader that his people were taking the artillery "in case Capt. McDonell would attempt to make use of them to stop us as we are now going to leave the country." Cameron had done his work well. He had succeeded in convincing a large body of the men and women Lord Selkirk had transported to Red River not only that their own interests would be better served if they abandoned the colony, but also that they were in some way justified in robbing and plundering their patron's belongings. Alexander McLean, the "one settler of the rank of a gentleman" whom Selkirk had encouraged with a grant of ten thousand acres back in 1812, was one of the few who attempted to resist the attackers, and for his trouble was choked by one of his former fellows. Cameron himself "with twelve or fourteen of his men, all armed, assisted the settlers in making their way into one of the colonial warehouses, and robbed it of its artillery," Archy McDonald wrote later. "He shook hands with the ring leaders of the thieves, and distributed drams to the whole of the banditti."

Of the settlers who remained to defend the colony, the majority were the older men and their families. McLean stayed. George Sutherland, senior, came to McDonald — "the old man in tears" — protesting his desire to help him and the governor and "that his shame hung over him . . . for some time back that he would acquaint me of the barbarous intentions of his countrymen. . . ." Alex Sutherland was anxious to stay, to see "whether his parents may come out next fall," and John Matheson as well, both these young men newly married to girls who had been with them on the walk from Churchill. John Bruce, a man of over sixty years, determined to stay behind and Archy McDonald guaranteed him a piece of land "near at hand . . . with seeds & provisions sufficient to support you untill you can raise them out of your own land."

But at the same time John Matheson, senior, Andrew McBeath and Alexander Gunn went to the North West fort, "muskets on their shoulders going to get dogs & sleds to take the women." At about six o'clock that night "3 dogs & sleds & 2 horse sleds passed to the NW" with some of the settlers' baggage and a strong guard of eight or ten men with "screw bayonets."

Two days later an armed party of more than seventy men, led by George Campbell, Cuthbert Grant and William Shaw, the two latter Métis sons of North West partners, descended upon the settlement, forced their way past the sentries and broke into the mess room, where McDonald, White and McLean were questioning Donald McKinnon, a Hudson's Bay Company indentured servant who had abandoned his post for the North West fort and who had been taken prisoner that evening on orders from the governor.

"Campbell & Grant were the two first faces that I saw," McDonald recorded in his diary, "at the same time presenting their pistols to me & threatening vengeance against us all three. . . . they now entered the room as many of French & settlers as possible, every one exclaiming against us & not a single one of them capable of addressing us with law or reason. Grant asked me where was my authority to apprehend McKinnon. I told him . . . that I had my superior officer's authority for it at the same time took up his contract and said that that was sufficient power to bring him into custody. Damn your contract, say[s] Grant." The "prisoner" himself told them to "show no violence on his account" and after about fifteen minutes of threatening "fury & madness" and brandishing of arms the invaders "marched off" to the river bank where they fired several aimless volleys into the night air.

In two days there were only about eighty settlers left at the colony village. The remainder were crowded into makeshift quarters at the "French" house at Fort Gibraltar. The governor returned from Pembina within days of the exodus to find the remaining small band still determined to resist. Regular guards were mounted to keep watch for marauders, and Macdonell organized his forty able-bodied men into a company. "Captain McLean, Lieutenant McDonald and Ensign Bourke," and a volunteer, John Richard McKay, each headed a "division" which thereafter practised military manoeuvres twice daily in a comic opera show of strength and bravado. It was hardly enough to intimidate the hundreds of people assembled at Fort Gibraltar, or the rallying band of Métis gathered by Alexander Macdonell, Cuthbert Grant and William Shaw at Frog Plain.

But even so feeble a resistance as this was too much for Cameron to tolerate. He had orders to destroy the Red River settlement and nothing but total obliteration would do. As soon as travel became possible after the spring breakup, he planned to send the deserting settlers with the North West brigade to Montreal, but he was determined that those who still remained loyal to the colony should be driven away and that he would take their governor prisoner. The steady campaign of night attacks, galloping ponies and war cries in the neighboring woods, and a further erosion of the loyalty of the few people who remained at Fort Douglas continued through the month of May. "Some families of the settlers were even dragged as prisoners out of their houses, because they refused to go to Canada, in the canoes of the North West Company. . . . Cameron himself threatened to put some of them in irons for the same reason." Early in June, when the North West Company had moved the settlers under their wing to the Métis camp at Point Future (Frog Plain), Alexander Macdonell led his Métis in a raid which resulted in their carrying off the colony's few cattle, slaughtering the bull and feasting on it around their campfire that same night. Miles Macdonell was taken prisoner and later released, but it was evident that even more violent measures were necessary to achieve the North West Company's aims.

From Archy McDonald's daily journal, June 10, 1815:
About three o'clock in the morning a large body of men singing a war song . . . passed down behind our dyke. . . . they are constantly riding up & down in twos & threes all day. . . . about 10 at night the war whoop was again put up behind our ditch, all hands turned out. . . . after the elapse of about ½ an hour seeing that they were determined to remain in ambush with some evil intentions Mr. McLean & I with 4 men went up to challenge them, but they would make no answer & at

last we saw & heard them making ready for fire — so immediately the action commenced between them & us six only, as our men from the houses could not have fired at them without hurting us. After the discharge of a few rounds we retired under cover of the houses & then our artillery began, so they soon desisted. . . .

It was scare tactics of a most miserable sort, but the following day matters became more serious. "Sunday AM our men fired at not far from the house." Alexander McLean and Duncan Macdonell were both wounded, and John Warren was fatally injured, though he was to lie in agony for weeks before he finally succumbed. "The Enemy consisted of about 40 & I believe the composition was of all nations, viz. natives, half bloods, Scotch, Irish, English & Canadians. . . . the Hudson's Bay Company's men fired not a single shot tho' their House was marked thro' with no less than 10 or 12 balls. . . . In consequence of the havoc they made our men are willing to surrender."

Next day, however, they found fresh courage. Miles Macdonell was still in residence at government house and his people agreed to try to hold out. Cameron and his fellow officers at Fort Gibraltar promptly issued a series of letters claiming they had a valid warrant for the governor's arrest on charges that he had stolen the North West Company pemmican the preceding year, and demanding his surrender. It was a feeble band of frightened men and women who huddled together at Fort Douglas to decide the best course to follow.

"The state of affairs this evening is miserable," wrote McDonald on June 14, "the livestock & other preparations made here for some years back are in a declining state. Our horses have been stolen & shot with arrows, our pigs worried by dogs, our cattle slaughtered, & part of our cultivated fields still without the seed in the ground. The lives of the few families we have under our protection have been threatened . . . all this at the instigation of the N.W. proprietors."

McDonald's orderly mind was offended too by the chaos existing in the provisions and accounts of the colony. Through most of the winter he had spent all his spare time trying to put the books in order, sorting out the untidy accumulation left behind by John Spencer, and keeping up to date with the debits and credits of his own people as they came and went. He was well aware that the deserters were going off to Canada owing considerable sums to Selkirk: "The little labour they did on the Establishment . . . goes but a little way in settling the debt." To add to this, the stores were in a "shocking" state. "The Bale & all the soft goods are laid about forming Batteries to the walls of the Houses. The Grocery & Ironwork are equally bad, everything is thrown out of its place, which will occasion the greatest confusion & trouble when the inventory is to be made out."

In spite of the hopeless outlook, the little group were determined to try to preserve their lands. The settlers met with Cameron and his fellows trying to negotiate a truce of some sort, but the colony's arbiters were unaware that the Nor'Westers had no intention of honoring any agreements they might make. And while conferences were going on between the officers of both camps, the Métis and the more aggressive settlers continued to intimidate the remnant of people who remained at the colony. On the evening of June 15 plans had been made for the wedding of John McIntyre to Catherine Sutherland, and when friends went down to the village to bring the bride-to-be back to government house for the ceremony they found that some of the settlers had been taken prisoner by the deserters. McDonald went down to investigate and as he approached the house where the girl was, he was surrounded by a group of armed men who attempted to take him in charge. "I . . . drew my sword & took out a pistol, steped [sic] backwards till I got myself supported behind by a high bank & then was able to keep them off. All the messengers I had sent down came now out & some more of the Irish lads who were down seeing Mr. Warren. . . . I told them all to hould out and not surrender, says they, you better surrender also for they are numerous & all armed." The resistance was crumbling and McDonald was left alone to push his way through the crowd. The governor wrote in his journal that night that his young friend had "cleared his way with his dagger, by his swiftness he got off — a shot was fired at him which missed."

The following morning the enemy had moved their camp to within half a mile of Fort Douglas, where the settlers had their headquarters, and the colors of the North West Company were flapping boldly in the light June breezes. Cameron sent a constable and three men with an order for White, McDonald, Sutherland, and Fidler to deliver "the prisoner" Miles Macdonell.

There were further negotiations, and finally the governor himself went out halfway on the plain between the two camps to meet Kenneth McKenzie, a North West partner who had arrived from Montreal earlier in the month, to try to find an "honourable" way out. He returned to his people convinced that he had no alternative but to surrender, assured by the Nor'Wester that the settlement would no longer be molested if he did so. He walked to the North West fort before breakfast on June 17 and gave himself up to Duncan Cameron.

It was not to end there. "Peace is now established," wrote Archy McDonald in his journal. "We would have been in the field but the misfortune is that we cannot muster a single horse." Not only were their horses gone; the Métis had taken possession of their farmyard, the barn and the mill; they had plundered the farmhouse, burning their fences and trampling the nearby fields. Any idea that the Nor'Westers intended to give up the fight now that the governor had been taken into custody was immediately dispelled by the arrival of a further decree from the enemy camp. "We were astonished to hear ourselves & the H.B.C. warned to leave this river in the course of five days," wrote McDonald. "Our situation is worse than ever." Miles Macdonell sent a message from his captivity, urging them "to hold out to the last," but the people finally acknowledged the hopelesness of their situation.

On June 21, Miles Macdonell was carried off, a prisoner, in one of the Montreal-bound North West canoes. Accompanying the brigade was "Captain" Duncan Cameron, and part of the flotilla was made up of canoes bearing one hundred and forty of Selkirk's settlers, between forty and fifty families, who were transported to York (Toronto), later to make their homes in Upper Canada (Ontario), some in Gwillimbury Township, south of Lake Simcoe, and some in the district south of London. Alexander Macdonell remained behind, in charge of the North West post and the Métis camp at Frog Plain, determined to tidy up his mission and drive the remaining settlers away from Red River for the last time.

That evening, in a strangely sad ceremony, Archy McDonald read the belated marriage rites for two of his faithful. "As John McIntyre & Kitty Sutherland have been disappointed in being married by the Capn [Macdonell] before he went off, &

there being no other Justice of the Peace in this country, I have this evening joined them together before witness." At ten minutes past two next morning the last siege began. Buoyed up by the effects of the victory celebrations, Alexander Macdonell's Métis corps descended upon the sleeping settlers, firing on their houses for twenty-five minutes without a single shot fired in return. There was no point in resisting. Most of their arms and ammunition had been confiscated, and their numbers were small against so formidable an assault.

It was only a matter of days before the last survivors of the settlement moved off toward Jack River. As they gathered together what possessions they could manage to transport and made preparations for their departure, word came that the two Saulteaux Indian chiefs were on their way from the Indian village at Netley Creek at the foot of Lake Winnipeg, "to take up our cause." It was too late for any reprieve. McLean's comfortable dwelling and outbuildings were already in flames and others of the settlers' houses being put to the torch by Alexander Macdonell's men amid shouts of joy and triumph. When the familiar figures of Peguis and the old Arrowleg chief appeared at the settlement followed by thirty-five of their young warriors, they paraded two by two past the still smoking ruins. The brave little band of settlers hoisted their flag in greeting and led their guests into the mess room "to smoke our pipes & talk upon the proceeding of affairs."

In the courteous and leisurely Indian tradition the haranguing began. McDonald, Fidler, Doctor White and James Sutherland represented the settlers' views:

We are in great mourning & we have sent for you to tell you of our griefs, your friend our Chief when he was taken from us told us that if we wanted protection to send for you, he told us to tell you that we were sent here to do good to Indians to feed them & cloath them & not to make war upon them — Our great father told us never to redden the lands with the blood of his children, & in order that we may live in peace your friend gave himself up to the Canadians, but it seems now that nothing but our blood can satisfy our enemies. They have told us that we must leave these lands, never to return, they have taken our horses from us, & destroyed some of our cattle, you see the smoak arising from our burnt Houses. They have killed one of our brothers, wounded another, & deprived another of the use of his arms and one of his legs. They hide themselves in the bushes every day & continually fire upon us, — we could return that fire if your friend had not told us to be careful of the blood of our father's children — you see us with sorrowful hearts tying up our goods in order to leave these lands, but we could not leave these lands without sending for you that you might tell us to leave them, because we consider those who are driving us away from your lands as having no right so to do — half of them were not born upon these lands, & the greater part of them are the sons of slave women. We know these lands are yours, if you tell us to leave them we are ready to do so, but if you tell us to remain here we will not leave these lands, but you must make peace for us with these people, we think that they want to spoil your land & then return to the lands from whence they came, we have repeatedly asked them to come and smoak the pipe of peace with us, but their answer always is that we must go away, or they will take our property and burn our Houses over our heads — We do not send you to make war on these people, we only want you to make peace for us . . . we are full of grief, we love these lands, we love our Indian brethren, and our hearts are swelled with the thoughts of our separation. . . . Tis not our custom to talk bad of anybody — you know our enemies, & have known them from your childhood, you all know they could never bear two fires upon their land, for what reason we know not. . . . Last night our wounded brother was driven from his house you now see it in ashes, we have another dying brother that they desired us to remove or they will burn him in the House, this is very hard, they treat us more cruely than the Sioux would do, they will not even let us dye in peace. . . .

The silent Indians listened attentively, puffing intermittently on their pipes. When the settlers' representatives finally reached the end of their addresses Peguis rose to his feet:

We thank you for your speech; What is the matter with these people? You do not trade skins from us, why then are they always quarreling with you? They always had greedy hearts & jealous minds, and always drove away those who brought us our necessaries — when your messenger came to our Tents, he found my Brother Chief and our young men assembled in order to come to your assistance as we had been told that the Canadians had carried off our Brother — We will offer these people the Pipe of Peace, and if they will not smoak with you we will not restrain our young men more, but shall join them in the Cry of War — What do these people mean by driving you from these lands? Had we no other support than what they give us, we might freeze in our tents, die of want and be at the mercy of our enemies . . . nor have we forgotten how pitiful and poor we were before your arrival here. . . . I have always loved the white people, and have always taught my young men to be kind to them . . . the hearts of my young men are vexed and inclined to war, it is with difficulty we can restrain them — I hope to procure you Peace — but if my land must be reddened with your blood — my blood & that of my children shall mix with yours and like a stone we will sink together.

Peguis turned to his warriors and motioned them to follow him. Half of them he directed to remain with the settlers while he led the others to the "French house" to try to make peace. Four hours later he returned with his men to the waiting crowd.

My children my heart is grieved — I return with shame — Those people have no Ears to listen to the words of Peace — they say you must leave these Lands — they are very strong — They have big Guns and their Fort is full of men — we are too few to contend with them at present — never mind, go you to Jack River and collect a force, and we will send word to the Chiefs of the Red Lake and elsewhere — had they known of this business they would have been here before this, because they do not love you less than us. . . . Take courage; muster strong — and make haste to come back, for as soon as the young Duck flies — you will find all your Friends assembled at the bottom of the River to conduct you to your gardens — when you embark, myself and young men, will sit down in your Boats, for I fear these peoples hearts are bad and perhaps they would pillage you.

On June 27, with the two wounded men Alexander McLean and John Warren each occupying a boat, a few horned cattle in another and the colony's remaining sheep in another, the forty settlers (thirteen families) still loyal to the settlement set off for the Indian village at Netley Creek, accompanied by Peguis and his band. On the river banks, thirty young Métis on horseback, headed by two of the North West Company clerks, watched them embark.

"We have been driven from a country whose fertile soil, wholesome climate, natural productions & beautiful scenery promised to us and our children *ages* of *happiness*," wrote Archibald McDonald in his journal that night.

CHAPTER FOUR

The Outrages Have All Been on One Side

1815 – 1816

Even as the last of the loyal settlers were embarking at Red River to abandon their fire-blackened farms, Selkirk was gathering yet another group in Scotland to set out for the colony that summer. He had found another governor to take Miles Macdonell's place, and Robert Semple, the Boston-born British businessman he had chosen, was full of confidence that he would be able to overcome all the problems that had proved too much for his predecessor.

Neither he nor Selkirk had any idea of the desperate state of affairs in Assiniboia. They believed that the eighty-four new colonists would arrive at a thriving village and strengthen the hand of the original settlers against the opposition of the North West Company. Selkirk had been warned by Colin Robertson, the disillusioned old Nor'Wester who had recently joined the Hudson's Bay Company, that Duncan Cameron would stop at nothing to achieve the aims of his Montreal partners, but back in England he had no conception of the lawlessness of the Indian country and he put his faith in the "benign protection of the laws of England."

As early as February 1815, after he had received word that the North West Company had "organized a plan for destroying the settlement," Selkirk applied to the Colonial Office to supply a military force to protect his people, and a few weeks later Lord Bathurst, the Colonial Secretary, wrote that he had given instructions to the Governor of Canada to provide "such protection to the settlers on Red River, as could be afforded without detriment to His Majesty's service in other quarters." For Selkirk, that word was enough, and he went confidently ahead with his plans for enlarging the colony, and even decided to take his own family to Canada so that he could go to Red River himself and personally direct its progress.

Meanwhile the Hudson's Bay Company had decided to step up its opposition to the Canadian traders in the rich Athabasca territory. The Napoleonic Wars had caused a falling off in fur sales in Europe, and dwindling profits made both companies anxious to improve their trade. The Hudson's Bay Company had traditionally been less aggressive than their rivals. It had been their practice to wait at their forts along the Bay for the Indians to bring the pelts to them, while the Canadians struck into the interior and actively sought out the fur hunters. When Colin Robertson came into their midst, he provided the leadership for a strong expedition to go into the Athabasca District and compete with the Nor'Westers. As Archy McDonald and his group of settlers were moving north on Lake Winnipeg toward Jack River, Robertson and his party were already on their way from Montreal.

On July 22 Robertson arrived at the fugitive colonists' camp near the Hudson's Bay post at Jack River. Two days earlier John Warren had died of the wounds received in the attack at the settlement on June 11, and the remaining settlers were still confused and undecided about how they were to make their way back to re-establish their village. Robertson was warmly welcomed by Thomas Thomas, an old Hudson's Bay officer who had been appointed governor of the Northern Territories and successor to Miles Macdonell pending the arrival of Semple. Thomas was glad to turn over his authority for the colony to the newcomer and Robertson was sure he knew where the others had gone wrong. "I cannot help thinking but that Major White & McDonald could have made a better defence," he wrote to Selkirk at the time, "but such was the influence of the N.W. Co. over the minds of these young men that they hardly thought themselves safe at Winipic settlement. The N.W. Co. owe the success of their depredations entirely to a want of energy on the part of their opponents." Such were Robertson's views. He stepped in with enthusiasm, and after meeting with Alexander McLean and a few of the other settlers drew up plans for their future with but little consultation with McDonald, White or Fidler.

McDonald had spent the weeks since his arrival at Jack River completing his work on the account books and preparing his notes for a statement of events at the settlement to take back to England. He was determined to return on the Fall boats and report first-hand to Selkirk, and though he resented Robertson's interference and his officious attitude, he was relieved to have someone to take over the charge. Thomas appointed Robertson to manage the colony, leaving the Athabasca Brigade to go west in charge of his second-in-command John Clarke, and McDonald began his preparations to set off for the Bay — and home.

On August 27, McDonald arrived at York Factory, just two hours after Robert Semple disembarked his eighty-four new settlers from the *Prince of Wales*. The newcomers had already had time to hear the disastrous tales of the destruction of the colony and the scattering of their friends and relations, but their dismay was tempered by McDonald's accounts of the determination of the remaining settlers to re-establish their homes, and they were soon restored to "their former good spirits . . . and ardently wished to proceed to the settlement." Reluctantly, McDonald volunteered to return to Red River with the new governor and his party, but knowing the young man's desire to go back to England, Semple decided that it would be wise for him to continue on.

Semple, like Robertson, thought the colony's leaders had been timid and wanting in confidence. He had nothing but scorn for Miles Macdonell and considered "his removal a benefit to the settlement which . . . could never have flourished under his auspices." At the same time he acknowledged the need for some sort of military force at the colony to augment the authority of its civilian leaders: soldiers were "absolutely requisite for the stability of any colony . . . a strong party is not necessary . . . an old sergeant and 20 men with muskets & great coats to act *au nom du roi* are all that would be required," and he advocated a more aggressive and forceful reaction to the North West Company. Time was to reveal the rashness of his attitude.

Of the others he had words to say too, putting his views in a letter he gave McDonald to take home to Selkirk. White he dismissed as a "slave to liquor"; McDonald he thought "by no means . . . yet worthy of extensive powers" but he was "happy in having Mr. A. McDonald to whom I can refer Your Lordship for every detail. . . . It is true he is not disposed to think anything amiss of his former Chief, but that is as it should be. No doubt Captain McD. was frank and polite in his manners, pleasing in his conversation and liberal to his friends. How natural it is for a young man to conclude that he who possesses these good qualities must also possess every other."

There was the usual bustle and confusion of late summer at York Factory. The Company ships being loaded with furs for the return trip, Hudson's Bay servants awaiting orders to proceed to the interior with the winter's provisions, and the newly arrived settlers with their worldly goods (and some of the possessions of the earlier parties which had been left behind for want of transport) — all contributed to the scene of disorder. The fur traders took it in their stride. To Semple and his charges the jumble of "boxes, bales & casks . . . hardware lying upon cloth and the wet dropping through parts of the roof" was an undreamt-of sight. Their ten days at the fort was an unexpected initiation into the world of the British fur trader in the Indian country.

But it was not only their bewilderment at the strange ways of this land they had adopted that was bothering them. Many of the new arrivals were relatives of the settlers who had defected with Duncan Cameron to Upper Canada. They had come expecting to find homes prepared for them by their sons and daughters. Instead, they discovered that the young people had gone off, leaving unfulfilled obligations and debts behind them. Along with the "circumstantial narrative" and "mass of documents" that McDonald took with him when he boarded the *Man of War* in late September was a deposition asking him to "use all the means he possibly can to return back to Red River our friends & children by representing their conduct in the late disturbance at the colony in as favourable a light as possible to the Earl of Selkirk." It was signed by James Sutherland (X), Angus

Matheson, Alexr. Murray, John Bannerman (X), George MacKay (X), William Bannerman (X) and Widow Gunn (X).

Unknown to McDonald as he sailed out through Hudson Strait, the Selkirks were already on board a Liverpool ship well on their way to New York. He arrived back in England on November 5 to learn that he had missed his patron by two months. He went instead to the headquarters of the Hudson's Bay Company on Fenchurch Street in London, and it was Andrew (Wedderburn) Colvile who received the detailed reports from the colony. The earl himself heard the news of the destruction of the settlement in New York, just before setting off for Montreal in mid-October.

In spite of his disappointment, there was work for McDonald to do in Britain. The word of one who had been there was an important weapon in the campaign to get the Colonial Office to provide support and protection for the colony. The North West Company had influential friends in London and it was no easy task for Selkirk's supporters to rouse public opinion against the outrages at the settlement.

"The case is already so strong that Govt. will not allow it to pass by without serious investigation," Selkirk wrote to Colvile from New York. "When the circumstances which did take place are combined with the threats which have been uttered for these four years past, they afford evidence of such a systematic & determined defiance of law, as no civilized govt. can allow to triumph in success & audacious impunity." He was wrong. Even when he got to Montreal and wrote repeatedly to Sir Gordon Drummond, the acting governor of Canada, warning him that "if you persevere in your intention to do nothing . . . there is . . . every reason to expect that . . . many lives may be lost," no action was taken. Drummond, whose information on the Indian country came primarily from William McGillivray, the most influential of the Montreal partners of the North West Company, wrote back in April 1816 that both fur companies must abstain from their "mutual outrages." To which Selkirk replied: "the outrages have not been mutual but all on one side."

While Selkirk struggled with officialdom in Montreal, and his agents at York amassed provisions for the strong party that he planned to take to Red River in the spring, his friends in England did what they could to call attention to the plight of the colony. Archibald McDonald went north to visit family and friends in the Highlands, stopping to see Alexander McDonald of Dalilia and his wife and daughters at Callander and then going on to Glencoe, where he visited his father's grave on Eilean Munda, the McDonald Burial Isle, and comforted his old mother who had been widowed that summer. In the villages and towns he passed through he told the tragic story of the Kildonan settlers and roused sympathy for Selkirk and his colonists. The "circumstantial narrative" he had written before leaving Hudson Bay was turned over to a printer in London, and in March of 1816 the little sixteen-page *Narrative respecting the destruction of the Earl of Selkirk's Settlement upon Red River in the Year 1815* appeared on the London scene to be distributed wherever interested men and women could be found to bring support to Selkirk's cause.

That same month, in Montreal, Selkirk was being attacked in print by an unexpected assailant, the Reverend John Strachan, D.D., Rector of York (later Bishop of Toronto), whose open *Letter to the Right Honourable the Earl of Selkirk, on his Settlement at the Red River, near Hudson's Bay* was a vicious personal onslaught. Strachan's information, based largely on material supplied by his friends in the North West Company, was causing a stir in Canada, and as McDonald prepared to sail for New York that spring, a copy of the *Letter* reached his hands in London. Whether at the suggestion of Colvile and John Halkett, another brother-in-law of Selkirk and an influential Hudson's Bay stockholder (Halkett was married to Selkirk's sister, Lady Katherine Douglas), or on his own initiative is not known, but McDonald undertook to reply in kind. It was the beginning of the active phase of the "paper controversy" that surrounded the Selkirk settlement.

"There are few controversies in Canadian history on which more contemporary printer's ink has been spilled than the struggle between Lord Selkirk and the North West Company over the Red River settlement," wrote Dr. W. S. Wallace later. Selkirk's own earlier publications, *Observations on the present state of the highlands of Scotland, with a view of the causes and probable consequences of emigration* (London, 1805) and *Sketch of the British fur-trade in North America, with observations relative to the North-West Company of Montreal* (London, 1816), had already been widely read, and the latter particularly had shocked its readers with the accounts of methods used by the Canadian company in its trade with the Indians, although no defence was forthcoming to the accusations it contained. Strachan, though he had never been anywhere near Hudson Bay or the Forks of the Red and Assiniboine rivers, represented the North West view, and although he later asserted that "in this contest I was neutral" and that his "motive was entirely disinterested & had nothing to do with the Rivalship with the North West company or the propriety of the fur trade," it was well known that he was a close friend of William McGillivray, and other Montreal fur merchants, and that his wife, the widow of Andrew McGill, had North West connections.

When Alexander Macdonell sent him a copy of Selkirk's "prospectus" (*Sketch of the . . . fur-trade*), Strachan wrote to McGillivray for information on the geography of the Red River area, transportation routes, Indian attitudes and any "other local circumstances worth mentioning [that] may occur," saying that he intended to write "a public letter on the subject as I conceive the whole to be a gross imposition on the nation and calculated to divert the stream of emigration from the Canadas." Strachan was convinced that the settlement would eventually become part of the United States, and that the Scots settlers who would be so welcome in Upper Canada would be swallowed up by the Americans. His ignorance of the local conditions brought forth criticism of the quality of the "sand and gravel" soil and the length of time it would take to clear the land, and he predicted that the settlers would all be massacred by hostile Indians before they had time to establish themselves. He called up statistics provided by McGillivray to illustrate the remoteness of the settlement, reducing the length of time the rivers from the Bay were open for navigation to eighty-three days, while the more usual time, as in the year of his writing, was 174 days. "We may very safely say," he wrote, "that no British colony will ever approach nearer than twelve or thirteen hundred miles" of Lake Winnipeg.

More hurtful than all his remarks about the practicality of the settlement were Strachan's accusations that Selkirk was a mere "land speculator" seeking personal gain. It was an unfair blow when it was only too painfully clear to Selkirk himself that the settlement was likely to cost him his fortune. Already he had invested thousands of pounds in the scheme, and in Montreal that spring he was forced to order the sale of lands he held in

New York to provide cash to outfit his expedition to Red River that summer.

Archy McDonald rushed to defend Selkirk's name — and his own, for Strachan had accused him of being "harsh and unkind" to the settlers in his care, and he was "desirous of clearing my own reputation, and those of my friends, of the stain you have attempted to fix upon them." In a series of four long letters which appeared in the *Montreal Herald* in May and June of 1816 and were later published in pamphlet form, he discussed point by point the criticisms levelled by the churchman in a literary style that was to disappear with the coming of the laws of libel. Strachan himself admitted to being "dreadfully cut up" in the exchange, but McDonald felt justified in replying to his "uncourteous attack"; since the rector had "voluntarily stepped out of the pulpit and thrown aside the restraints which a regard for the decency becoming your office as a Clergyman, might have imposed, the freedom with which I reply requires no apology." He expressed amazement that a man of the cloth should support the actions of the North West Company — "acts of unparallelled barbarity. . . . the attempt to ruin the Colony, was entirely the work of the partizans of the North West Company, employed for that purpose, under the superintendence of their agent, Mr. Duncan Cameron. That statement is grounded on facts, which all their counter-assertions cannot weaken, nor all their falsehoods overturn."

McDonald had the advantage of having been there. Strachan soon realized he had made a mistake in meddling in affairs of which he had no first-hand knowledge and he withdrew into silence on the matter of Selkirk and his settlement, but not before he had interviewed some of the settlers who had been brought to York in the North West Company canoes, and according to McDonald "employed your well-known rhetorical powers to embellish the statements of which the emigrants only furnished the groundwork." The depositions appended to Strachan's pamphlet appear to have been written by him after meeting Alexander Matheson, John McPherson, Andrew McBeath and William Gunn, and McDonald discussed their complaints at length. "Notwithstanding Macbeath and Gunn's complaints about the prices [of provisions from the colony stores] . . . I have to inform you, that never was a penny paid by either of them." In fact, Mc-

Donald asserted, although McBeath was credited in the account books for labor to the amount of £1 14s 6d (three shillings and their food for one day's mowing) and Gunn and his father (Sandy Gunn) with £5 7s 8d, "the Dr. sides of their accounts are much more considerable."

To Strachan's remarks about the poor quality of the soil, McDonald replied that "the fertility of the soil at the Colony, surpassed any that they had ever seen . . . they had only to plough the ground and put in the seed . . . our returns were beyond any that I ever heard of in any part of Scotland. Had the crops not been trampled down by the men and horses employed as cavalry by the North West Company, our returns last season would have been such, as to render us independent of all supplies of those articles from any other quarter." In fact, McDonald told his correspondent, "at the time you were despatching your Epistle, [the Colony had] risen from its ashes, being so far re-established, that although the houses had been burnt to the ground, and as much done as our enemies thought necessary to destroy the standing crops; yet that by the end of September, the settlers, with the assistance of the native Indians (whose imagined hostility you take such pains to describe) had secured and housed in 1500 bushels of wheat, besides other grain and potatoes."

For the colony had "risen from its ashes." Colin Robertson had led the remaining settlers down from Jack River in the fall to find that John McLeod and the three Hudson's Bay men who had remained at the Forks had erected a few crude buildings and encouraged the trampled crops back to life in preparation for their return. Robertson promptly moved in on Fort Gibraltar, retrieved two of the cannon which had been stolen from Fort Douglas, and took Cameron prisoner, releasing him only on condition that he cease his opposition to the settlement. He then exercised his considerable charm and influence on the Métis, bringing them around to a state of almost friendly truce with the settlers. All was calm when Robert Semple arrived with his new party of settlers in November, and although these two strong personalities were to clash during the winter months with resulting rash decisions, it seemed for the moment at least that the problems were near to being solved.

In the spring of 1816, when McDonald returned from England to find Selkirk in Montreal readying his impressive expedition for their westward journey — with a large band of recently retired Swiss mercenaries, of the de Meuron regiment, engaged as soldier-settlers — the colony again appeared strong and hopeful. As the vituperation flew back and forth on the printed pages, the more practical business of re-establishing the settlement was steadily going forward. Unfortunately, the period of calm was to be short-lived. The Nor'Westers had been concentrating their trouble-making on the Athabasca territory where sixteen of John Clarke's party who had come west with Colin Robertson had starved to death that winter. They were about to renew their assaults on the settlers at Red River.

Cuthbert Grant, the Métis leader, had withdrawn to Qu'-Appelle for the winter months, and at the instigation of Alexander Macdonell, the Nor'Wester, he was gathering his followers from as far west as Fort des Prairies (Edmonton) to descend upon Red River in the spring. "A storm is gathering to the northward," Macdonell wrote to Cameron, ". . . little do they know their situation last year was but a joke — the new nation under their leaders are coming forward to clear their native soil of intruders. . . ." As Miles Macdonell set off in May from Montreal with the advance party of Selkirk's expedition, Grant, with his new title "Captain-General of the Métis," was rallying his men for a move to Frog Plain from the opposite direction.

At the colony, relations between Robertson and Semple had deteriorated to the point where Robertson was ready to abandon the settlers to their fate and return to England. In March he had seized the North West Express and intercepted an exchange of letters between Cameron and Alexander Macdonell which left no doubt of their plans for a violent attack on the colony in June. He led an assault on Fort Gibraltar and again imprisoned Cameron, in an attempt to immobilize the opposition who were dependent on their post at the Forks for the safe passage of the annual provisions for the interior. Had Robertson been on amiable terms with Semple and his men he might have remained to see them through the difficult time ahead. With Fort Douglas a hive of ill will, threats of duels and actual physical assaults, he decided to depart.

Semple sent his men to dismantle the empty North West fort and float the usable lumber downriver to strengthen the stockade at Fort Douglas. Nothing would have deterred the Nor'Westers in their openly avowed aims, but events of that spring at Red River gave them the excuse of provocation. Semple's actions could only aggravate the opposition, and he should have realized the foolhardiness of his behavior, knowing as he did that Alexander Macdonell was about to dispatch the Métis force. In fact they were already on their way, having attacked and captured the Hudson's Bay post at Brandon House en route. Even the Indians were watching and waiting for the assault. On June 17 they sent two emissaries to warn Semple that Grant and his men were nearing the settlement, offering their support to the colonists. Still believing that it would be possible to negotiate a lawful peace, Semple refused their help.

In the late afternoon on the 19th the line of horsemen was first sighted from the watchtower at Fort Douglas. In minutes many of the settlers gathered within the stockade. Semple himself took the spyglass and counted what appeared to be a band of about sixty or seventy men riding through the woods to the west in the direction of the colony village. He called for volunteers to go with him to meet the intruders and ask their business, and more than twenty men accompanied the governor as he walked out of the fort and followed the mounted party down toward the grove of Seven Oaks near the settlement. They had gone less than half a mile when they met a group of terrified men and women running helter-skelter from the fields, seeking the protection of the fort. Already some of their companions had been taken prisoner by the intruders, they reported, and on hearing this Semple sent John Bourke, his storekeeper, back to the fort to bring out a cannon.

By this time Grant's horsemen had seen Semple and his party advancing toward them. At a signal they wheeled around and encircled the helpless settlers in two wide wings, looking down on them from their excited mounts. One of them, Boucher, galloped forward, shouting at Semple. As he came near, Semple grabbed the horse's bridle and almost simultaneously a shot was fired. There was disagreement later about where that first shot came from, but it brought forth a general rattle of gunfire that felled Semple and nineteen of his men, while only one of the Métis lost his life. Semple was wounded in the hip and, according to an eyewitness account, his men gathered around him to see how serious his injury was. "While they were thus collected, in a small body in the centre, the party of horsemen, which had formed a circle around them, fired a general volley amongst them, by which the greater part were killed on the spot."

Grant came forward then and attempted to protect the wounded governor from further injury, but the frenzy and hysteria of the attackers was such that there was no stopping them. One of them murdered Robert Semple as he lay, and the whole frantic band went on to mutilate and plunder the bodies of their victims. When Peguis and a few of the Indians encamped nearby got permission from the Métis commander next morning to bring some of the bodies back to the fort for burial, the scene of carnage and devastation was horrifying. Stripped of their clothing, pierced with stab wounds, in some cases torn limb from limb, the dead lay scattered along the banks of the Red. Among their number, along with the governor and two of his principal aides, were Alexander McLean, Selkirk's one "gentleman" settler, and Dr. White.

Back at the fort, after a night of wild victory celebrations, the Métis made ready to drive the settlers once again from their lands. Stunned and sorrowing, the wives and children of the murdered men gathered up their meagre possessions, and with their fellow survivors prepared to board the boats that would take them (about two hundred in all) to Netley Creek. Two days out from Fort Douglas they met Archibald Norman McLeod, with eight other North West partners, and an armed band of about one hundred men in nine or ten canoes from Montreal, all jubilant to hear that the Métis force had been so successful in their attack on the settlement. The Nor'Westers had carefully avoided the actual clash, though many of their clerks and employees were involved, but they left no doubt in the minds of the watchful settlers that they knew well the plan of attack. McLeod asserted his authority as "magistrate" and conducted a search of the settlers' possessions, seizing the effects of the governor which were in their boats, including papers and documents relating to the colony. Cuthbert Grant had already taken over all of Lord Selkirk's property at Fort Douglas, when he banished the colonists from their homes.

Archibald McDonald, en route from Montreal with Selkirk, heard the disastrous news weeks later at Sault Ste. Marie. Miles Macdonell and his advance party were within a day's journey of

Fort Douglas in late June when they learned of the massacre. Immediately they turned back to intercept Selkirk, knowing that his flotilla bearing the de Meuron soldiers and the reinforcements for the settlement would be nearing the vast open waters of Lake Superior. From this vantage point it would seem that Seven Oaks signalled the point of no return for the settlers. To Selkirk it was the red flag which increased his determination to put down the lawless Nor'Westers. He refused to believe that British justice could continue to condone their deliberate attacks on what he regarded as a peaceful farming community. Convinced that he was on the side of the right, he determined in his capacity as a justice of the peace to take the law into his own hands, to proceed with his strong force to Fort William, hub of the North West empire in the West, and issue warrants for the arrest of William McGillivray and whichever of the Canadian partners he found at the fort.

He had the strong support of his two de Meuron officers, Captains Frederick Matthey and P. D'Orsonnens, to bolster him and he paid little heed to the objections of his doctor, John Allan, who knew the weakness of the earl's consumptive constitution, and Miles Macdonell, who feared that the opposition would not stop at murder to put Selkirk out of their way. Within days the great canoes were gliding swiftly past the north shores of Lake Superior. Selkirk got to the mouth of the Kaministikwia River first, paddled past the North West fort and set up camp about a mile upstream to await the rest of his guard. Within hours, the full force had arrived, twelve boatloads of the de Meurons in their scarlet tunics, canoe after canoe moving past Fort William under the astonished gaze of the North West servants and the Indians and Métis gathered around the post. They had not long to wait for the action they knew was inevitable.

Selkirk sent a messenger to McGillivray asking him why he was holding prisoner six men who were either fugitives from the settlement or employees of the Hudson's Bay Company. McGillivray replied that the men were not prisoners, and sent four of them to Selkirk's camp immediately, informing him that two had already gone on to Montreal. The four who were able to tell their story to Selkirk included one who had actually witnessed the massacre at the colony. The other three testified to events leading up to Cuthbert Grant's departure from Qu'Appelle with the

Métis corps, and the jubilant reactions of A. N. McLeod and other North West partners when they heard the news of the rout. Their stories bore out all that he had already heard, and they left no doubt about the complicity of the North West Company in the whole horrible affair.

Selkirk lost no more time. He had the first-hand evidence he needed. A constable was dispatched to arrest William McGillivray with a warrant charging him with treason and conspiracy, and as an accessory to murder. The earl had decided to match strength with strength. He was sure that the Nor'Westers could no longer be immune from the law.

Unfortunately, however righteous he may have felt, however right he may have been, Selkirk went on from there to stretch his actions beyond his magistrate's powers. It did not matter that the North West partners had been issuing and enforcing illegal warrants in the Indian territory for years. When the whole matter was brought to the courts in the months to come, Selkirk was judged on all sides to have been, at the least, hasty, and without doubt to have overstepped his authority.

For what he did was not only to arrest William McGillivray; he also imprisoned the two partners, Kenneth McKenzie and Dr. John McLoughlin, who accompanied the "Lord of the Northwest" when he was brought to answer the summons before Selkirk. The earl then sent Captain D'Orsonnens and twenty-five of his men to serve warrants on all the other partners then at Fort William. A struggle ensued and the de Meurons entered the fort and manned the guns that covered the stockade entrance. Selkirk's men had taken over the North West bastion. Although the partners were later allowed to return to their quarters — an ill-advised move as it turned out, because it gave them an opportunity to burn and destroy most of the papers and documents in the fort — they were humiliated in front of their own servants and the Métis and Indians they had impressed for so long. The proud, arrogant Nor'Westers were never quite the same again.

Next morning, August 14, 1816, word came to Selkirk that men from the North West fort had slipped past the de Meuron sentries in the dark, carrying out a quantity of arms. A search warrant was issued and Selkirk's men found a large cache of guns and ammunition hidden in the hayloft of a barn outside the fort, and near a swamp a few miles away eight barrels of gunpowder.

Whatever thoughts the Canadians had of resistance, there was no questioning Selkirk's strength. The partners were all housed, under guard of the numerous de Meuron sentries, in their own bunkhouse. Selkirk conducted an official court of inquiry, but it was a mere formality, an opportunity for him to come face to face with the formidable McGillivray. Within days the partners were sent off to Montreal to be dealt with by the authorities there. Not for a moment did Selkirk doubt the legality of his own behavior.

On August 18 three canoes under the command of a de Meuron officer, Lieutenant G. A. Fauché, carried off the prisoners — McGillivray and all but one of the arrested men — leaving Selkirk in charge of the most important post in the whole North West command. He was to learn much as he searched for evidence after their departure, a search that turned up, among other things, stolen packs of furs with the Hudson's Bay Company mark still faintly visible though superimposed with the brand of the North West Company, and, even more incriminating, a list in Alexander Macdonell's hand of the Métis who were to be rewarded for their part in the affair at Seven Oaks. The very fact that the partners had stayed up all night to destroy as many papers as they could proved that they knew they had much to hide.

With the North West partners on their way to Montreal and so much important evidence in his hands at Fort William, Selkirk decided to send Archy McDonald in the wake of Fauché and his prisoners to tell the tale firsthand to Lady Selkirk and his legal advisers in Montreal, and to deliver to them letters and papers documenting the seizure of the fort. Before he reached the east side of Lake Superior, McDonald heard that one of Fauché's three canoes had overturned just west of Sault Ste. Marie and that nine men had drowned, including Kenneth McKenzie, a de Meuron sergeant, and an Iroquois chief. McKenzie's body had been taken on to the Sault to be buried, but not all the victims had been recovered. As McDonald's canoe passed the site of the accident they found two more bodies, the Indian chief whom they recognized, and another Iroquois, and buried them on the spot.

Later that day, September 1, when he arrived at Charles Ermatinger's imposing stone house at the Sault, McDonald learned that McGillivray was well before him in the race to Montreal and, more than that, even though a prisoner, he had somehow managed to dispatch an express canoe in advance of Fauché's party to take his own account of the events at Seven Oaks and of Selkirk's "violent measures" at Fort William ahead of him, in an attempt to draw sympathy to the North West cause.

When McDonald arrived in Montreal in mid-October he was in time to hear news of the governor's appointment of a royal commission to travel to the Indian country to investigate the disturbances. It was a move Selkirk had been urging for months, and Lady Selkirk had herself been quietly working to bring about through her new friendship with the governor, Sir John Sherbrooke, and his wife. Even the North West Company, threatened as they now were by Selkirk's actions at Fort William, welcomed the news. Although one of the appointees, an undistinguished police magistrate from Quebec named John Fletcher, was to prove worse than useless, and finally had to be removed, the other, the Honourable William Coltman, a member of the executive council of Lower Canada who had legal training, was regarded as a fair and sensible person, and in a community where almost everyone had opinions about who was at fault in the much-talked-about fur trade war, he was as impartial a man as could be found.

Delighted as she was with Sherbrooke's decision to send his investigating team to the West, Lady Selkirk soon discovered she could not rest on her laurels. Rumors began to fly about Montreal that McGillivray, who had been released on bail immediately on his arrival back home, was organizing a secret force to retake Fort William. Through the weeks of October and November canoes were being dispatched singly or in pairs with orders to rendezvous at Sault Ste. Marie, where McGillivray would join them to lead the attack. He had applied for warrants for Selkirk's arrest on charges of theft of the guns at Fort William and he looked forward to turning the tables on his adversary at their next encounter.

Lonely and discouraged, longing for an opportunity to be with her husband and to talk over their mounting problems, Lady Selkirk turned to McDonald. He could go back, report to the earl on all the behind-the-scenes activities in Montreal, take her personal and private messages, and warn him of McGillivray's gathering "armada." The November days were getting

73

colder and there was already a hint of snow in the air when he set off to cover once again the 1,500-mile journey by canoe to the head of the lakes.

Coltman and Fletcher had begun their investigations at York, and McDonald followed them there and then went on to Nottawasaga on Georgian Bay. There he learned, as did the commissioners, that no more boats would get through that season. The ice had sealed the northern lakes and they all turned back to the East to await the coming of spring. McGillivray, too, was thwarted in his plans, and Selkirk was left to spend the winter quietly at Fort William.

In January, when he sent Miles Macdonell with D'Orsonnens and a party of his men over the snow to Red River, their arrival was so unexpected by the Nor'Westers that Selkirk's men took back Fort Douglas with ease and began to make ready for the return of the settlers and the coming of Selkirk that spring.

CHAPTER FIVE

They Cannot Take
From Us Our Good
Conscience

1817 - 1819

In Montreal, Lady Selkirk knew she had to continue actively to represent her husband's interests. Her friendship with the Sherbrookes did not blind her to the fact that the North West Company held all of that great fur trade city in its hands, and as the winter wore on she became more and more aware that the influence of the McGillivray family had spread into the Colonial Office in London, where Simon McGillivray had the ear of Henry Goulbourn, secretary to Lord Bathurst, and the facts of the Seven Oaks massacre and of Selkirk's move on Fort William were being twisted and distorted to the Nor'Westers' advantage.

Even the birth of a second daughter, Katherine, on January 4 did not keep the countess from her self-appointed task. Though she knew that the family fortunes were being steadily reduced by the great sums of money Selkirk was pouring into the settlement, and she worried about the future of Daer, the little boy who would one day be the sixth earl, she felt it was absolutely necessary to provide strong support for the move back to the settlement. Through the winter months, with the help of their lawyers

James Stuart and Samuel Gale, she devoted her days to gathering together another force of de Meurons, all of them interested in settling at Red River, but also experienced soldiers who would provide the military strength that appeared to be necessary to protect the colony. Archy McDonald was to have charge of the group and take them to join their officers at Fort William.

William McGillivray had already set off with an imposing North West brigade and the avowed intention of reoccupying his old headquarters when the commissioners made their first move. "Major" Fletcher went on ahead, being a slow traveller and so caught up in the consequence of his new appointment that he seemed determined to cause a stir along the way, arrayed as he was in the specially created braid-bedecked scarlet uniform of his new commission, with his fourteen-man military guard. Samuel Gale, who was to accompany Coltman's party as Selkirk's legal observer, cooled his heels and waited impatiently to be on his way. Early in May, McDonald, gathering his party at Lachine — forty-eight de Meuron settlers with forty-five of their wives, and fifty-five men engaged for the service of the Hudson's Bay Company — was suddenly forbidden to proceed. The North West partners in Montreal had convinced Coltman that the de Meurons were armed for war, though the only guns they carried, except for a couple of fowling pieces, were eight wooden cases of trade guns which were the property of the Hudson's Bay Company.

"Archy McDonald was sent back here for orders," wrote Lady Selkirk from Montreal, ". . . and arrived as I was dropping asleep thinking the bustle was over. I sent him to Stuart, & sent them both out by break of day on Monday morning to Lachine to get it settled. . . . Archy in a fit of despair offered to undergo any punishment if they could find a single man to vary in the story; then they called in the sergeant, and the sergeant's wife, & examining them declared themselves satisfied, and our men went off in high glee. . . . I plume myself much on them as they are my throw entirely."

But the North Westers did not give up easily. All the way, as the eleven canoes travelled along the Ottawa and the French rivers, through the north channel of Lake Huron above Manitoulin Island and on to Sault Ste. Marie, McDonald met rumors of further obstructions. As they neared the Sault he was warned that

Fletcher was waiting for him there, determined to stop his party from going on to join Selkirk at Fort William.

Coltman had already moved west when McDonald and his flotilla put in to Point Meuron, about ten miles east of Sault Ste. Marie, but Samuel Gale decided to wait behind when he discovered Fletcher's intentions. That McDonald might need a legal adviser was in no doubt. Fletcher, when not drinking in his tent, was out on the square drilling his troops (all fourteen of them), preparing to stop the de Meuron force *en militaire* and leaving all who witnessed it to wonder if he was mentally deranged. In spite of the ludicrous nature of the commissioner's threats, Gale wanted to be sure that the de Meurons did nothing to provoke him and instructed them all "to act with the most Christian patience."

As it happened, Fletcher was hard put to find anything to criticize. McDonald's party arrived unarmed without even bugles to herald their coming, and "all extremely submissive and well-behaved." Gale was there to greet them, but the welcome was barely over and he and McDonald conferring in his quarters when Fletcher arrived with his military guard and ordered them to turn over all their arms. McDonald sent some of his men to bring out the eight cases of trade goods containing guns and merchandise, "the whole being intended for the commerce of the Interior." Immediately Fletcher ordered his soldiers to confiscate the property, called McDonald's party before him and forbade them to continue their journey. Protests of Gale and McDonald fell on deaf ears. "I act *en militaire*," said the pompous part-time major as he strutted off to raise another glass in his tent.

It was difficult to take him seriously, but in spite of his irrational behavior, Fletcher was still one of the two commissioners appointed by the Crown to look into the many grievances in the Indian country. Gale and McDonald were only too aware of the need to give no cause for complaint against Selkirk's men, and McDonald sat down to compose a written protest to Fletcher. They all knew that large numbers of well-armed North West canoes had already passed by the Sault that spring. What could possibly justify Fletcher's detention of the Hudson's Bay servants and the "peaceable and unarmed settlers" bound for Red River? McDonald demanded the return of the trade goods and announced his intention to "proceed as speedily as possible."

77

Fletcher had acted "in contempt of the Prince Regent's Proclamation," he said.

Fletcher waved it all aside. When McDonald went in person to present his views, the besotted commissioner sat in his tent and refused even to read the letter of protest, let alone return the eight chests. Frustration mounted, and McDonald finally decided to attempt to move on with several of his canoes without Fletcher's permission. It was just what the commissioner had been waiting for. At the head of the first portage, between Point Meuron and Fletcher's headquarters, they were met by the "Major" himself with his soldier band, arms primed and at the ready, and were ordered to lay down the packs of provisions and goods they were about to carry across.

Fletcher took McDonald into custody, along with two of his men, and announced his intention of sending him as a prisoner to Quebec, but that night, after only a few hours under guard, the bewildered young man was released without a word from his captor. Fletcher's behavior was so irrational that it seemed impossible to know how to deal with the situation. McDonald wrote another official protest, and to strengthen their case, Gale put his legal mind to work and took his turn at putting pen to paper, demanding "that you do immediately deliver to Archibald McDonald . . . eight chests or cases . . . that you with strong hand, forcibly, violently, & illegally seized . . . likewise demand . . . that you cease to . . . hinder, molest or retard the settlers." All to no avail. Gale's attempts to keep it all on a legal plane were dismissed by Fletcher with the remark "that he could not talk law at the head of a Battalion." Indeed, Gale said later, "If there were any magistrates in this country I could get the affidavits of Col. Dickson & several others to state that they believed him [Fletcher] mad."

There was certainly an element of farce in it all, but it did not alter the fact that the days were passing and there seemed no way around the impasse. To act in defiance of Fletcher's commission — had they been equipped to do so — would have seriously jeopardized Selkirk's cause. There was nothing to do but to try to convince the foolish "Major" that he should revoke his decisions, return the seized property, and allow the party to proceed. It was easier said than done.

Gale's protestations brought forth a further strange response from the Crown's appointed commissioner. McDonald was sharing Gale's tent when the lawyer was roused between two and three one morning by a pair of armed men, both North West Company clerks, who handed to him a letter from Fletcher stating that only one canoe would be permitted to depart before he was ready to move on himself, and that one "without arms of any description . . . baggage subjected to inspection . . . accompanied by yourself or . . . other person of equal rank & responsibility."

In vain Gale pointed out that "the men whom you have forcibly detained *are not* under my orders . . . the crew only of the canoe in which I came is. . . . as law agent for the Earl of Selkirk I have advised them that no law prohibited them from proceeding — these servants & settlers have not been in possession of arms since the commencement of their journey." It did not matter that the Hudson's Bay Company provisions for the interior were being delayed so that they might not get to Red River in time for the winter shipments. Fletcher was adamant, and for ten days longer they remained under his orders at Point Meuron.

It was June 20 before McDonald's canoes were allowed to proceed to Point aux Pins, a few miles past the Sault at the entrance to Lake Superior. There they waited a further two days for Fletcher to make his majestic move, a signal for them all to proceed along the north Superior shore to the mouth of the Kaministikwia River. On July 4 when they arrived at Fort William, McGillivray was back in command. Selkirk had joined his settlers at Red River two weeks earlier, and Colonel Coltman, pursuing further evidence for his commission, was somewhere between the two.

It was fortunate, at least, that Coltman was taking his mission seriously, because Fletcher showed no signs of improving his behavior as he moved on. Two days after their arrival at Fort William he was sitting in his tent "taking a glass" with the officer of his guard and several others when McDonald was called from a nearby tent and asked to join them. He found Fletcher in full feather, bragging of the "high and unprecedented power" conferred upon him by the Prince Regent's proclamation. Suddenly the commissioner turned on his astonished guest and said violently, "I can cause you to be hanged in an hour from a gallows eight feet high." McDonald asked mildly what he had done to displease him, and Fletcher promptly ordered him out. When Mc-

Donald rose to leave, followed by Colonel Robert Dickson, one of the other officers, Fletcher called for one of his sentries to take McDonald into custody, repeating his gallows threat, and adding "I can have you shot, I will put you in Irons, I will have you tied hand and foot, and flogged, seven dozen . . . in the true camp style, with the strop of a Musket."

On second thoughts, the inebriated commissioner decided that the flogging ought to take place then and there, outside the tent. At that the other officers protested. When Colonel Dickson "remonstrated with him on his conduct" it only enraged Fletcher further. He turned on the colonel saying, "What Sir, do you say I am wrong!" and called instantly for the Fort William guard, to take Colonel Dickson prisoner as well. By the time the soldiers paraded over, followed by a collection of curious North West Company partners and servants who were drawn by the commotion, Fletcher had calmed down. He turned to his prisoners again and asked them to return to his tent where the "matter might be explained." When McDonald recalled the incident later in Montreal, after Fletcher had been brought back east and his appointment revoked by an embarrassed Governor Sherbrooke, he wryly remarked that he had declined the invitation, "deeming it imprudent . . . to accept."

Fletcher fumbled to maintain his dignity — he was not even capable of writing out a warrant to legalize the arrest he had ordered and finally as the guard tried to find out what he wanted done with the "prisoner" Fletcher exclaimed, "Take him to Hell." McDonald and Dickson were taken off to the North West fort and held overnight, but next morning, in the bright light of day, Fletcher ordered them released, saying that he never wanted to lay eyes on McDonald again.

For McDonald, the whole episode was an unsettling experience. With all its ridiculous aspects, it began to seem that he himself was the target of Fletcher's persecution, and that as long as he remained at the head of the de Meuron settlers their progress would be hindered at every turn. More than that, Fletcher's antagonism was of such proportions that McDonald actually feared for his life, and he agreed with Gale that the wisest course would be for him to return to Montreal and leave the settlers to go on to Red River with their own leaders. Samuel Gale continued westward to carry on his observation of the commission's inquiry on Selkirk's behalf, writing back to Lady Selkirk, "Perhaps it may be considered . . . that I have been violent. The truth is that I believe if His Holiness the Pope himself had acted as Major Fletcher did, I would not at the moment have used any milder language than is contained in these strange papers."

McDonald's light canoe returned to the Sault in time to pick up Colin Robertson on his way back to defend himself against the North West Company charges in the courts of Canada, and together the two traced the now familiar Huron waters to the French River–Ottawa route, covering sixty and seventy miles a day when the weather was favorable, slowing up for the heavy winds on Lake Nipissing and the difficult portages on the Ottawa, to reach Montreal in mid-August. Lady Selkirk was at Sorel holidaying with the Sherbrookes when he arrived back, but she returned to Montreal shortly to be regaled with Archy's account of Fletcher's behavior. A few weeks later she was able to write to her brother in England that Fletcher, too, had come back to Montreal, "in consequence of receiving a letter from Sir John to inform him that as a major in the Indian department he had no military rank, & had no right to put the officer of the escort under arrest."

On September 24, after making a long deposition before a justice of the peace detailing his experiences with Fletcher, McDonald boarded the steamer for Quebec to return to London and report to the Committee of the Hudson's Bay Company. The courts of Canada were buzzing with the charges and counter-charges of Selkirk and the North West Company partners, but all awaited Coltman's report before pursuing the actions.

For McDonald it was a relief to escape from the turmoil. When he appeared before the committee at Fenchurch Street in November, he was asked to spend some time in the Highlands in the spring recruiting young men for the Hudson's Bay service. He was delighted to comply, for it gave him an opportunity to spend more time with friends and family in Inverness and Argyll.

It was March when he headed north from London, but by the time he reached Callander to spend several days at the home of his old friend Alexander McDonald of Dalilia, spring was on its way. Yellow broom lined the roadside and early lambs clustered by their mothers among the clumps of fresh daffodils.

McDonald had always been charmed by Dalilia's four

daughters; mention of "the young ladies" was frequent in his letters to their father. On this occasion only one was left at home to direct the housekeeping while the two youngest girls visited their married sister in France. It was Jean McDonald who was free to entertain their guest, to roam the lovely Perthshire hills and explore the rocky crags that rose back from the tiny village. Together she and Archy wandered along the banks of the river Teith gathering wildflowers while the traveller amused his companion with tales of his adventures in the Indian country. In that romantic setting it was not surprising that they should fall in love, although both McDonald and the girl realized that the suit would not please her father — at least not as long as the young Highlander's future was attached to the uncertain fortunes of Selkirk's flagging settlement and the rough life of Rupert's Land. In spite of that, by the time he moved on to Inverness they had pledged themselves secretly, and the determined suitor went off resolved to take steps to provide a way for himself that would bring Dalilia's approval. Those idyllic days remained long in his heart — were his prospects "even more gloomy and disadvantageous than they are, still our resolutions are fixed," he wrote.

When he again boarded a ship for York Factory in late June he had decided to take his case to Lady Selkirk and enlist her aid in providing "something decent" for his future. "As for the fur trade I have got no kind of relish for that sort of life," he told her, "and to continue a mere clerk at Red River is a more contracted scale of employment than my ambition at this stage of life would readily yield to." He was now twenty-eight years old, anxious to marry the girl of his choice and to settle down in comfort for ever after.

In mid-August 1818, when the *Prince of Wales* put into York Factory with McDonald again a passenger, Selkirk was in York preparing to move on to Sandwich (Windsor, Ontario) for hearings in the courts there. The preceding winter had seen a frustrating series of indictments pass through the courts of Lower Canada with results that caused James Allan to question, with others, the "integrity of the bench." In June the hearings were moved to York and thence to Sandwich.

Back in Montreal that season, Nor'Westers in jail awaiting trial on charges arising out of recent events at the colony flouted authority by feasting and roistering at all hours of the night and day. "Even the prison of Montreal had become a place of public entertainment," Colin Robertson wrote to a friend, "from the circumstances of it holding within its walls partners, clerks, and other auxiliaries of the N.W. Co. Every other night a ball and supper is given, and on these occasions a highland piper is employed, as if the sound of this martial music would deafen the voice of public censure. . . . You will naturally ask for what crimes are these men committed, for debt or petty misdemeanor, No! bills of indictment have been filed against them for murder, arson, and robbery," and Selkirk later complained to Governor Sherbrooke that "some idea may be formed of their effrontery from their complaining of the conduct of the Sheriff because he has not allowed a Billiard table to be placed in their apartment."

It was all representative of the climate that Selkirk had to contend with. In the corridors of power walked the North West partners and their friends. The chief justices of both provinces had close ties with the Canadian company, and as time went on it became more and more evident that there was little hope for truth to emerge from the convoluted proceedings that went on for months — delays causing witnesses to disappear, prisoners to escape, new charges to be laid, and all the while the enraged but bewildered Selkirk struggling to overcome the obstacles and gradually realizing the futility of his cause. Coltman, in his report, had shrugged it all off as a "trade war" and decreed that both parties should share the blame. The courts seemed reluctant even to assess the responsibility.

At the end of August when Archy McDonald was writing from Hudson Bay seeking some assurance that his "future prospects" with the colony merited his returning there, Selkirk was too immersed in the legal tangle unfolding around him to give thought to any individuals in his service. As it turned out, he might well have wished that McDonald was at his side, for within two days of the young Highlander's setting off from York Factory for Red River, a surprise was sprung in Sandwich. Instead of hearing two minor charges involving Selkirk's refusal to respond to what he regarded as an invalid warrant at Fort William in 1817, the attorney-general decided to proceed with a charge against Selkirk and nineteen others of "conspiracy to ruin the trade of the North West Company."

It was totally unexpected and although the Crown was prepared with forty witnesses, most of them partners or clerks of the North West Company, many of those who could have given first-hand accounts of Selkirk's side of the story were far from the scene of the hearings, among them Archy McDonald, whose name was one of those on the indictment.

Mr. Justice William Dummer Powell presided over the court, but after several days of hearing evidence he summarily adjourned the case while the grand jury was still hearing testimony of defence witnesses, to the dissatisfaction of both sides. Selkirk protested in open court at what he regarded as not only unfair but corrupt proceedings, and the attorney-general replied in kind. "The controversy was so warm that the court with difficulty preserved order by silencing them both," the *Dumfries & Galloway Courier* reported in a dispatch.

Powell's decision was to move the hearings back to York, but when the cases resumed there in October Selkirk, his health seriously undermined, even his mental attitude somewhat twisted by the dispiriting experiences of the past months, had decided it would be fruitless for him to appear, and that he should return to England and attempt to vindicate himself through direct approaches to the government and the Colonial Office there. He was convinced, and with reason, that there was no hope for justice in the courts of Canada.

Pleading with him not to destroy his health completely by persevering in the fight, Lady Selkirk wrote: "Let the wicked flourish. They cannot take from us our good conscience." She gallantly agreed to remain behind in Montreal to represent his interests, but the following spring when she learned that his health had deteriorated badly, she abandoned all else to return, with the children, to his side.

Within months they had retired to the south of France where Selkirk spent the last days of his life in bitterness and frustration. Back in the courts of Canada, one after another of the charges was dismissed or just forgotten, in a mockery of the much vaunted "British justice." Even as Archy McDonald returned reluctantly to Red River in the fall of 1818, the court at York was acquitting the two Nor'Westers charged with the murder of Semple at Seven Oaks. (Cuthbert Grant, after being bailed on the same charge, had escaped to the Indian country some months before and was beyond the jurisdiction of the courts.) The reputa-

tion of an admired and respected British nobleman counted for
nothing against the hard influence and the unscrupulous manip-
ulations of the North West partners.

With the disintegration of Selkirk's brave plans went Archy
McDonald's hopes of bettering his own situation, and he again
took up his responsibilities at the settlement. In November, when
Attorney-General John Beverley Robinson was writing to Samuel Gale to say that McDonald headed the list of witnesses he
wanted to call to testify on the charges against Duncan Cameron
but that he was "ignorant where he is," the missing witness was
unknowingly setting off on an expedition to the Missouri territory to the south, lands of the Mandan Indians, where he hoped
to procure horses for the colony, and in fact made his first venture into the fur trade.

He left Fort Douglas on November 10, and on the 18th
moved on south from Pembina with ten men, three horses and
two carts. Heavy snow hampered their progress and finally, with
all the horses "knocked up," McDonald decided to take off for
Brandon House with one of his men, Pisk Kippling, leaving the
rest of the party with the trade goods to await their return with
dogs and sleds to enable them to carry on with their mission. On
December 2, returning with five sleds and fifteen dogs, he was astonished to find that the rest of his party had "decamped" and
the trade goods had disappeared.

Describing the excursion to Selkirk he wrote:

Soon after I fell in upon an Indian Encampment where I
found a Soulteau Indian & family who had conveyed the
goods & everything to their camp a few days before. By all the
information I could collect from them, they said that the white
people got alarmed at seeing them in the woods, & must have
taken *them* for Stone Indians, and on the other hand they asserted, that the body of people they saw at first sight, in the
edge of the big plain, appeared to them to be Sioux Indians
and consequently both parties got alarmed at each other.

After 25 days unremitted exertion to get on with this little
expedition, I found myself as far back as the first day . . . came
to the resolution of proceeding to the Mandans with four men,
five sleds and all the goods. Pisk & Angus Matheson from
Bran. were two of the number — a young half breed whom I
engaged in the plains was the third, and a Souteu Indian was

the fourth, he was to act the part of guide, & interpret Stone Indian should we fall in with the Ossiniboians. After two days journey . . . the Indian would not venture any further on account of the danger he dreaded from some bad Indians & very deliberately took his leave of us behind the Turtle Mountain on the 5th. I then determined to persevere with the three men & myself, and got to the banks of the Missourie on the forenoon of the 12th and the disk [*sic*] of the evening brought us to the Upper Village. Having met with every civility & friendship I spent six days among them there. The horses were not so cheap or numerous as I had reason to expect at first, however I traded nine fine able horses (exclusive of one Kippling bought) and 170 Beaver besides other little matters. . . . with the ten horses & five sleds and a considerable quantity of the goods which remained on hand . . . reached Brandon House on 26th. Having . . . allowed the horses to remain for a few days' rest I left Brandon Ho. on 28th and safely arrived at the Forks to the agreeable surprize of everyone on 31st Decr.

The consternation into which everyone in the place was thrown, from the moment the report was carried home to Pembina by the deserters, to the time of my return was so excessively alarming that different parties were sent out in various directions but could hear no tidings of myself or even find out the place where the goods were abandoned. Some of the men were examined before I returned home. One said he had seen from 10 to 15 Indians, another would say he saw from 30 to 50, a third saw upwards of 100 — but old LaGrave & others saw *300* all painted, with feathers stuck up in their heads & could distinctly see the Bows & Arrows and the whole saw more or less of Horsemen! — The conduct of these people was not only infamous in the extreme on this occasion, but some of them had actually mutinied against me before I was two days from Pembina. . . . I trust the impropriety of their conduct will be duly considered.

To McDonald the "impropriety of their conduct" was such that he was not about to trust them on the next horse-trading expedition, proposed for the Saskatchewan in February. "I think it would be desirable to have a person of some responsibility to conduct them thither. Rather than go without I shall offer my own services, for the loss of 50 or 60 horses, if they could be effectually

86

guarded from the Indians, would be worth the attention of a Gentlmn. from here."

In spite of his lack of "relish" for the fur trade, McDonald finally bowed to fate and took a hand in it. He remained at the settlement more than a year longer. In the summer of 1819, having had no word from Selkirk that season, he determined to leave but en route to York Factory was convinced by Governor Williams and Colin Robertson that his services were badly needed in view of "the critical and uncertain situation in which . . . the colony is placed."

On September 8 he set off on the much travelled route from York Factory, again conducting a band of newly arrived settlers down to Red River, "aware that the destitute state of the settlement this Winter requires the influence of all to reconcile the settlers to their fate, and more especially the newcomers."

His decision was made, however. His hopes of returning to Scotland to claim Jean McDonald as his bride had gradually diminished. There had been a brief flurry of optimism when Jean's father discussed with him a suggestion made by Selkirk that Dalilia take up an allotment of land in Assiniboia and establish a settlement there in his own name. McDonald had reason to believe that the old man might let his daughter come out in such circumstances. But by March 1819, when Dalilia wrote to the earl to confirm his interest in the proposal, Selkirk was back in England, too ill and careworn to have energy to spare for any considerations but his approaches to the British government over his own troubles. Nothing came of Dalilia's scheme, and when no other opportunities arose, Archy McDonald finally faced the fact that his future was in the fur country and there was no place for Jean McDonald in that way of life.

When he officially entered the service of the Hudson's Bay Company in the spring of 1820, it was not with enthusiasm but with a sense of resignation.

PART II

The Waiting Wilderness

CHAPTER SIX

Two Novices in the Fur Trade

1820 – 1821

In the year 1820 when Archibald McDonald made up his mind to enter the fur trade, another young man a few years his senior was in London preparing to embark for Hudson Bay and a career with the "Gentlemen Adventurers." George Simpson, also a Scot, a native of Ross-shire, had attracted the attention of Andrew Colvile while serving with his uncle's London business firm in which Colvile had an interest. He had been appointed to go out for a year to act as "locum tenens" in the event that Governor William Williams was forced to go to Canada to answer indictments in the courts there. Simpson was totally inexperienced in the fur trade, had never even been to the Indian country, but he possessed certain qualities of strength and decisiveness, along with sound business sense, that were much needed at this crucial stage in the affairs of the Hudson's Bay Company.

The long years of bitter competition had taken their toll of both companies. Neither could afford to continue the fight, and the impracticality of two firms bartering for furs side by side in the same locations all over the vast territories of British North

America was evident to all. Disregarding Selkirk's unflinching opposition to the scheme, Colvile and other senior Hudson's Bay partners spent months meeting behind closed doors with a small group of influential Nor'Westers, trying to hammer out the terms of a mutually agreeable merger between the two firms. In the field, especially in the Athabasca territory, the toughest of the old-line wintering partners of the Montreal firm were prepared to keep up their campaigning against the Hudson's Bay men until the bitter end.

In truth, the two groups made strange bedfellows, and that was one of the biggest problems the new firm would have to face. When the decision was made to send Simpson across the Atlantic, it was realized that if anyone could draw the Nor'Westers and the Bay men together to work in harmony, it would have to be a stranger with no past associations with either. If George Simpson shaped up in his first season, the great sprawling fur empire might well be his prize.

George Simpson was an unknown quantity to the hundreds of sceptical, experienced traders watching and waiting by the sidelines, observing suspiciously what most of them regarded as an impossible attempt to blend oil and water. He was small of stature, of no imposing mien, but from the moment of his arrival in the Indian country his authority was established. His inexperience was acknowledged, but he brooked no attacks on his command. Colvile had sent him out with wide powers, and although none of the men in the field in either company knew just exactly what they were, they soon learned that George Simpson was a figure to reckon with. While he never achieved any measure of popularity with his confrères, and all but a few of his contemporaries in the fur trade regarded him more with respect than with affection, a quelling glance from his blazing blue eyes, a chilling comment from his eloquent repertoire, was enough to keep them all in line, and it was not long after his arrival in Rupert's Land that these facts were recognized. That a figure of such firmness and decision was required in the uneasy early days of the union between the traditional enemies is in no doubt.

Simpson sailed from Liverpool early in March and arrived at Norway House by way of New York, Montreal and Fort William in midsummer. On his meeting with Governor Williams at Rock Depot he learned that Colin Robertson had been captured and taken off to Montreal by the Nor'Westers, leaving the captaincy of the Athabasca campaign vacant. The possibility of Williams's removal to Lower Canada had passed, and it took little time for him to decide that Simpson could take over Robertson's job. The newcomer agreed to the change in plan, to go west with the canoes bound for the interior and take command at Fort Wedderburn on Lake Athabasca, where the North West Company was expected to mount its strongest opposition.

Archibald McDonald had arrived at Norway House that summer too, another newcomer to the fur trade, but one whose credentials as a prominent leader of the ill-fated Selkirk settlement were in favor neither with Hudson's Bay sympathizers nor Nor'Westers. Many long years were to pass before fair-minded men began to see events at the colony in their true light. In 1820, with many cases still before the courts arguing the pros and cons of the whole affair, the influence of the Montreal company in Canada was still such that little quarter was given to any of Selkirk's followers.

McDonald was at a disadvantage, but he had already proved that he was not one to shirk responsibility and that he could face up to any challenge that came his way. Whatever reluctance he felt on entering his new career was pushed aside, and he undertook to introduce himself to the ways of the fur trade by going over all the past season's records of Île à la Crosse, the post he was destined for, before setting off for the Athabasca territory with Simpson's party on August 17.

This was to be the first of many journeys McDonald and Simpson made together in the western wildernesses — the beginning of the memories they shared years later as they both neared the end of their days back in the East. Theirs was a close association that was to span nearly a third of a century, Simpson always the dominant figure, but nevertheless dependent to an extent on the qualities in his friend that he could never muster in himself. For McDonald possessed a joie de vivre, a gift for friendship and loyalty, that Simpson could not match; a devotion to family and a delight in children and young people that charmed everyone in his circle throughout his life; a geniality and warmth, a humanity, that was missing in Simpson's makeup.

In his often quoted "Character Book" written secretly in 1832, Simpson employed the same contradictory mixture of good and ill terms to discuss McDonald's character as he did all the Company's officers in that strange document, but as time went by a geniune friendship built up between the two men that is clearly evidenced in their surviving correspondence. It is well known that at the time Simpson wrote his "Character Book" he was himself ill and discouraged, his wife unwell and despondent at the death of their infant son, and this malaise is reflected in the general tone of all his assessments in his coded character studies. Even his close friend and confidant, John George McTavish, came under fire, being described as "rather strong in his prejudices" and "over fond of good living . . . getting into habits of conviviality and intemperance."

McDonald fared better than some, on the plus side being portrayed as "a shrewd, clear-headed man" who "expresses himself tolerably well on paper and is better informed, and would make a better figure at our Council board than many of his colleagues or even than the majority of those now seated there." But Simpson mused that it was possible that he "would be overbearing if in power" and suspected that he might "become addicted to Liquor if exposed to temptation and not under restraint," both suppositions that proved over the years to be quite erroneous. McDonald's being "fond of conviviality" made Simpson suspect him of overdoing it, although McDonald himself, writing to Edward Ermatinger in 1839 of Frank Ermatinger's visit to Colvile when they toasted absent friends in a "bumper" of brandy, assured him that "this kind of manifestation of good fellowship does not often occur with us . . . what I in days gone bye conceived a glorious merrymaking I now look upon as beastly. . . ."

Simpson's suggestion that McDonald was "rather inactive and 'tis thought does not possess much nerve" loses its force when we look at the record of his journeyings back and forth through the Rocky Mountains and up and down the Fraser, the Thompson and the Columbia rivers which continued right up until his retirement to Lower Canada in his fifty-fifth year. But Simpson was not clairvoyant, and his "Character Book" notations in general have not stood up to the test of time. As he set off with McDonald and the rest of the party for his first journey into the interior, he knew none of these men and had nothing on which to base any judgment of their capabilities in the fur trade.

Canoes and York boats had been leaving with men and supplies for the interior for several days before they embarked. The Athabasca and Peace River brigades were already on their way, leaving "twelve Canoes navigated by sixty men, contg. two hundred and fifty-four pieces" for their inaugural voyage into the fur country.

They set off that windy morning at five, Simpson with Robert Miles in a canoe manned by nine strong Canadians, accompanied by John Clarke, Archibald McDonald and Louis Pensonnant in another with the same complement of men. Simpson was to take charge of Athabasca, Clarke of the Île à la Crosse District, and the stormy weather that prevailed throughout the journey was symbolic of their relationship in the days to come.

The weather continued to be "boisterous" as their canoes made their way along the northern waterways, and it quickly became obvious that John Clarke, the seasoned veteran of the trade, was obstreperous too. Clarke, a former Nor'Wester, had a record of extravagance and a cavalier disregard of Company rules, but his ability to draw the Indian hunters and his experience in the country for the most part outweighed his self-willed arrogance. Even before setting off on the journey, Simpson complained in his journal, Clarke had taken the "flower" of the people and far more than his share of goods and provisions for his own district and ten days later he observed that "Mr. Clarke daily loses ground in my estimation. . . . to indulge his incorrigible vanity, self importance and ambition, I verily believe he would sacrifice the Company and all their affairs." They were uneasy travelling companions, but Simpson felt it would not "be judicious to quarrel with him as yet . . . as I believe he is sufficiently mercenary to change sides immediately, and from his influence with the Canadians and Indians, and his indefatigable zeal in the cause of revenge, he would be a very dangerous enemy."

All along the route Simpson found signs of inefficiency and mismanagement, and he quickly began making notes of his suggestions for improving the conduct and economy of the Company's affairs. He admired Francis Heron's garden at Cumberland House and saw that if every outpost cultivated a plot of land there would be less call for the expensive long-distance transport of provisions. He complained about the extravagance of carrying men, and sometimes their families as well, back and forth from their winter posts when they could remain in the interior year round.

It was early in the journey, less than a week out from Norway House, when they first heard rumours of Selkirk's death in France on April 8, but Simpson refused to believe the reports, even though the news was repeated over and over as they came up with other parties travelling along the way. Not until February did he receive confirmation of the sorrowful news in a letter from Governor Williams, and no one in the fur country mourned the loss more than Archy McDonald, who remained ever grateful to Selkirk for his early kindness and help and was loyal and affectionate to Lady Selkirk and the children all his life.

Clarke and Simpson parted at Île à la Crosse, and Simpson went on with his clerk, Miles, to the headquarters of the Athabasca Department, arriving at Fort Wedderburn on September 20. To McDonald fell the task of serving as Clarke's assistant, a difficult position where even Clarke's friendship was a mixed blessing. Intrigue and gossip surrounded Clarke and McDonald wanted no part of it. He offered his services to Simpson for the Mackenzie River post for the following year, willing to accept any assignment that meant moving on.

Clarke remained uncooperative and unmoved when Simpson sought his help — at Lac la Loche Simpson was told that they had been "instructed by Mr. Clarke never to render any assistance to the Athabaska Department." It was not enough to contend with the militant Nor'Westers, Simpson, like McDonald before him, discovered; even his supposed ally was in opposition. From late September on, Simpson struggled to induce Clarke to forward to him supplies and provisions that had been left at Île à la Crosse awaiting transport. Clarke's refusal to send them on resulted in severe deprivation at Fort Wedderburn as winter wore on, and it was not until February when McDonald took it upon himself to go up to Lac la Loche to send them on their way that Simpson got his shipment.

Another bone of contention between the two was Clarke's inclination to bribe the Indian hunters to trade in his district by paying higher than the agreed rate for their furs. Finally Simpson wrote to his neighbor on February 9, "I find that nearly all the Indians belonging to this district are migrating to Isle à la Crosse, they have heard of your unbounded generosity . . . it is scarcely necessary to remind you that we are not sent here to op- pose each other but our avowed Enemies."

The heightened opposition of the North West Company in their final season, the shortage of supplies and near-starvation at some of Simpson's Athabasca outposts, the intrigue and bickering among the Hudson's Bay men, and the refusal of Clarke to ac- cept Simpson as his superior officer all contributed to the miseries of that winter — the season that was both Simpson's and Mc- Donald's introduction to the fur trade. Clarke had already set off for Cumberland House with his furs when Simpson joined Mc- Donald at Fort Superior, just below Île à la Crosse, on the way back to Norway House at season's end. It was June 6, 1821, and Simpson and his men were again close to starvation. "Our people are nearly worn out with hunger & fatigue, indeed myself & the other Gentlemen are in the same state having had little or no sustenance for eleven days." After a day of repose Simpson was on his way again, but not without taking the opportunity of dis- cussing with McDonald his plans for the future.

Although it was unknown to the "winterers" in the interior, the coalition agreement had been signed by the Hudson's Bay and the North West companies on March 26, and George Simp- son, whose life was to take on a new direction as a result, did not hear the news until he approached Norway House nearly two weeks after parting from McDonald. One of the most significant terms of the merger was that while Williams retained control of the Southern region, Simpson was to take over as governor of the Northern Department. He grasped the reins firmly and lost no time in putting to use the lessons he had learned during his long, hard winter in Athabasca.

One matter he had little to say about was the appointment of the chief factors and chief traders created by the merger agree- ment. Of the one hundred shares that made up the new compa- ny, forty were set aside for these senior officers in the field, and the coalition gave fifteen of the twenty-five chief factorships, and seventeen of the twenty-eight chief traderships to former Nor'- Westers, an event that caused a certain amount of chagrin amongst old Hudson's Bay men. Colin Robertson was one who voiced his dismay: ". . . will wonders never cease! In throwing my eye over the appointments as they stood in the Deed Poll I saw A. McDonald chief trader, and forthwith began to congratulate the friends of one Archd. McDonald on his appointment to half a share . . . what was my astonishment when I found the A. Mc-Donald was my old friend of Fort Wedderburn. . . . In my humble opinion Archy was more entitled to a share than this man."

George Simpson was even more displeased to hear that John Clarke was made a chief factor, and it took several years of moves from post to post before Clarke was finally dismissed from the Company's service. Others whom Simpson regarded as superfluous did not last as long. Within three months of taking over the Northern Department he decided to discharge "at least two hundred and fifty men" in order to save £15,000 of the £60,000 spent on wages. Many of these moved with their families to the Red River settlement, giving new heart to the little community which had sunk even further into despair on the death of its founder. At any rate, the move had the desired effect of streamlining the Company's operations, reducing waste and increasing its efficiency. Simpson put into practice some principles of plain good housekeeping: sound management, thrift, and tidiness. He had a strong sense of order and applied it to the reorganization of the long network of fur posts that stretched across the continent, eliminating some, combining and consolidating others, encouraging all to cultivate agricultural products where they could for their own consumption, making sure that each man had a job to do and did it.

There was one area in the new empire that Simpson knew nothing about. The Hudson's Bay Company had never ventured west of the Rocky Mountains although since the first decade of the century a small band of Nor'Westers — Alexander Mackenzie, Simon Fraser, David Thompson among them — had been competing in New Caledonia and in the Columbia District and Oregon territories with the American and Russian fur hunters. Under an act of parliament passed at the time of the merger of the two companies, the British government granted the new Hudson's Bay Company exclusive trading rights for twenty-one years in all British North America between Rupert's Land and the Rocky Mountains and the sole British trading rights in the Oregon country, where a Treaty of Joint Occupation with the Americans had been in effect since 1818. A reliable Hudson's Bay man was needed to go out and assess the situation, and Archy McDonald was Simpson's choice for the assignment. On

September 8, 1821 he wrote to Colvile: "We possess little information about the Columbia. . . . [I] have sent Archibald McDonald thither . . . to give a full and accurate report of it which will be transmitted to the committee." At the same time Simpson mentioned his "good abilities" and recommended that his salary be doubled — to £100 per annum.

McDonald had been well-schooled in Simpson's views on economy and their application in the fur trade. The new governor was confident that his emissary would carry the message beyond the mountains where profligacy was said to run rampant.

CHAPTER SEVEN

A Sense of Separation

1821 - 1825

McDonald went west with Chief Trader John Lee Lewes, the first two Hudson's Bay men to cross the mountains after the merger, setting off from Norway House in late summer to follow the great Saskatchewan River westward to the Athabasca Pass through the Rockies.

With them was John Dugald Cameron, a former Nor'Wester who was one of the two chief factors appointed to the Columbia District. (Chief Factor John Haldane was already there, as was Chief Trader James McMillan, both old Nor'Westers.)

They arrived at Fort George (formerly Astoria) at the mouth of the Columbia River on November 8, and within days McDonald and Lewes had begun the inventory — a document that was to reveal to the committee back in England that such fineries as ostrich plumes, such delicacies as led Simpson later to say "they may be said to have been eating gold," such extravagances as they had not conceived, were all stockpiled at this remotest outpost of them all. They found quantities of provisions wasted: casks of flour, corn and sugar gone bad; pease eaten by weasels with just the shells left to reveal the loss; bad pork and bad beef improperly stored in the damp climate that defied its preservation. Systematically Lewes and McDonald examined the stores of the headquarters at Fort George, and then moved on to the records of other forts in the district, Walla Walla, Spokane and Thompson's River, to do the same. And back to Governor Simpson went the reports the following spring clearly showing that a major cause of the lack of profits in the Columbia District was the indulgence in large quantities of costly European provisions. There was no doubt that a revolution was in order. Only the length of time that it took to communicate back and forth delayed the hour.

The inventory completed, McDonald stayed on as accountant at Fort George, supervising the Indian store and keeping records of all the Columbia transactions. It was a free and easy life, far removed from the other districts of the Northern Department, and the great wall of the Rocky Mountains seemed to create a sense of total separation from the old days and the old ways.

Even the native people on the coast differed greatly from the familiar Indians of Assiniboia, from the Saulteaux, the Cree, the Mandans and other tribes he had come to know during his years in Rupert's Land. Here at the mouth of the Columbia were the Chinooks and the bands in the immediate vicinity lived in settled villages and built wooden lodges decorated with monumental carved house poles. The men wore conical woven hats and robes of muskrat or beautifully woven blankets flung over their shoulders; the women wore girdles of loose cedar bark, much like hula skirts, down to their knees. They were fair of skin, fine-featured, quick-witted — and impressively lazy. The salmon they caught with so little exertion was their livelihood, and except for a flurry of activity during the annual summer run when the fish were netted and dried for winter use, they spent much of their time engaged in simple gambling games. They were indifferent hunters, though keen traders, and only exerted themselves in that direction because contact with Europeans had made them "accustomed to the produce of the civilized world."

Richest and most powerful of the chiefs of the Columbia region was old Comcomly, whose imposing lodge stood directly across the river from Fort George. He had been a great friend of Astor's men when the Americans were trading out of Astoria, and when McDonald arrived on the coast he had so established his position that few of the neighboring bands dared trade directly at the fort, but did their bartering through "King" Comcomly, the intermediary. He also served as river pilot when the Hudson's Bay Company ships arrived each spring, sighting their arrival from a lookout high on a cliff above his lodge and quickly signalling twenty of his slaves to launch the colorful royal canoes and paddle him out to meet the incoming vessels.

Comcomly, whose exploits were recorded in the journals and writings of all the literary travellers who passed his way, was chief of the Chinooks, a band of Flathead Indians, so-called because of the practice of binding their babies' heads in a wedge-shaped wooden frame to leave their foreheads permanently flattened as a mark of aristocratic distinction from their myriad round-headed slaves. His fame had spread far and wide by the 1820s and his power over the other tribes was such that he was a valuable friend to his fur-trading neighbors. He was very proud of the association and had already taken steps to strengthen it by marrying off one of his daughters to Duncan McDougal, a former Astor partner. Political considerations were all-important to him, and he was delighted when the prospect arose of his pretty youngest girl, Princess Raven, becoming the bride of Archibald McDonald, one of the senior officers at the Hudson's Bay Company fort. Walled off from civilization by the impenetrable ridge of the Rocky Mountains, McDonald made his decision. His future was here in this wilderness and there was no turning back.

No contemporary account of this wedding exists (McDonald's son, Benjamin, in later years set its date as September 12, 1823), but there is a vivid description recorded by Ranald McDonald, the only offspring of the union, as it was told to him later in life by an eyewitness, the captain of an American vessel from Salem, Massachusetts, who was trading on the northwest coast at the time. Comcomly spared no pageantry for the ceremonial:

> The royal residence was, in the fashion of the country, a long, one-story, gothic-roofed, very large house of wood with doors and windows and other conveniences, and adornments outside, including a monumental totem pole by way of royal flagstaff. All about — quite a town — were houses on a scarcely simpler scale, for accommodation of all the retinue — at least five hundred men — of the King. Add to that some of his subjects . . .

settled there — for they were not of nomadic habit — a population, altogether of probably four or five thousand.

The locality was a striking one. . . . In the rear was the grand forest of densely fronded lofty Douglas pine and other such arborage. In front the gently sloping beach, tide laved, of golden sand and pebbled shingle.

From water marge to the King's court, where in open heaven, the ceremony was to take place — a distance say of about three hundred yards — was a path of golden sheen, of richest *furs, viz.* of prime beaver, otter (sea and land), nothing less! . . . Along this golden path way, as a guard of honor, were three hundred of the slaves, so-called, of the King.

On the arrival of the bridegroom and his party . . . they walked the furried path; the yeomen of the guard (all warriors taken captive in battle) retaining their statue stand, arrived at the King's gate. With little preliminary of ceremony, the King, with royal grace and dignity, in silence, handed over the evidently not unwilling bride; not unwilling, for her true love in his young manhood was of the handsomest of the sons of men — and *debonair*; eagle-eyed, and with the thews and éclat of his mountain race; of most magnetic touch, and look, and tongue; a truly princely man. . . .

To crown the occasion, soon as the last foot of the whites had retrod the fur path on their return, the whole was picked up by the three hundred slaves in waiting, and piled, at the boats on the river marge, and presented in *gift*, pure and spontaneous to the bride's man. There was, of course, "cakes and ale" — Potlach in plenty for all. . . .

There can be no doubt that this is a somewhat exaggerated account of the proceedings. None of Comcomly's biographers ever suggested that his village ran to a population as high as five thousand souls, though it is well known that he was the wealthiest and most influential chief on the coast, and probably the total number of people in the tribes over whom he held sway would reach that. Governor Simpson recorded at the time of his visit to the Columbia in 1824–25 that Comcomly had one hundred male slaves and seventy female, and he estimated the number of free residents of the old chieftain's village at three hundred and fifty men and two hundred women. It can be assumed that they were all on hand for the big event, and probably, along with them, the two hundred or so Indians from the Chinook settlement on the south side of the river, as well as others of their language from the Columbia and Willamette river basins. It is known that years later Ranald McDonald felt that he had been "robbed" of his birthright when the carpet of furs that was presented as the bride's dowry to the bridegroom was turned over to the Hudson's Bay Company, to become part of the annual returns for the year, according to the firm rule that officers and servants of the Company could in no circumstances carry on any "trading" as individuals or accept gifts from the Indians.

The marriage was doomed to be short-lived. The following summer — "the salmon running time" — shortly after Ranald was born to "Princess Sunday" (the name she had taken at her wedding) at Fort George, the young mother died and McDonald allowed Comcomly to take his infant grandson to his nearby lodge to be cared for through babyhood by an aunt, Car-cum-cum. The young widower was left in solitude to mourn his loss.

That was a year of decision in the Columbia. Fort George was on the alert awaiting the arrival of the governor, who was already making his way across the continent, inspecting all the posts along the way but primarily intent on revamping affairs beyond the mountains. With him came Dr. John McLoughlin, another experienced Nor'Wester, who was to take charge of the district and put teeth into whatever edicts Simpson issued for the improvement of the trade.

When George Simpson arrived at Fort George on November 8 (having accomplished the journey from Hudson Bay in eighty-four days, twenty days less than anyone who had preceded him), his men dressed in their best and bedecked with gaily colored ribbons and sashes singing lustily to the paddles' rhythm as they approached the fort, the governor found it worthy of remark that the first sight that met his eye as their boats approached the widening of the river was that of the chief factor, Alexander Kennedy, and his accountant, Archibald McDonald, "amusing themselves Boat Sailing." The arrival marked the end of their holiday for the time being. It meant down to work, and a reformation of the casual ways they had fallen into.

The trade on the coast was "unquestionably worth contending for" Simpson decreed, and he settled immediately to map out a plan for driving the American traders from the area and turning the Columbia District into a profitable enterprise. Until his arrival there had been some doubt that it was worth the effort, though the committee in England felt it was incumbent on them to preserve the British claims to the Pacific coast regions, and at the same time protect the rich fur territories northwest of the Athabasca that had as yet hardly been tapped.

With Simpson's presence on the scene, the Hudson's Bay Company adopted a competitive spirit that had previously been lacking in their conduct of the Columbia trade, and in a few short years the district was transformed into an efficient, productive operation, not only increasing appreciably the returns from the fur trade, but experimenting with lumbering and fisheries and, after establishing farms to supply their own needs, developing these agricultural pursuits sufficiently to be provisioning the Russian outposts to the north within the next decade.

One of Simpson's first moves was to reduce the size of the establishment. He found at Fort George "a large pile of buildings covering about an acre of ground well stockaded and protected by Bastions or Blockhouses, having two Eighteen Pounders mounted in front and altogether an air or appearance of Grandeur & consequence which does not become and is not at all suitable to an Indian Trading Post." Indeed, he noted, "Everything appears to me on the Columbia on too extended a scale *except the Trade*," and then he went on to say that "mismanagement and extravagance has been the order of the day. It is now however necessary that a radical change should take place and we have no time to lose in bringing it about." The first step was to cut by one-third the number of men employed at the fort, and within months the headquarters itself was moved to a new site, Bellevue Point, about seventy-five miles inland on the north side of the river at its junction with the Willamette, a move calculated to preserve the Company's claims to the territory north of the Columbia, while unofficially recognizing that the American government's rights extended at least to the south bank, although they were already showing signs of holding out for a boundary settlement at the 49th parallel.

The site chosen was a beautiful one "as may be inferred from its Name and the Country so open that from the Establishment there is good travelling on horseback to any part of the interior; a Farm to any extent may be made there, the pasture is good and innumerable herds of swine can fatten so as to be fit for the Knife merely on nutricious Roots that are found here in any quantity and the Climate so fine that Indian Corn and other Grain cannot fail of thriving."

Here was a chance for the governor to prove his point. It was entirely possible for these remote outposts to provision themselves — to grow their own grain and mill their own flour, to cultivate vegetables and fruits, to raise cattle and sheep and pigs to augment the natural diet of fish without requiring expensive shipments from afar. Fort Vancouver, as the new post was called, became the first farm in the Columbia, and it was quickly followed by Fort Colvile, a lovely fertile valley at the high point on the Columbia near Kettle Falls, a location that could serve the inland trading posts, and Fort Langley, created at Simpson's suggestion a few miles inland from the mouth of the Fraser River. At both of these forts, in succeeding years, Archibald McDonald was to play a key part in developing and expanding the grand design. But meantime there was work to be done to set the Columbia house in order.

About eight hundred miles' journey to the northeast from the new headquarters was the lonely outpost of Thompson's River, also known as Kamloops, from the Indian word *Cumcloups* — "meeting of the waters." In terms of profits, Simpson felt the site should be abandoned, but it provided a necessary link with Fort Alexandria and Fort St. James in the New Caledonia District to the north, and he felt that with proper management it should bring in enough furs from the neighboring Indians to justify its existence. For two years its fortunes had been in the hands of Chief Trader John McLeod, the same McLeod who with a handful of men had brought the Red River settlement back to life after it was first overrun by the North West Company in 1815. He was older now, burdened with serious family problems, and unable to adjust to the ruggedness of life west of the mountains. He was in terror of the neighboring Indians and in Simpson's ruthless judgment "useless": "I concieve [*sic*] that an Indian trader who cannot obtain personal influence and secure himself the respect and esteem of the Indians he has been in the constant practise of dealing with . . . is unworthy the title he bears and unfit for the situation he holds." It was decided to give McLeod permission to recross the mountains with his family, and Archibald McDonald was appointed to the charge of Thompson's River.

"This young gentleman has not had much experience as an Indian Trader, but from his manner and address I think he would very soon gain popularity, he knows the value of property and I have every reason to believe would turn it out to the best account; he appears thoughtful, steady and discreet and I am satisfied he will spare no pains or exertion to put things on a proper footing and give satisfaction & we may depend on his following instructions implicitly . . . ," Simpson wrote to McLoughlin.

The Columbia revolution was well under way when the governor departed from the new headquarters on March 19, 1825. His last action there at sunrise was "to hoist the Flag Staff . . . and in the presence of the Gentlemen, Servants, Chiefs & Indians I Baptised it by breaking a Bottle of Rum on the Flag Staff . . . and repeating . . . in a loud voice . . . I thereby name this Establishment Fort Vancouver. . . ." He then "Gave a couple of Drams to the people and Indians" and at 9 A.M. was on his way, accompanied by Chief Factor Kennedy who had turned over command of the district to Dr. McLoughlin.

Simpson continued making last-minute adjustments and reformations in the Columbia arrangements as he proceeded east, spending some time at Spokane House and Fort Okanagan ironing out problems in the interior, and stopping at Kettle Falls to select the site for the new Fort Colvile. He was well pleased with his year's work when he arrived back at York Factory on July 11.

Ten days later he dispatched the Express for the Columbia and with it two brothers who were to serve as clerks in the district — Edward Ermatinger, to take over Archibald McDonald's duties as accountant at headquarters, and Francis Ermatinger, who was to be McDonald's companion on many memorable occasions in the next twenty years. The Ermatingers, grandsons of Lawrence Ermatinger and nephews of Charles Ermatinger, two well-known figures in the fur trade, had arrived at Hudson Bay as apprentice clerks in August 1818, taking passage on the *Prince of Wales* with Archibald McDonald, who was then returning to Rupert's Land after taking reports of Selkirk's activities to the Hudson's Bay committee in London.

When the Express from York Factory — two boats and forty

men — arrived at Fort Vancouver on November 18, McDonald was delighted to greet these two congenial friends. Good-fellowship was what the gregarious young Highlander craved most at the remote wilderness outpost. His naturally sociable disposition cried out for the warmth of a wider circle of friends than the limited society of the dour Scots traders at Fort George, many of them old Nor'Westers disillusioned by the loss of their former strength and power. The appearance of the fun-loving Ermatinger brothers did much to assuage his loneliness and cheer the scene.

But the death of his young bride the preceding year had left an emptiness in McDonald's life that the society of the fur trade fort could not fill. He was at heart a family man, and to find himself in his early thirties still alone with no wife to console and befriend him, deprived of the company of his only son, was difficult to bear. The likelihood of a suitable young woman appearing on the scene in this faraway place was remote, and he had little hope of it happening.

Whether McDonald had met Jane Klyne back in the mountains when she accompanied her fur trader father on one of his forays to Boat Encampment at the Big Bend of the Columbia where the trail from the Athabasca Pass meets the river is not known. Somehow she was there that summer of 1825, slipping onto the scene as unobtrusively and confidently as she was to live out the rest of her remarkable life. The two fell in love — the record of their later years attests to this — recognizing in each other a response, not only to their need for companionship in their isolation, but an answering gaiety and a mutual love of the wild freedom and beauty of the wilderness that held them both captive.

Jane Klyne, who had grown up in the Northwest, was barely seventeen when she came into McDonald's life. She was the daughter of Michel Klyne, a former Nor'Wester who had recently come down from Lesser Slave Lake to take over as postmaster at Jasper House, the Rocky Mountain post at the headwaters of the Athabasca River where travellers traditionally abandoned their canoes and took to horseback to cross over to Boat Encampment on the west side of the mountains. Her mother was a native of the country and her father, a Dutch-Canadian, had served in almost every capacity from canoeman

Archibald McDonald descending the Fraser River in 1828: "certain death in nine times out of ten" according to his travelling companion, Governor George Simpson *(from a painting by A. Sherriff Scott for the Hudson's Bay Company)*

Thomas Douglas, fifth Earl of Selkirk, founder of the Red River colony *(Public Archives of Canada)*

Sir George Simpson, Governor
of the Hudson's Bay Company,
1821-1860 *(Public Archives of
Canada)*

Edward Ermatinger retired in
1828 after ten years with the
Hudson's Bay Company and
settled in St. Thomas, Ontario.
(Courtesy Elgin County Museum)

"King Comcomly's Burial Canoe" painted by Paul Kane in 1847.
Comcomly's daughter, Princess Raven, married McDonald at the Chinook
village at the mouth of the Columbia River in 1823. *(Courtesy Stark Museum of
Art, Orange, Texas)*

"Indians Playing at Alcoloh" by Paul Kane, 1847. These Columbia River
Indians are intent on one of their favorite gambling games. *(National Gallery
of Canada, Ottawa)*

Chief Factor Archibald McDonald from a daguerreotype in the possession of
the author *(British Columbia Provincial Archives)*

Sketch map of the Thompson's River District drawn by Archibald McDonald in 1827; the first map of the interior of British Columbia *(Hudson's Bay Company Archives)*

Jane Klyne McDonald, an outstanding example of a model fur-trade wife *(Public Archives of Canada, Ottawa)*

Jasper House, key post of the Hudson's Bay Company in the Rocky Mountains, where Jane Klyne lived with her family before her marriage to Archibald McDonald in 1825 *(Paul Kane, 1847)*

Return of a war party, Pacific Coast, a scene often repeated during McDonald's tenure at Fort Langley, 1828-1833 *(Paul Kane, 1847)*

Tshimakain Mission, home of the Rev. Elkanah Walker and the Rev. Cushing Eells and their families near Fort Colvile (*Paul Kane, 1847*)

Fort Edmonton. The cross (upper right) marks the burial place of the three little McDonald boys who died of scarlet fever on the family's last journey east from the Columbia in 1845. Painted by Paul Kane the following year.

John McLoughlin, Chief
Factor in charge of the
Columbia District, 1824-1845.
*(Public Archives of Canada,
Ottawa)*

Dr. William Fraser Tolmie,
physician and fur trader in the
Columbia District. He later
played a prominent part in the
affairs of the Crown colony of
British Columbia. *(British
Columbia Provincial Archives)*

and boat builder to gentleman's servant and interpreter in the North West Company since before the turn of the century. He had proved himself so useful that he had been appointed that year as postmaster, the highest rank a noncommissioned officer could hold in the Hudson's Bay hierarchy. The Klynes were well-known to all who crossed the mountains, but how and when Jane and Archibald met is not recorded. What is known is that their marriage was a model in fur trade annals — a bond of strength and mutual affection seldom equalled in any of the records that now exist.

McLoughlin had delayed McDonald's move to Thompson's River, awaiting the arrival of Edward Ermatinger, the new accountant from the East who must be instructed in his duties. "We have them [the accounts] now in order & we ought to endeavour to keep them so," McLoughlin said, setting McDonald to the task of passing on his methods to the newcomer.

It was not until January 7 that McDonald left Vancouver to take up his new charge. And when he made the move, with him went his new bride, Jane Klyne McDonald, whom he had wed "in the custom of the country" sometime that fall.*

The prospect of being established with the command of a post of his own created a vision of family life that McDonald had long been seeking. His young wife was willing to take over the care of Princess Raven's baby, Ranald, and accustomed as she was to life on a northern trading post she had no fears of her neighbors, or of the loneliness that was the lot of residents of such a remote, if romantic, spot.

---

* Their son Benjamin later gave the date of their marriage as September 1, 1825. Ten years later, on June 9, 1835, when they were at last together in the presence of a clergyman, Jane and Archibald McDonald were united in matrimony in an Anglican service performed by the Reverend William Cockran, at the Red River settlement.

PART III

West of the Rockies

CHAPTER EIGHT

Along the Skirts of the Mountains

1826 - 1828

The move to Kamloops was a happy one. Responsibility sat well with McDonald and he adopted his patriarchal role in the small community with ease, his concern embracing not only the officers and men of the fort and their families, but extending to the Indians of the neighborhood who gathered at the gates waiting for a glimpse of the new trader, ready to size him up and decide whether or not to extend their friendship and cooperation.

The season was nearing its end when he first arrived at the district headquarters in February. John McLeod and his family were still there, preparing to move east with the Express as soon as spring cleared the rivers, so McDonald left his little family at Okanagan and continued on to Kamloops to take over the charge and pave the way for the coming of Jane and young Ranald later in the year. The winter had been mild so far, but by the end of the month the river was choked with ice, and the flatlands as well as the neighboring mountains were covered with a thick blanket of snow. To McDonald, who thought "nothing can be more congenial to man than the Winter," it was an agreeable scene. He found Kamloops "perfectly free from that raw and heavy atmosphere so common to other parts of the country west of the Rocky Mountains" and he looked forward to establishing himself and his family in the primitive officers' quarters when the McLeods made their move.

First, though, he must make himself known to the neighboring Indians. Nicolas, the Okanagan chief, whose tribe spread itself along both sides of Big Okanagan Lake, and Tranquille, the Shuswap chief, who lived with his people to the east, were both near at hand, ready to welcome his friendly overtures. Farther off, along the upper reaches of the Fraser River, the more remote tribes seldom came near the fort. With only a few short weeks before it would be time to take the season's furs down to Fort Vancouver, McDonald decided to set off to visit them and on the way explore the unknown territories to the northwest. Whether cultivating an attachment to this group of Indians would increase the dwindling fur returns of the Thompson's River District remained to be seen, but at least the effort must be made.

Thompson's River, in spite of its name and of the extent of its surrounding waters, relied largely on overland communication; the stock in trade were strong, healthy horses, grazing in the neighboring ranges in large numbers to be called on whenever men or furs or trade goods and supplies had to be transported to or from the New Caledonia District to the north, or headquarters to the south. While throughout most other areas of the British fur trade water transport was predominant, at Kamloops the business of the establishment revolved around its horses. The horse park was carefully maintained to keep a constant supply of the animals ready at hand. Two or three men of the post were assigned to their care: bathing their sore backs with potash and water to heal the lesions caused by carrying the heavy packs over long, difficult trails; and in winter tending their special needs when "the poor horses suffered much, tumbling in the hills head over heels like as many wool sacks."

On returning from his first short exploration, McDonald immediately sent his men to organize the pack train for the trip south with the Thompson's River furs, seeing to it that there were still plenty of fresh vigorous horses in the corral to bring the New Caledonia furs on down to Okanagan when Chief Factor Connolly made his appearance from the North. By mid-March he was again on the trail, leaving Francis Ermatinger at Kamloops to see the New Caledonians on their way.

After a reunion with his family at Okanagan, McDonald with Edward Ermatinger and John Work was accompanying the Express canoes the short distance to the Forks of Spokane when disastrous news reached him from the North. The New Caledonia Brigade had been stranded at Alexandria, an "unaccountable mortality" among their horses leaving them without transport even as far as Thompson's River.

Failure of the salmon in the neighborhood of Fort Alexandria had caused starvation and suffering among the Indians, leaving them in no condition to help. McDonald left his friends and returned immediately to Okanagan to send twelve of the best horses he had brought down in his pack train two weeks earlier along with eighteen others from that fort back to Kamloops with orders for Francis Ermatinger to procure what horses he could from the Thompson's River Indians and dispatch them all to Alexandria. It meant a long delay in getting down the furs, but McDonald would go ahead to Vancouver with those from his own district and hope that the brigade from New Caledonia would arrive at the Columbia before the ships set sail for England. Meanwhile, plans must be made to gather a large number of horses to fill their future needs.

On April 20 he said farewell to John Work at Okanagan and set off with his deputy, Francis Noel Annance, Edward Ermatinger, twelve engagés and two Indians, carrying "12 packs furs, 15 bales salmon, 4 bales Appechimons, 1 bale saddles, 1 bale leather, 1 bale cords, & 3 cassettes," to proceed by boat as far as Walla Walla and thence on horseback overland to Fort Vancouver. It was nearly two months before Chief Factor Connolly made his way down from New Caledonia, and when he and Mc-Donald met in mid-July at Walla Walla they agreed that the only solution to the shortage of horses was an excursion to the Indian horse fair at Nez Percés Forks, one hundred and fifty miles distant, a colorful but unpredictable gathering of such numbers that as a rule it was firmly avoided by the fur traders. In this emergency there was no alternative, and McDonald cast about for the strongest party he could muster to accompany him on the journey.

James Douglas (later Sir James Douglas, the first governor

of British Columbia) was there, newly arrived in the Columbia, and Francis Annance, and with John Work, the clerk in charge at Walla Walla, an interpreter, twenty-eight men and an Indian chief named Charlie they embarked in two boats for the journey up the Nez Percés (Snake) River. To McDonald's delight, also accompanying them on their mission was a travelling botanist, David Douglas, who had arrived on the Company's ship the preceding summer, sent out by the Horticultural Society of London, England, with the protection of the Hudson's Bay Company. McDonald, an enthusiastic amateur naturalist, had met Douglas earlier in the year at Fort Vancouver and the opportunity of assisting him in gathering specimens of the flora and fauna of the Columbia to send back to Britain was a welcome one.

To the fur traders, the constant journeying about by boat or on horseback was no novelty. They bore the inconvenience and the discomfort without complaint, and when they did remark on any unusual events in their travels it was generally to call attention to an oddity or to record an amusing incident. In fact, the mood around the campfires was one of happy conviviality, and if Edward Ermatinger was on hand, there was always music to brighten the scene. He never travelled without his flute and, if he could carry it, his violin as well, to provide a fuller-bodied accompaniment for the singing and dancing. For dance they did, and much to Douglas's astonishment, on one occasion when travelling with Ermatinger the men engaged in a particularly lively promenade in his honor. "I could not do less than endeavour to please by jumping, for dance I could not," he wrote in his journal.

The horse fair provided the wandering botanist with more wonders to describe for his sponsors back in England. The journey along the river took nearly a week, with temperatures ranging from 98 to 108 degrees Fahrenheit, travelling from daybreak till early afternoon when the sun was at its height, and then later in the cool of the evening continuing on for another fifteen or twenty miles. "Except that good water may always be obtained," he wrote, "there is nothing to render this country superior, in summer, to the burning deserts of Arabia." Occasionally they purchased a few fish from Indians they met along the way, but for the most part they dined on horse flesh, either boiled or roasted over the fire on the end of a stick.

Sharboni

They found six hundred men gathered at the Forks when they arrived at their destination — "a camp of three different nations . . . the Pierced-Nose Indians, the Chawhapton and the Chamniemuchs" — and that evening their chiefs arrived at the visitors' camp to sit with them till the night grew late and present them with gifts of some of their favorite horses. Next day it was down to business, but the parleying seemed endless to Douglas, who was impatient to explore the surrounding territory and search out his seeds and samples. His protectors held him back, however, unsure of the mood and temper of their Indian hosts, and it was not until the third night, after an amicable day of "singing, dancing, haranguing and smoking, the whole party being dressed in their best garments," that McDonald agreed to let him leave the encampment, sending with him one of his own men as a companion and guide.

When Douglas returned to the fair two days later he found a different atmosphere prevailing.

A misunderstanding having arisen between our interpreter and one of the Indians chiefs, the latter accused the former of not translating correctly, and words failing to express sufficiently his wrath, he seized the poor man of language, and tore off a handful of his long jet hair by the roots. On being remonstrated with for this violence, the Indian set off in a rage, and summoned his followers, seventy-three in party who came, all armed, each with his gun cocked, and the arrow on the bowstring. As, however, every individual of our camp had done all that was possible to accommodate matters, we took things coolly, and apparently careless of the result, stood, thirty-one in number, to our arms and asked if they wished for war? They said "No; we only want the interpreter to kill him, and, as he is no chief, this could not signify to us." But our reply was, that whether chief or not, each individual in our camp, though he were only an Indian, was entitled to our protection; and if they offered to molest him, they should see whether we had ever been in war before or not. The coolness, which we took care to show by our countenances as much as in our speech, had the desired effect, and they earnestly begged for the peace which we were certainly quite as glad to grant. Many speeches were made on the occasion, and, to judge by the gestures of these children of nature, and the effect which their harangues produce, some of them must possess oratorical powers of no mean description. The affair ended, as usual, by an interchange of presents.

On the sixth day the horse-trading was completed. The speech-making, the singing and dancing and smoking came to an end, and the Hudson's Bay men set off with a train of seventy healthy new horses to distribute among their posts. McDonald descended the Columbia River to Vancouver, anxious the while about Jane, who was awaiting the birth of their first child at Okanagan. When he arrived back there with Connolly on August 10, he found his new son, Angus, born on the first day of the month, waiting to greet him.

Connolly hurried to get his New Caledonia brigade in order for the long northward march, and Francis Annance, who was to serve as McDonald's clerk at Kamloops, moved off with an advance party to prepare for McDonald, who would follow a few weeks later with the other men and the wives and children. Young Angus was less than four weeks old when he started on this first of his many long journeys in the Northwest, carried by his mother on horseback during the two-week trek while two-year-old Ranald stayed under his father's wing. With them were Mrs. Annance and her little son, who, with her husband, were to share the officers' quarters at the outpost with the McDonalds.

The McDonalds arrived at Kamloops on September 9 at the head of a train of fifty horses carrying the annual Outfit for the post, and accompanied by the eight men, seven of them with families, who with Annance and two others who had gone ahead with him made up the complement of the establishment. In their absence the key to the fort had been left with Nicolas, the Okanagan chief, but the nearer neighbors, Tranquille and his Shuswaps, insulted at not being trusted with its care, had broken in during the summer and helped themselves to whatever they could find. "Several hundred dried salmon & a few old saddles and appèchements belonging to N. Caledonia is the net loss sustained — & the store lock, which the Shewhaps removed to render the key & Master Nicolas' charge of very little consequence."

The whole was soon put to rights, the small crop of neglected potatoes and barley harvested, a quantity of salmon dried and put aside for winter, and McDonald turned his attention to the trade, only to discover that fur-bearing animals had almost disappeared from the Thompson's River area: "even the name of a Beaver is scarcely heard among the natives," he noted. "A person can walk for days together without seeing the smallest quadraped, the little brown squirrel excepted." It was obvious that something must be done to extend the trade, and that meant further exploration of lands not as yet reached through their local hunters.

The Thompson's River District ran north from the Columbia River in the area of its confluence with the Okanagan River (Ermatinger's post) "along the Skirts of the Mountains till it embraces all the waters falling into North River; and then in a S.W. direction towards . . . Frasers river."

McDonald had already discussed with McLoughlin his proposed investigation of the Thompson River to its junction with the Fraser, and his plan included forays into the hitherto unexplored territories surrounding its banks. When Nicolas, the Upper Okanagan chief, arrived with his furs ("his whole trade is 27 large & small Beaver") a few days after McDonald's party returned to the fort, a conference was held with him. McDonald was anxious that this favored chief should accompany him, and though Nicolas was at first cautious about the scheme, holding out no "flattering prospects of finding an easy navigation," he finally agreed to go along, and he returned to his lodge arranging a meeting three days later "where the Coutamine [now the Nicola River] empties itself into the Thompson's river."

The object of the expedition was not only a new source of furs. It was well known that the Americans were pressing their claim to the land north of the Columbia and Governor Simpson was convinced that a communication might be developed via the Thompson and Fraser rivers, should the eventual boundary settlement exclude the Hudson's Bay Company from the Columbia route. That these rivers had never been run in the years that fur traders had been roaming the territory, and that the Indians firmly avoided many parts of them did not discourage him in his view. He was eager to hear first-hand reports, and although McDonald's exploration was made on horseback and not by water, it encouraged the governor to think that this alternative was possible.

This river to the mouth of the Coutamine is not bad, & indeed to the little rivulet Nicaumchin there are no very dangerous places: but from there for about five miles down, even when I was there and when the water was greatly fallen, it was nothing but a continuation of cascades & strong rapids — Earlier in the season it would of course present a more formidable appearance, but if this place was the only obstacle it could with additional exertion be overcome at any time — The fact is, that the nature of those two rivers, rolling down with great rapidity in a narrow bed between immense mountains generally speaking render their ascent most laborious, & in places in the main river perhaps impossible except at low water.

Just how impossible McDonald learned two years later when, en route from Hudson Bay to the Pacific with Governor Simpson, they followed this waterway in a boat with twelve paddlers, encountering "a number of minor rapids . . . a little below passed a dangerous one . . . below which was the Rapide de la Grosse Roche, which ought to have been taken on the left side, as we took in much water by running close to the rock on the right hand . . ." and on through other swirls and rapids until "we were nearly swamped, for in three swells we were full to the thafts, and the danger was increased by the unavoidable necessity of running over a strong whirlpool while the boat was in this unmanageable state."

George Simpson was less sanguine:

The whole of these Rapids we shot down, and only lightened at two of them, where it was necessary to run altho' dangerous, as there was no possibility of making a portage: at another which our "Boutes" did not examine with sufficient attention, we had a narrow escape, the water coming over the Thofts at the first plunge, and the Boat in this unmanageable state entering another, which we did not observe, until on its brink, out of which, however, we providentially got all safe, altho' the whitened countenances of the boldest among us, even that of our dark Iroquois Bowsman who is nearly amphibious, shewed that we felt anything but comfortable. . . .

When the next day the party proceeded on down the Fraser River, Simpson without question abandoned his hopes of a communication system through these waters: "bad as Thompsons River is . . . the Frasers River is infinitely worse."

McDonald's overland exploration with Nicolas failed to reveal the dangers so evident from the water and therefore prolonged the optimistic views of the governor, who had not yet, in 1826, visited the tumultuous rivers in question. In his second object, the excursion was more successful. Though he was accompanied by eight of his own men, it was the close association with Nicolas that cemented their friendship and provided access to the Indian tribes along the way who were the chief's friends. At the junction of the two rivers (Lytton, British Columbia, today) he left Nicolas and four of the men encamped and went off with his interpreter and three men "for the span of about 8 miles," questioning the Indians they met about the condition of the river on toward the sea, and hearing from them tales of beaver in plenty in various directions around them.

During the trip we had the good fortune to see but few Indians — their salmon fishing was over, and by that time they were back in the Mountains after Deer. Some however more anxious to gain our favour represented all the absentees as off for Beaver. Nicolas showed himself among them very jealous for the Whites — he exercised his rhetorical fancy among them two or three different times & as I was told much to the purpose: above all things to avoid quarreling with us. I have advised this Indian to continue his friendship with the two Chiefs from below & to bring them to the Fort next time they come his way . . . we may soon make a very favorable impression upon the numerous tribes of Indians in the lower part of the river —

In all, the expedition took only a week, but McDonald returned to the fort with careful measurements of sufficient accuracy to enable him to draw the first map of the interior of British Columbia. Apparently his studies in London had included some cartography, and he was able to send off a sketch map to McLoughlin with his next report on the journey, saying, "I had a few good observations for the Lat. and I have reason to suppose that the Long: of the Forks cannot be far wrong — This place is about the same meridian with Okanakan which the inland travellers have placed on or about 120° & I believe the mouth of Fraser's river is not far from 123[°] of Vancouver's surveys of the coast. . . ." On another occasion he took the latitude of the fort "with a small sextant & a saucer of molasses. The Index gave 39′ − 38′ and if the Instrument & Observation be correct our Lat. is about 50 − 40."

In the *Historical Cartography of British Columbia* McDonald's map is reproduced and described by A. L. Farley. "It is not surprising that few maps were made by the fur-traders, and the sketches that were made lacked the precision and quality of the trained cartographer. Even with precise observations, the intricate drainage patterns and generally difficult topography associated with what is now British Columbia rendered the mapping especially complex. Small wonder that the delineation of the interior British Columbia was so long in the making.

"An exception is found in the work of Archibald McDonald. . . . Much of the area was already familiar to Company men and McDonald unquestionably made use of information from other traders. Unlike others, however, he was apparently interested in mapping and possessed no mean ability as a draughtsman."

McDonald's other scientific interests included botany and zoology. He had already in the spring of that same year packed up "a box or two of curiosities and preserved Birds" to send home on the Company ship for John Halkett to pass on to his scientific friends at the British Museum. This interest was to continue through all the years McDonald spent west of the Rockies, stimulated by the visits of such travellers as David Douglas who came his way and encouraged him to continue his hobby.

The nature and behavior of the native people he came to know fascinated him as well, and he frequently noted his observations in his journals, summing up his conclusions in a style both graphic and methodical. In his report on the Thompson's River district written for the Governor and Council of the Northern Department in the spring of 1827, he included a full discussion of the Indians of the neighborhood, including a population count of the thirty thousand square miles in his charge. He interviewed all the chiefs he came in contact with and kept careful records of the information they provided.

"They furnished me with a small stick for every grown man of their community, with few exceptions each has a wife, seldom more." The total count indicated an unusual proportion of adults to the numbers of children, but he accounted for that because "the lists of young hunters and married women are swollen up with children of 10 and 12 years old."

In the territory McDonald numbered eleven tribes, listed the names of sixteen chiefs or "principal men," with a mere 3,400

Indians over all the lands. He found them an entirely different breed from the Chinooks, Kootenay, Cayuse, Flathead, and Nez Percés tribes to the south, and equally far removed in their habits and customs from the people east of the mountains. Only a few of the tribes, and these mostly to the north, showed any interest in fur hunting. The others made their contact with the traders by bartering the dried salmon that were the winter staple food, along with the few potatoes grown at the fort and berries and root vegetables gathered nearby.

The Salmon tribes are of a very indolent habit — during the summer & autumn they live quite exposed along the rivers, & in winter burrey up themselves in circular pits under ground — Their covering for the most part is the skin of the small deer with the hair on — that & the quiver with his Bow & Arrows constitute the whole costume of one of our Indians unless he is provident enough to secure bits of dressed leather to cover his legs — The tribes in question are also much given to gambling — a consequent evil attendant on their sedentary life — The Salmon, they take with scoop nets in the Edies [*sic*] along the high cliffs, but in the neighbourhood of Kamloops where the water is less intercepted, they use the dart & Toarch at night — Throughout this part of the Country they are remarkably superstitious & have the most implicit faith in the good or evil virtue of what is termed *Medicine* among themselves — They have no slaves & a plurality of wives not prevalent. — Nothing can exceed their fancy for Tobacco — to appearance they indulge in Smoaking, with no other view than that of gratifying the passion: but I believe it is also combined with strong motives of devotion — deaths, Sickness, Scarcity of Salmon, bad luck in the chase, or any other misfortune is immediately attributed to the want of Tobacco — the most inexorable heart (according to their way of thinking) must be cured by Tobacco, and when the *heart* is good no evil can follow — Rum they know nothing of.

McDonald had an opportunity to observe this phenomenon at close hand. Three of the neighboring chiefs — Nicolas, Court Apatte and Cadarotte — called at the fort seeking his support in "a grand turnout against the northern Indians" to avenge the death of Nicolas's father three years earlier. To their host it was a "mere talk war," and after giving his "entire acquiescence in their schemes of warfare & by so doing avoid the obligation they think they have imposed upon us by relinquishing a war expedition in which they are anything but serious themselves," he presented each with a yard of tobacco and they retired to enjoy it.

Eight days later they were "still hanging about the house" and McDonald was tiring of their presence. "From such long visits they not only become troublesome & fall in our estimation, but they themselves lose the little dignity with which they arrive — they are immoderately fond of tobacco, but they will not admit this love proceeds from a mere wish to gratify their desire of smoking — Nicolas very ingeniously maintains that he and those among them of any good sense smoak tobacco for a *much different* & better motive, that which moves the white people to look in the Great Fathers Book: for the moment *he* takes his pipe, he cannot help thinking of the great question of the world and the number of good things done for their benefit the Indian cannot understand. . . . I never saw a savage that seems more concerned in the power of a Supreme being."

Scarcely had the two Okanagans been seen off the premises when McDonald's attention was turned to Court Apatte and his people. For days Indians had been slipping into the Shuswap camps from the North River and Upper Shuswap Lake. Court Apatte and the Lower Shuswaps had invited them all, along with the Coutamines, to a "Grand entertainment" and after months of planning the preparations were now complete and the appointed time had arrived. It was mid-December and snow was thick on the ground when the last of the guests, those from the Upper Lake, arrived to join in the smoking and dancing. They paid a formal call at the fort, bringing their beaver skins to trade, before going to join their friends at "the house of merriment & feasting." After several days of preliminary celebrations, Court Apatte appeared at the fort to invite the HBC men to his "grand banque." McDonald and one of his Canadian servants agreed to attend.

It is much to be regretted that the object of this kind of jubilee (not uncommon among the natives here) is not better understood by the Europeans, & am sorry to say, that I am not likely to throw any additional light on the subject — not a word of the native language here can anyone attached to the Compa-

ny's service speak. All our little dealing with them is done thro'
the medium of the Okanakan —

On arrival at the Camp I saw for the first time the cabin
which the chief had constructed for the express purpose of this
entertainment — its dimension at base is 45 feet square with
an upright wall of about 4, and then the roof running to a
point in the centre, to answer the purpose of a door — to this
aperture is fixed up nearly perpendicular, a stout stick of about
18ft. notched at convenient distances to serve as ladder. . . .
gang of stark naked fellows actively engaged in lowering down
by means of slings from 20 to 25 of their waterproof baskets,
smoaking hot with thin soups, none of them less than 10 gallons & some considerably more. In mean time as many were
already busily employed below cutting up most excellent dried
Beaver & venison laid up at the expence of much labour &
privation to themselves solely for the purpose since the autumn
— Bear's fat both raw and melted was also partining [sic] out
& roots of every description . . . ready for distribution.

The guests near upon 300 men sat upon the ground as thick
as they could [word illegible] round & round this subterranean
habitation leaving very little space for the attendants, who by
the by let it be observed were not the most contemptible of the
Shewhaps & even Court Apatte himself was by no means an
idle spectator altho his labour did not extend beyond mere
superintendance. Every man was furnished with the cheek
bone of salmon for his spoon, & the soup kettles, consisting of
berries — roots — grease — pounded fish — salmon roe etc.
etc being planted here & there among them they fell to & soon
emptied their dishes — These spacious reservoirs, the Shewhaps Chief other personnages in attendance, made it a point
to taste a portion of each before the hungry visitants commenced the attack — The next course was each a lump of suet
— after which the Beaver & venison with a raw piece of Bear's
fat; & lastly the roots — This ceremony occupied about two
hours, when I enabled them to resume the pipe, which being
some time indulged in, the devouring organs were again called
to action & to continue alternately with the pipe for at least 24
hours. It is a universal rule with them on such occasion that
the guest must eat all put before him, & if this task be too
much another is imposed — that of carrying it with him —

This (being liberally supplied with the most substantial part of the eatables) was unluckily the case with myself today, but the constant dry salmon at home rendered it more agreeable than painful. Those who come from a distance are by this law much beholden to their good appetite & to their still better powers of digestion, but I believe before the feast is over seldom is the latter found capable of performing its functions, & the consequence is what naturally might be expected. This heaving up scene affords the host (evidence absolutely necessary) the most convincing proof of their being treated to their hearts content —

They have been dancing for the last 48 hours, which I believe necessarily carries with it a system of fasting. During the dance presents were exchanged. The Coutamines gave 3 or 4 horses — guns & Hayques. The Shewhaps returned the compliment with Guns — Robes — Beads & a few Beaver Traps — I observed hung up in the Banquet Hall what they told me were appendages belonging to some of the deceased relations of Court Apatte & friends, which in the progress of the dance were often saluted with loud peals of mourning & lamentation. During this rendezvous it is also an object with them to pledge their friendship with each other, altho religion no doubt is the primary consideration. . . . The rest of our people crossed to the camp in the evening — None of the Okanakans attended & but very few of the Schimilicameach.

It was several days before the visitors had sufficiently recovered from this orgy to make their way back to their own camps, and soon after, Court Apatte and his local Indians had an opportunity to observe the Europeans' feast day — Christmas at Kamloops, 1826. Francis Annance with six men and an interpreter had left two days earlier for the Coutamine on one of his frequent excursions to procure salmon from the Indians there to provision the fort. "The two men at home with me were regaled with a good fat Dog & their three dried salmon each — Our little flag was hoisted & the Indians were at a loss how we could have two Sundays running as it deprived them of another day's smoking . . . the flag on Sundays is used as a subterfuge to keep the natives from the Fort that day which they obey with surprising strictness." Next day they gathered round in large numbers "making up for their lost ground for two days past —"

New Year's Day was marked in the Scottish tradition, the most important celebration of the year. "Went thro' the usual ceremonies with the few men at the Fort — five — after exchanging compliments of the season, a Flaggon of spirits was produced on the occasion, which with a couple of fat dogs with their dried salmon completed their regale for the present — The Ladies (double the number of the men & as many children) next made their appearance in the Bourgeois' Hall . . . & with equal modesty put up with a single Flaggon of wine." When Annance and his party returned to the fort on January 4 it was time for another feast. An unmanageable horse was committed to the kettle. "This luxury & each a pint of rum made them forget the miseries of a whole twelvemonth —"

Time then to stoke the fires against the bitter chill of winter's coldest months, to catch up on correspondence, to prepare reports for McLoughlin, Superintendent of the Columbia District, and others for the Governor and Northern Council in time to send them east with the express canoes in early April. The pace slackened and there were moments to enjoy the little boys and to relax by the hearth with his pretty young wife. There was a welcome visit from Frank Ermatinger, who made his way up from Okanagan over thick-crusted snow to bring letters forwarded from Fort Vancouver and to remain for a convivial ten days while Annance took care of the post below. And then it was mid-March and again time for McDonald to pack up the horses with the year's collection of furs and lead his party down to Okanagan to meet the eastward-bound Express and send the returns west to the ships at the mouth of the Columbia.

He arrived at the rendezvous before the travellers from Fort Vancouver, and was continuing south toward Walla Walla in hopes of meeting them when he came upon his botanical friend, David Douglas, who had walked the whole distance from headquarters while Edward Ermatinger, in charge of the Express, and others in the party from headquarters moved along by boat and on horseback.

An opportunity to further his scientific knowledge was just to McDonald's taste and he spent the next five days wandering along the Columbia River, studying the early spring wildflowers that were already shooting up in the rocky crevices along the south side while snow still covered the northern banks. Douglas

was on his way back to England, planning to accompany Ermatinger as far as Hudson Bay and board one of the Company ships
there. He had little time left to gather specimens from west of the
mountains, and this last-minute walk gave him a chance not only
to fill out his collection of plants and birds but to pick up bits of
minerals as well, samples of marble and granite from the steep
rocks that rose high from the river's banks, fine pebbles from the
flat gravelly patches. He had acquired a handsome fine-plumed
male grouse a few days earlier, and with McDonald's assistance
found a hen bird to complete the pair. By the time the two joined
their companions at Okanagan they were fast friends, absorbed
in their mutual interests, and McDonald was happily committed
to continuing his investigations of the local flora and fauna and
forwarding what specimens he could gather in the future to the
Horticultural Society in London.

Douglas set off for the East, his prized pair of grouse carefully wrapped in oilcloth, expressing his warm gratitude to Mc-
Donald for his "information, assistance and hospitality" and his
hopes of returning again to the Columbia. It was only days before a message was carried back from Colvile. Douglas had lost
his birds, a "great misfortune" in his eyes, and he wrote to Mc-
Donald to try to get him another pair before the ship sailed from
the Columbia for England. The grouse had been devoured, "the
skins torn to pieces by the famished Indian dogs of the place. Although they were closely tied in a small oilcloth and hung from
the tent-poles, the dogs gnawed and ate the casing, which were
leather thongs. Grieved at this beyond measure," Douglas recorded in his diary.

McDonald returned to Kamloops to spend a quiet summer
with his family, making the most of the opportunity to expand
the gardens, encourage the cultivation of a larger quantity of potatoes and grains and experiment with a few other hardy vegetables that might be put by for winter to vary the everlasting diet of
dried salmon. In October he was at Okanagan when Edward Ermatinger returned from the East, bringing welcome first-hand
news of Jane's family, with whom he had travelled from Fort Assiniboine to Jasper House. There was time to discuss arrangements for McDonald's own trip back to York Factory next
spring. His long-awaited commission had at last come through,

and the new chief trader was to travel eastward across the continent to attend his first meeting of the Northern Council in July.

Back at Kamloops, the winter went on much as before, the Indians taking up their hungry vigil at the gates, parties journeying forth regularly to the more provident tribes near the Fraser River to bring back provisions, and sometimes furs. Jane's second son, Archibald, was born early in February, and less than six weeks later McDonald was making ready to take the returns south to the boats on the Columbia River, his cassette packed for the eastward journey. He was accompanied by Chief Trader Joseph McGillivray with the New Caledonia furs, who was to join the party bound for Hudson Bay. Edward Ermatinger was again in charge of the Express from Fort Vancouver leaving the Columbia for the last time, planning to retire from the fur trade and take up a business career in Upper Canada.

The two parties, fourteen in all, met at Okanagan and went on together to Fort Colvile where they remained with John Work until April 20, the date they set off by water for Boat Encampment northeast of Kamloops at the base of the Rocky Mountains. From there in the early days of May they proceeded on snowshoes through the difficult Athabasca Pass, "gentlemen" and servants alike carrying their own packs of clothing and provisions. David Douglas described his similar experience the year before: "I can hardly imagine what a stranger would think to see nine men, each with his load on his back, his snowshoes in his hand, starting on a journey over such inhospitable country, one falling, a second helping him up, a third lagging behind, a fourth resting smoking his pipe. . . ."

At Jasper House, Michel Klyne had their horses waiting, and after a few days' rest with his wife's family McDonald, with Ermatinger and McGillivray, went off ahead of the main party, leaving their baggage to follow them to Edmonton, carried in train by thirteen horses. From there it was three weeks' journey by canoe to Norway House where they met George Simpson in mid-June, and continued on with him to the council meeting at York Factory.

CHAPTER NINE

Certain Death in Nine Attempts out of Ten

1828

McDonald had waited seven long years to have a part in the decision-making of the Northern Council. To be one of the four chief traders invited to attend in the first year of his appointment was flattering, and he took his place at the table with fresh confidence and enthusiasm. The conviviality of the week-long gathering and the festivity around the bountiful board each evening appealed to his gregarious nature, and the exclusiveness of joining with the eight chief factors at the business sessions chaired by the governor contributed to the sense of importance that his new commission gave him.

The deed poll of 1821 had created a special class in the chief factors who set themselves far above any other rank in the hierarchy, but though several of those present were new to him, some, at least, were old friends, among them Colin Robertson, John Rowand from Edmonton, and J. G. McTavish, chief at York Factory (whose granddaughter would later marry one of McDonald's sons). It was ironic that one of the memorable acts of that annual meeting was the creation of the title "Warden of the Plains" at a salary of £200 per year for Cuthbert Grant. The thoughts of Colin Robertson and Archy McDonald at seeing the leader of the Seven Oaks attack so rewarded are not recorded in the minutes.

What is recorded is that it was at this session of council that the Standing Rules and Regulations were drawn up, to be printed in permanent form for the guidance of officers and servants of the Company throughout its far-flung territories. Many of the provisions included in the document were repetitions of items in the minutes of preceding years, but the object was to establish a permanent guide to the position of the Company on such routine matters as transport and handling of the annual Outfits, salaries, contracts and other matters pertaining to personnel, conduct of the trade itself, prices of furs and trade goods and dealings with the Indians.

Beyond the stipulations regarding business affairs, the Standing Rules went on to set out a pattern to be followed in relations with the Indian people — "encourage industry, repress vice and inculcate morality," said rule number 15, and treat them "with kindness and indulgence." At the same time the Indians were to be asked to the regular Sunday reading of divine service at the various outposts to join with "every man, woman and child" on the establishment, who were required to attend. The Company would furnish appropriate religious books.

The families of "gentlemen" and "servants" alike were protected and controlled. While living on the posts they were to receive regular instruction in their A B Cs and catechism from the father, and if any of the men wished to leave women and children behind in the Indian country on their retirement, they were required to make provision for the future maintenance of the families so abandoned.

The week was stimulating and one to remember in the long months and years of what McDonald himself referred to as "exile" in the wilderness west of the Rocky Mountains. It was to be six summers before he would again take part in the council meetings, and he savored his brief moment at the hub of the Company's affairs in the Northern Department. More than that, he was to have the added distinction of accompanying the governor west to the Pacific coast at the end of the sessions.

Simpson had in his few years in the country acquired a formidable reputation as a traveller, driving the hand-picked crew of his canoe to ever better records for speed in covering the thousands of miles of waterways he traversed. He was impatient to be off, and after winding up the business of council on the afternoon of July 11, allowed time for only a few hours' rest before embarking. There was not a man at York Factory who was unaware of the governor's fondness for pomp and ceremony, and in spite of the hour — it was 1 A.M. when they made their departure — the entire establishment gathered at the river's edge to see them off on their historic journey. Fourteen commissioned officers led the three cheers that sent them on their way, and a salute of seven guns from the garrison filled the air, drowning out the voices of the eighteen paddlers singing a familiar voyageur air as the two light canoes swept round the point against the strong current of the Hayes River.

As they set off with such a flourish, gliding in comfort in gaily painted craft manned by the best paddlers in the country, each "gentleman" with a personal servant to look after his needs, McDonald's mind must have turned back to his first journey up this river — the weary, inexperienced young Kildonan settlers plodding along the icy river banks or crowded into the heavy York boats, struggling with rough waters — and how his own fortunes had changed.

The officers of the Company did travel in some comfort, though they were as exposed as anyone else to the discomforts of the weather, the long walks over portages and the torment of the flies and mosquitoes that were synonymous with the North, particularly in spring and early summer. Food was rough, but while the paddlers kept up their strength on a diet of pemmican and an occasional dram of spirits, the "gentlemen" supped on cold meat and a glass of wine. When fresh fish was available along the way or a hunter had luck with geese, ducks, partridge or an occasional deer, there was a feast for all, but the double standard was well marked and observed without question on both sides. The old voyageur who said after twenty-four years as a paddler and forty-one years in the fur trade, "Were I young again, I should spend my life the same way over. There is no life so happy as a voyageur's life," apparently spoke for them all. The pride that the French-Canadian canoemen felt in their work and in themselves, the joy and vigor they applied to every part of their lives, were eloquent testimony to the fact that theirs was a chosen profession.

Simpson described the routine of a typical voyaging day:

Weather permitting, our slumbers would be broken about one in the morning by the cry of "Lève, lève, lève!" In five minutes, woe to the inmates that were slow in dressing; the tents were tumbling about our ears; and, within half an hour, the camp would be raised, the canoes laden, and the paddles keeping time to some merry old song. About eight o'clock, a convenient place would be selected for breakfast, about three quarters of an hour being allotted for the multifarious operations of unpacking and repacking the equipage, laying and removing the cloth, boiling and frying, eating and drinking; and, while the preliminaries were arranging, the hardier among us would wash and shave, each person carrying soap and towel in his pocket, and finding a mirror in the same sandy or rocky basin that held the water. About two in the afternoon we usually put ashore for dinner; and, as this meal needed no fire, or at least got none, it was not allowed to occupy more than twenty minutes or half an hour.

Such was the routine of our journey, the day, generally speaking, being divided into six hours of rest and eighteen of labour. This almost incredible toil the voyageurs bore without a murmur, and generally with such a hilarity of spirit as few other men could sustain for a single forenoon.

The governor's movement across the land was marked with ceremony all the way. His own picked crew was, to a man, proud to be selected for such an honorable position, and came equipped with the most colorful of sashes and ribbons and the finest of feathers in their caps to mark the distinction. Their singing of the vivacious voyageur songs was lustier, and the quiet airs more poignant, than any of their fellows, and as they approached the principal posts along their route their talent for the theatrical was almost as important as their skill with the paddle.

Simpson encouraged the practice of dressing up for arrivals, and a few hours before they came to the newly rebuilt Norway House near what McDonald had known as Jack River in his Red River settlement days, a stop was made to allow the men to change into their most colorful raiment. McDonald and the third "gentleman" of the party, Dr. Richard Hamlyn, who was on his way to take up duties as surgeon at Fort Vancouver, sat together in one canoe with a bugler to herald their approach. A young piper, Colin Fraser, newly arrived from the Highlands, took his place beside the governor, ready to accompany the party as they made their way up to the fort from the river's edge. And along the river the paddles dipped with precision in time to the songs of the voyageurs.

John McLeod and his companions at the fort heard them before they saw them and gathered at the gates to form an excited welcoming party. It was a short stop. Next morning at eleven they were on their way again, the governor having dispatched some last-minute correspondence and taken on fresh supplies, including a few delicacies such as ham and cheese and pork, and a number of kegs of Madeira and port wine.

The westward journey began in earnest. Simpson had decided to follow the northern route via Île à la Crosse: along the Athabasca and Peace rivers, and crossing the mountains at the Peace River Pass to Fort St. James, rather than taking the usual Express route by way of the Saskatchewan to Fort Edmonton, Jasper House and the Athabasca Pass to the Columbia River Boat Encampment. It provided an opportunity to inspect all the northern posts along the way and to look over the New Caledonia District before coming down via Kamloops and the Thompson and Fraser rivers to the newly established Fort Langley not far from the Fraser mouth.

The days soon fell into a regular pattern. In spite of almost incessant rain (both Simpson and McDonald noted in their journals that from the beginning of their journey up to the end of August they had only three fair days), the camp was roused before 2 A.M., McDonald and the doctor standing watch in turn to give the morning signal.

Simpson was not the easiest of travelling companions, his naturally critical nature being tested to the ultimate by the constant close companionship over the three long months the voyage would take, but it became his practice to invite one of his companions to join him over "dinner" — the midday stop for a cold collation and glass of wine — and to take him into his canoe for the afternoon run. The doctor he quickly despaired of. The governor thoroughly enjoyed his mode of travel and found all around him "delightful country." It was difficult to understand a man who "complains of the portages, discovers no beauty in the scenery & wishes himself back at the Factory." McDonald, on the other hand, apparently tried too hard to please. His "laugh & small talk" which were acceptable in the early stages of the journey became "abominably insipid" ten weeks later, when Simpson wrote to his friend McTavish that he had "tired of the voyage and my fellow travellers."

In fact, by this time he was not only tired but ill, and although Simpson does not mention it in his record of the trip, McDonald's journal through the last days of September repeatedly notes that the governor was "very unwell" even though he continued to travel on. His impatience with his companions extended to his servants: Fraser, he said, proved to be "a piper and nothing but a piper," and on one occasion he even had a "dust" with his best paddler, who developed a sore throat and could not sing; Simpson castigated him in no mild terms and "brought forth music in a twinkling."

But in spite of these relatively minor differences, the journey appears to have been for the most part an interesting and reasonably congenial one. At every post along the way they dressed up for the traditional ceremonial arrivals accompanied by bagpipe, bugle and the ringing voices of the voyageurs. And at each of these stops, when the neighboring Indians gathered to greet the visiting governor, Simpson harangued them in his best dramatic style and distributed tobacco and small gifts to encourage their continuing friendship.

The party's musicians held a special fascination for the Indians, and the governor, always ready to take advantage of their wonderment, made a point of entertaining them with a round of the bagpipes and a bugle call or two at every opportunity. Their admiration knew no bounds when he produced his musical snuff-box to baffle and amuse them further; they were all astonishment, "especially when it was made to appear to be the Governor's dog that performed the whole secret."

It was as well that there were these lighter moments, for the journey was an arduous one. Even though it was midsummer, the weather was cold and miserable through most of the 3,261 miles they travelled together from York Factory to Fort Langley. (On August 10, while in the governor's canoe, McDonald describes a half-hour storm pouring down "hail stones of at least the size of a small pistol ball.")

There were the inevitable difficult portages — the longest of them the marathon Methye Portage between Lac la Loche (now Methye Lake in northern Saskatchewan) and the Clearwater River, where they enlisted the assistance of a band of Chipewyan Indians to help with the lift. As a general rule, canoes were not carried over this gruelling twelve-mile stretch. In the ordinary conduct of the Company's business, parties from the East brought supplies and trade goods as far as the east end of the portage, while the furs from the Mackenzie River were brought down from the north and an exchange made, so that only the packs had to be carried. Seldom did a party, as Simpson's did, go all the way carrying their canoes with them.

McDonald's journal describes the episode:

Friday, (August) 8th, — About four o'clock a.m. made a start. The eight "bouts" (. . . steersmen and bowsmen . . .) carrying the canoes, and the other five men of each of the canoes . . . with the assistance of the ten Indians in carrying the loading, were able to remove everything in one haul . . . by a succession of "poses" of 500 to 600 yards each. We reached the south shore of Little Lake by nine, where we breakfasted . . . two thirds of the distance. We crossed it with canoes and baggage about eleven, and the last one-third took us till two p.m., but the canoes and Indians did not arrive before four. We gummed [repaired the canoes] for three quarters of an hour, and again embarked. Made the whole of the Mud portage by seven, and encamped, that the men may enjoy two or three extra glasses of spirits tonight, which they would have had in making the portage had we had no Indians about us.

Even the welcome stops at the Company's forts did not always offer better fare or greater comfort than they had along the way. At Fort Chipewyan, where they spent three days to allow the governor to close his eastside correspondence and to confer with Chief Factor Edward Smith who was returning to the Mackenzie River District after bringing their year's returns down to the rendezvous at Methye Portage, they found the buildings in a state of decay and the gardens meagre and unproductive. Across the mountains at Fort McLeod — "the most wretched place in the Indian Country" in Simpson's estimation

— they caught John Tod by surprise. He and his men had been "on short commons" because of the failure of their fishery all summer, and the bleakness and cheerlessness of their situation were temporarily brightened by the excitement of the arrival of the governor and his party. "I was made inexpressibly happy by . . . your kind letter . . . which was handed me by our gay old acquaintance Mr.Archd.McDonald, who, along with other bucks, arrived here in the suite of Govr.Simpson," Tod wrote to Edward Ermatinger later.

In between the two was the Peace River and the spectacular Peace River Pass: "remarkable for the beauty and grandeur of its scenery, the fertility of its Soil, the number of its vegitable productions, the variety of its mineral appearances and . . . its riches in Beaver and other Fur bearing animals," Simpson recorded.

To McDonald it was remarkable in other ways as well. The party had taken on an extra canoe at Dunvegan to ease the portages through the mountain pass, but the difficulties encountered were formidable, including "about a mile of the worst road in Christendom . . . with unspeakable misery to the poor men. . . . No people having passed this way for the last three years, and, of course, no clearance made in a road that at best must be an infamous one . . . whatever be the fate of the canoes and men by water, I think, of the two evils, they have chosen the least."

The following day they learned that the men with the canoes had indeed "had a most miraculous escape . . . the guide's canoe, with himself and three men, were within an ace of going to perdition over one of the most formidable cascades they had to encounter." And for those on foot the way continued hard. "With the exception of the first four hours today, the road was passable, but many of our pieces were most awkward, such as our taureau (pemican in bags) that were made almost round, and to mend the matter in parchment skins, so that to keep one on top of the other was next to an impossibility." In all it was thirteen days' journey from Dunvegan to Fort McLeod, and in spite of the difficulties of the passage there was time for hilarity when the guide Jean Baptiste Bernard, one of Simpson's favorite men, slipped while carrying his illustrious passenger on his back from the canoe to the shore and flung both of them into what then became known as "Bernard's River."

At McLeod's Lake the party abandoned their canoes and

set off on a hundred-mile overland march to Fort St. James, the principal New Caledonia post on Stuart Lake. The "road was exceedingly bad, no transport of any consquence having gone on . . . for the last three years, and no improvement or clearing away made" and the loads were carefully distributed amongst the men to make the long trek as comfortable as possible. At 5.30 A.M. on Saturday, September 13, the men moved off, walking in pairs to help each other in taking off and putting on their loads, each man carrying a piece assigned as follows:

1 keg Madeira wine	La Course
1 bag Tongues	DeLorme
1 Cassette, McD. and H	Anawagon
1 Paper Trunk, Governor	Martin
1 Cassette, Mr.McGillivray	Larante
1 bag Biscuit	St. Denis
1 Bed, Messrs McD. & H	Houle
1 keg Port Wine	Lasard
1 Cave (Travelling Case)	M——
1 Piece (two tents)	Charpentier
1 Basket	Hoog
1 Pemican	Desquilars
1 Cassette, Governor	Nicholas
1 Bed	Tomma
1 Pemican	Peter
Clothes bag, dried meat, shoes, two skins	Guide
Cooking kettle, tea kettle, saucepan, gum	Piper
Guns, great coats, etc.etc.etc. . . .	Servant

Four days later, on the 17th, after stopping for breakfast and the change to ceremonial dress within a mile of Fort St. James, the party reached the end of their long march. McDonald's journal records the arrival:

The day, as yet, being fine, the flag was put up; the piper in full Highland costume; and every arrangement was made to arrive at FORT ST. JAMES in the most imposing manner we could, for the sake of the Indians. Accordingly, when within about a thousand yards of the establishment, descending a gentle hill, a gun was fired, the bugle sounded, and soon after, the piper commenced the celebrated march of the clans. . . . The guide, with the British ensign, led the van, followed by the band; then the Governor, on horseback, supported behind by Doctor Hamlyn and myself on our chargers, two deep; twenty men, with their burdens, next formed the line; then one loaded horse, and lastly Mr. McGillivray* (with his wife and light infantry) closed the rear. During a brisk discharge of small arms and wall pieces from the Fort, Mr. (James) Douglas met us a short distance in advance, and in this order we made our *entrée* into the Capital of Western Caledonia. No sooner had we arrived, than the rain which threatened us in the morning, now fell in torrents."

Again it was time for a brief respite. Within hours of their arrival at Stuart Lake, Chief Factor William Connolly, head of the New Caledonia District, made his appearance, and the next day James Murray Yale arrived with the rest of his party. While Yale was sent on to Thompson's River to direct the building of a boat to take the governor's party through the whirling cataracts of the Fraser to Fort Langley, Simpson took time out to confer with Connolly on affairs of his district. The men remaining behind occupied themselves repairing two large bark canoes at Fort St. James to take some of the party on to Alexandria, and after a week's stopover they set off from Fort St. James "with the usual compliments of the garrison."

At Alexandria, where they again met Yale, the party split into two: Yale and fourteen men to go in two bark canoes to the Forks of the Thompson and Fraser rivers (Lytton, B.C.); Simpson, McDonald and Hamlyn to travel on horseback overland to Kamloops. They would all rendezvous twelve days later, to resume boat travel for their heroic descent of the Fraser River.

For McDonald, the arrival at Kamloops was something of a homecoming. Although his family was no longer there, Court Apatte and his Indian friends were lined up with Frank Ermatinger and others from the fort to greet him when the governor's cavalcade rode in, flag flying, pipes playing and the usual volley of shots marking the occasion. Simpson was anxious to meet Nicolas, having heard much of him from his travelling companion, but the favored chief was off hunting. When he failed to appear within two days of their arrival, it was decided to move on across the lake and into the Thompson River to descend to the Forks

---

* Joseph McGillivray and his family had joined the party at Dunvegan, bound for a posting in New Caledonia.

where it meets the Fraser, the stretch of the river explored by McDonald on horseback the preceding year. The turbulent waters and rock-bound cascades hemmed in by walls of steep granite served to prepare the party for the even more dangerous passage down the Fraser — a stretch of water that even its namesake Simon Fraser chose to skirt by scrambling along the rugged Indian trails along the high rocky cliffs that bank the river, rather than take his chances in the rapids and whirlpools below. When Simpson and McDonald joined Yale's party at the Forks they were able to congratulate each other on two remarkable feats: both parties had descended stretches of water that had always been "considered next to impossible" and had never been run before.

Their historic journey was nearing its end, but the last lap was to be the most dramatic. Simpson still had hopes that the Fraser would prove navigable, and he was determined to take the canoes and the newly built Columbia River boat down through the mighty canyons and treacherous falls and eddies that lay between the Forks and Langley. A large part of this section of the Fraser runs through a narrow gorge carrying the raging torrents of water down from the mountains. Towering heights of rock rise nearly perpendicularly in some places, and walls of stone zigzagging in and out form natural hazards that only the most skilled boatmen could avoid, and then only if luck was with them. Simpson was undaunted. A brief conference with Bernard — "the best judge of River Navigation in the Indian Country" — and they were off, Simpson in his own canoe at first, but later trading places with Yale and taking a seat in the boat with McDonald. They entered the south branch of the Fraser below the Forks shortly after noon on October 8 and with considerable difficulty, in a gale that seemed to increase in force as they went along, passed through a continuing series of rapids until they reached the night's encampment. Next morning as soon as visibility was clear they were under way again and were soon in a long rapid which they ran until encountering a strong whirlpool that forced Bernard to turn back and take to the opposite side of the river.

Down they continued, to the terror and amazement of the scores of Indians who peered out from their shelters in the caverns and chasms in the rocky cliffs. Simpson described the scene:

The banks now erected themselves, into perpendicular Mountains of Rock from the Waters edge, the tops enveloped in clouds, and the lower parts dismal and rugged in the extreme; the descent of the stream, very rapid; the reaches short, and at the close of many of them, the Rocks, (which at times assumed singularly grotesque & fantastic shapes on a most stupendous scale) overhanging the foaming Waters, pent up, to from 20 to 30 yds. wide running with immense velocity and momentarily threatening to sweep us to destruction. In many places, there was no possibility of Landing to examine the dangers to which we approached, so that we were frequently, hurried into Rapids, before we could ascertain how they ought to be taken, through which the craft shot like the flight of an Arrow, into deep whirlpools which seemed to sport in twirling us about and passing us from one to another, until their strength became exhausted by the pressure of the stream, and leaving our water logged craft in a sinking state. In this manner, the greater part of two Days was occupied.

As McDonald remarked in his journal, rather mildly it would seem in the circumstances, "This is a bad piece of navigation." He too described the speed of the current as the torrent of water raced through the "Gate Dalles" and the "great skill and vigilance" required of the men in manoeuvring their craft through the swirling waters. Farther on:

At least half the distance, the river is deeply imbedded in solid rock, and the other half is of bold rapids, with, however, plenty of water all over. The mountains in no part of this day's work, recede from the very edge of the water. . . .

The natives seem to use but few canoes, for in places we have observed, that instead of gaining access by them to . . . the water's edge to watch the salmon, they contrive *by many ladders* to descend from a considerable height, and return by the same hazardous communication with the fish. Foot paths if any, are very imperfect, and I believe, that when they do travel from tribe to tribe, they scramble on along the rocks and face of the mountains at some distance, the best way they can.

High up on the narrow rocky ledges far above the whirling waters of the mighty Fraser the naked Indians, cool-eyed, watched silently as the sturdy craft tossed about in the rushing, churning torrent below. No Indian would dream of attempting it. Yet before their astonished eyes, here was a boatload of ribbon-bedecked paddlers with two men in tall black hats in their midst shouting and singing as their boat plunged its erratic course through the untamable vortexes. The Indians gave these adventurers little chance of reaching calmer waters in safety. It was an impossible feat — inevitable that their boat would be swallowed up and dashed to pieces against the jagged rocks that lined the river's edge, the men lost forever in the swirling cascades.

The final serious hazard was at Simpson's Falls, where the river is choked up by a most solid rock of about half an acre in extent. Examined it along the west shore, but conceived the run on that side extremely dangerous, and owing to the immense rocks all over, to carry was impossible. The East lead was then determined upon, crossed, and run without landing on that side, by the Guide who rushed on with his bark canoe, and a safe arrival below was effected, but not without much risk in the whirlpools against the enemy [the rocks] that hung over us. The boat followed, but did not suffer by the eddies so much, as it did by being swallowed into the swell of the Fall, out of which the utmost power of twelve paddles could not keep it. The second canoe having the advantage of being behind, came on with greater precaution. A few hundred yards below this, we came to the next and last run, which was steep but uniform. Then the river began evidently to assume a different form. The water was settled, the beach flatter, and vegetation more profuse.

All this took place before breakfast on Friday, October 10, and when they landed for the morning repast, "which did not detain us forty minutes," shortly after nine they were still in the shadow of the lofty cone-shaped mountain they christened "Sugar Loaf." They were all eager to press on, and it was just half past three that afternoon when they met the tide from the Pacific Ocean.

At dusk they reached Fort Langley, Colin Fraser's bagpipes echoing up and down the great river as they neared the recently constructed wharf where an astonished Chief Trader James McMillan stood waiting to greet his unexpected guests. Only the sound of the voyageurs' voices as they sped their paddles' pace for the last stretch of the journey had warned him of their coming this hitherto untravelled route. Simpson's boatmen had set yet another record for the governor, having covered more than 3,200 miles in sixty-five days of travel by canoe and on horseback across more than half the continent and navigated parts of the savage Fraser never traversed by boat before or since. It was a jubilant occasion as they entered the gates of the palisaded compound amid handshakes and congratulations from the twenty-odd men of the establishment.

McMillan had been sent to the mouth of the Fraser River in June of 1827 to choose a site and erect the new fort that was intended to be the principal post on the coast in the likely event that the Americans took control of the Columbia waterway. When Simpson arrived there after his harrowing run through the Fraser's treacherous rocks and cascades he acknowledged that it could never be used as a trade route: "I should consider the passage down to be certain Death, in nine attempts out of ten. I shall therefore no longer talk of it as a navigable stream."

CHAPTER TEN

New Harvests in a
Mild, Lush Land

1828 - 1833

After crashing down in high falls and cascades through the towering walls of granite that bank its edges for miles, the mighty Fraser spends itself as it nears the sea and spreads out into a wide, peaceful stream. Broad alluvial plains take the place of tall rocky cliffs and the great river — almost turbid in places — quietly makes its entrance into the blue Pacific.

Here, on the flat lands, James McMillan chose to build Fort Langley, about thirty miles inland from the Gulf of Georgia. It was far enough from the river mouth to lessen the threat from the warlike tribes of Indians from around Vancouver Island, but near enough to the coast to be accessible to the sailing ships that brought the trade goods from Fort Vancouver and carried the furs back to headquarters. This was to be Archy McDonald's home for the next four years. Simpson had decided that the newcomer should take command at the post to allow McMillan to go on to the Columbia and proceed east on furlough.

McDonald was not altogether happy with McMillan's choice of site. The land was arable, true, and ready for the hoe —

in fact McMillan and his men had a large crop of potatoes ready for harvesting that October of 1828 — but there were frequent floods when the sudden coming of spring made the snow on the mountaintops melt too fast, and near the fort only about fifteen acres were under cultivation, while soon after his arrival McDonald found a larger plain on high land a few miles upstream where he could have greatly increased the size of the fields without any clearing whatever.*

But the fort was established, with its two tall bastions and high cedar palisades enclosing the houses and outbuildings. It was strongly built, with long galleries along the sides from which to keep watch, and within a month McDonald had enlarged the compound which he found too confined, extending it backwards 36 feet from its original 120 by 135 feet. There were two dwelling houses, one of two compartments each with its own fireplace, for the "gentlemen," and another of three separate sections for the men. In the large provision shed fires were kept going continually to dry and smoke the salmon hanging from the rafters, and another room housed stores of flour, grease, salt and sundry necessities.

The "Big House" intended for the chief trader and his family was still under construction, but Jane and the children were not due to move up from Fort Vancouver until the vessel from England arrived the following spring, and by then the partitioning and wainscoting would be completed and they could all make themselves comfortable in the two spacious rooms with large "garret" above, cellars below, and the big adjoining kitchen with its fine new bake oven and all the conveniences the Columbia District could provide. In all, McDonald was well satisfied with his lot, and he welcomed the challenge of establishing a scene of domestic comfort amid the continual turmoil that was characteristic of the Fraser River mouth.

The Indians of the gulf, hundreds of whom had made their encampments along the river banks near the fort, lived in a constant state of siege. Not for them the placid pace of the Shuswaps and Okanagans of Kamloops. Marauding bands of the formidable tribes of Clallam from Puget Sound and Yukulta (Kwakiutl) from the coast islands swept down with great regularity in their

* Some years later, when James Murray Yale had charge at Fort Langley, the establishment was rebuilt at the preferred site.

thirty-man war canoes, attacking the weaker tribes, murdering their men, and carrying off their women and children as slaves. Langley's nearest neighbours — a Cowichan band known as Kwantlens — clustered near the fort, seeking the protection of its handful of Hudson's Bay men.

Less than a year before McDonald's arrival, Alexander McKenzie, a clerk of the Company, had been murdered with four of his men by a band of Clallams on the shore of Puget Sound en route from Langley to Fort Vancouver. Dr. McLoughlin sent an avenging party of sixty well-armed men up from the Columbia headquarters to demonstrate to the Clallam tribes that the HBC traders would not stand by without a murmur and see their friends murdered and maimed.

This was fresh in the minds of Indian and Company man alike when McDonald took command at Langley. There was an all-pervading sense of restlessness and unease in the Kwantlen village nearby, and continual reports and rumors reached the fort of threats from the formidable Yukultas, the much feared traditional enemy from Vancouver Island.

The new Bourgeois looked back in the pages of the fort journal, noting the frequent tragedies and the even more frequent alarms. But he was a brave man, and a fair one. He had dealt with many Indians in his years in the country, and to him they were individuals with all the usual complexities of humanity. His equanimity appeared undisturbed by the threatening situation he found himself in. He had lived in close harmony with the native people for more than a decade, and although he was aware of the need to maintain a reasonable number of men at the fort to give some impression of strength, he was not at all fearful of the overwhelming numbers of restless Indians that surrounded him.

After all, the business he was concerned with was furs, and the American traders up and down the coast were making serious inroads in the returns. He must put his mind to keeping the peace among the tribes, not only for the protection of his own men and his Indian friends, but also to ensure an ever increasing trade in the prime otter and beaver skins that were the lifeblood of the Company.

At the same time, though, his own interests were broader, and his mind turned frequently to alternatives to the fur trade —

to extending the gardens in this mild, lush land west of the mountains and, perhaps, to capitalizing on the abundance of salmon that crowded up the rivers each summer and establishing an export fishery. It was fortunate that in these extra-curricular pursuits he had the solid support and encouragement of the governor. He well knew that any steps he might take to help make the Columbia District independent in terms of provisions and supplies would have George Simpson's approbation.

Simpson and McMillan set off on October 16 with their party bound for Fort Vancouver, leaving McDonald, with James Murray Yale as his second in command, Francis Annance as Indian trader, and seventeen men, some of them with families, to make ready for their long winter at Fort Langley. There were three fields of potatoes to be harvested, a bumper crop of more than two thousand bushels that McDonald boasted, when totalling his figures in mid-November, provided double the yield of the same acreage at Fort Vancouver. And throughout those weeks of October and November small groups of local Indians came almost daily to the fort to barter fresh salmon, hundreds at a time, for buttons, beads and scalpers. The rafters of the large drying shed were soon lined with long rows of fish curing in the smoke-filled interior, and the twenty men of the establishment were assured that there would be a bountiful supply of food to see them through to spring, whatever might be their concerns about the alarums and rumors of Yukulta attacks that frequently accompanied the Indians on their trading missions.

McDonald refused to give much credence to these frequently expressed fears, knowing that the rumors grew in magnitude as they were passed from tribe to tribe up the river. That is not to say that he abandoned all caution. When a young servant who was a member of Annance's household slipped out of the fort at night he was brought back and forced to "run the gauntlet, & among other displays of Corporal chastisement he was hung up to the Flag Staff . . . to impress upon him the enormity of his crime in opening the Gate during the dead of night. . . ." On another occasion, in the excitement of the New Year's celebrations, one of the men of the establishment "contrived to haul up an Indian woman by one of the port holes." The following morning he was called to answer for his crime before "two of the most credible men amongst themselves" and did not seem to think his sentence hard when told that "one-half his wages — Eleven pounds Stg. — should be the forfeiture of so unpardonable a Conduct and to taste no liquor from me during the present Year of our Lord."

There was good reason to be prudent and apparently it took stern measures to impress this on the men who had little to attract them to this lonely new outpost, surrounded by hostile Indians and cut off from communication with their fellows in all directions. McDonald realized that it might be difficult to sign them up for another year's service if some means were not found to make their lives more comfortable and contented, and in the early months of his tenure at Langley he encouraged them all to take Indian wives. As McDonald explained to Simpson and the Northern Council, "It has had the effect of reconciling them to the place and removing the inconvenience and indeed the great uncertainty of being able to get them year after year replaced from the Columbia. . . ."

McDonald spent that first lonely winter at Langley gathering his forces. The fort was snug and secure with food in plenty. The year's returns — fourteen hundred skins — were cleaned and packed to be shipped to Fort Vancouver when spring cleared the way for travel again. The buildings within the palisade were improved and in some cases enlarged and finishing touches were put on the chief trader's house and the big kitchen equipped in preparation for the arrival of Jane and the boys when the vessel appeared early in summer.

He had time to plan for the future, and what was to him most evident was that something should be made of the Fraser's teeming salmon. The impressive results of the fall run, well known to be inferior to the summer, were enough to encourage some exertion in this direction, and although he acknowledged the inexperience of his men both in fishing and in curing (not to mention barrel-making), he wrote to headquarters on several occasions during his first year urging McLoughlin to provide the necessary helpers and supplies to take advantage of the fishery. He set his men to building a large cooper's shop and a new storehouse fifty-five feet long in anticipation of his suggestion being carried out.

Early in March as the weather improved and the way was again clear to re-establish communication with the Columbia,

Yale, Annance and "ten of our best men" set off for Puget Sound
to proceed via the Cowlitz Portage to Fort Vancouver, carrying
the annual "packet" with the fort journal, accounts and correspondence, including McDonald's reports to McLoughlin and to
the Governor and Northern Council containing along with the
usual information detailed descriptions and population charts of
the fifty Indian tribes in the district. There were also requisitions
for much needed blankets, beads and other trade goods that were
being used up faster than ever in the face of the increased tariff
caused by the strong American opposition along the coast. The
plan was to do a little trading around the sound and while there
to find a trustworthy Indian to carry the papers on to Fort Vancouver.

Scarcely had they disappeared from sight when the Kwantlens reported that no fewer than thirty Yukulta canoes were
making their way up the river, twenty-five to thirty men to a canoe. The few men left behind made the fort fast and McDonald
issued firm orders that the women were to remain inside except
for twice-daily trips to the river for water, and prayed that it was
yet another false alarm.

A day or so later four or five small canoes came into view, a
far cry from the promised Yukulta army, but rumors persisted
that the enemy were in the river, and McDonald's anxiety
mounted when ten days passed and there was still no sign of the
absent men. How great his relief when the voyageurs' song was
heard a little before sunset on the 21st and the watchers saw
Yale's boat round the point, its briskly flying flag proclaiming all
was well.

That all had not been well that morning McDonald soon
learned. The dreaded Yukulta had waited in ambush for the
Langley party at the river mouth and only the brave stand taken
by the handful of men in Yale's boat had saved them. Nine Yukulta canoes, each with about thirty men, fanned the river to bar
Yale's passage, but after a brief skirmish on shore and an exchange of gunfire the Indians retreated to the gulf.

The matter was not to end there. A few weeks later an Indian lad "naked as the day he was born," his body covered with
scratches and lacerations, staggered out of the woods near the
fort with the news that his father, the Kwantlen "Doctor," a familiar and popular figure to the Hudson's Bay men, had been

[handwritten annotation: Prominent Indians important to the fur trade enter & leave the journals without ... with very limited identification]

murdered along with the rest of his family by the Yukultas back near the river mouth. The Doctor — "by far the most decent Indian . . . within this river" — had gone to the gulf a few weeks earlier to trade beaver in and out of the small channels that interlaced the mouth of the Fraser, and had been nearby when Yale and his men had their encounter with the enemy. Rather than make for the open sea, the Yukultas had returned with renewed force to the river and had fallen upon the unfortunate Kwantlen family.

Toward evening on the day after the boy's appearance — Good Friday 1829 — "a melancholy Cry was heard coming up the River, which soon brought all the Quaitlines [Kwantlens] to our wharf. . . . that all was not well . . . was immediately confirmed by the arrival of the other brother with the headless body of their Father — and a moving Scene it was — the poor Doctor . . . still in the prime of life . . . head, arms & legs cut off & in this state found by his poor son as he ventured back to the spot — [and] all by himself effected their Escape."

A week later the Sandish (Saanich) and Cowichan chiefs arrived with their furs and reports of more Yukulta attacks on the Indians of Puget Sound and Vancouver Island. After murdering the doctor and two of his companions "they continued their course along the coast to the southward and about the night of the 17th fell upon the Scadchads with the same brutality, carrying off a number of their women & children. . . . [it] did not end with the Scadchads, for about the mouth of this river, they again got hold of six or seven Cawaitchins [Cowichans] that shared the same fate."

These renewed attacks by the long-dreaded enemy drew all the neighboring Cowichan bands together, united in their determination to revenge the murders. And up to the fort came their principal chief, offering his furs in return for a new gun and three hundred rounds of ammunition to distribute among his followers. McDonald hesitated but briefly: "so much amm. to one man in this part of the world & at a time like the present may seem imprudent . . . but keeping our own immediate hunters & traders . . . in a defenceless state, will I presume appear equally impolitic. . . . Indeed from the general horror at present of the Yewkeltas by all the Indians we have to do with, I think the more we promote the ruin of that detestable tribe the more effectually we secure their good faith."

It was with good reason that McDonald feared for the safety of the Company ship he expected momentarily with supplies and trade goods from the Columbia. "'Tis to be hoped our people will be on their guard."

There was still a long wait for the ship to appear, and when it did come the *Cadboro* brought the explanation for the delay. In early March the Hudson's Bay Company brig *William and Ann* had gone down as she crossed the Bar at the Columbia mouth with the loss of her captain, crew and cargo, but although McLoughlin attempted immediately to send a message to McDonald via the Nez Percés Indians around Walla Walla, his letter never arrived at the Fraser River and Langley remained in isolation until early summer wondering why no word came from headquarters, and how they could compete with the American vessels trading off the coast when their supply of trade goods was dwindling so rapidly. Where one 2½-point blanket had previously purchased as many as five good beaver skins, the Americans were now willing to give one blanket for a single pelt and the native hunters, shrewd bargainers that they were, made every attempt to exact the same tariff in the better-quality Hudson's Bay blankets.

Meanwhile, with milder weather came time to think about getting the crops into the fields. One quiet Sunday, when the people were observing their Sabbath day of rest, McDonald with Annance and eight men paddled off upriver to explore the surrounding lands. He looked longingly at "a beautiful prairie of at least 3 miles in circumference & of uncommon rich soil" just a few miles from the fort and debated with himself whether he could send his people to work that far away in safety. Reluctantly he had to acknowledge that the risk was too great with the Indians in their present state of upheaval, and returned to the acreage adjoining the fort still dissatisfied with its limitations and wary of its susceptibility to flooding.

Nevertheless, the potatoes in storage were beginning to sprout, and he set the women to cutting seed for planting. Wheat and pease were put in the ground in late April, and the men then began clearing a kitchen garden and fencing the grain fields and an enclosure to house the livestock expected on the ship. Fresh sturgeon provided a welcome change from the winter's dried fish diet, and early in May the first salmon appeared — "the best tasted & richest I have ever seen in this country." By the end of June the grain and potatoes at hand were all planted, but there was still no sign of the ship and the seed for the kitchen garden had not arrived. It was July 7 when rumors first reached them that a vessel was at the mouth of the river, and the next day Mc-Donald, impatient to welcome Jane and the children after their long separation, set off in the boat with Annance and ten men to meet the *Cadboro* in the gulf.

There was a brief and excited reunion. Ranald, nearly five years old now, and tow-headed Angus, to be three in August, were both much changed since he had parted from them in the spring of the previous year; the baby Archibald, now eighteen months, was all but a stranger. In a few short days he would have them all back home with him in the comfortable quarters he had prepared at the fort.

Business came first, and he conferred with Lieutenant Æmelius Simpson, captain of the *Cadboro*, who brought the sad tidings of the loss of the *William and Ann* and the consequent news that all the Columbia would be short of trading goods, a particular blow to Langley where the main force of the American competition was felt. Even nails were in short supply and two hundred had to be borrowed from the *Cadboro* to make cases in which to ship the season's fur returns.

McDonald remained on board ship that night and returned with his men to the fort next day, sending Yale to the *Cadboro* with a smaller crew to bring back some of the newly arrived goods. It was five more days before Lieutenant Simpson came alongside the wharf at Langley and "landed me my little family, all well." Jane happily inspected her new home, while the little boys ran about exploring upstairs and down and a proud and happy McDonald beamed his approval.

The chief trader's wife and children quickly became the focal point of family life at Fort Langley. The fair-skinned, dark-eyed youngsters were favorites with the French-Canadian voyageurs and the gentle Owhyhees (Sandwich Islanders) alike. They lived with a variety of languages: French, their mother's native tongue; English, the language of all the Hudson's Bay Company posts; as well as the Gaelic which, John McLeod asserted, was closer to North American native dialects than any other. The friendly little boys had the run of the fort and their natural curiosity and rather quaint courtesy made them welcome companions to the men of the establishment as they went about their daily tasks.

In their home they were secure in the warmth and fondness of their indulgent parents, but they knew discipline as well. McDonald lost no time in establishing regular hours for study and was soon writing to his far-flung correspondents that he had a "thriving school" going at Langley, and not only were "the little Archies . . . quite smart" but their mother too had become an "excellent" scholar.

Jane McDonald, quiet, dignified, untutored and still in her early twenties when she came to Langley, patiently struggled with her ciphering and her catechism under her husband's critical gaze. "I already feel the benificial effects of the Govr. & McTavish's marriages [both George Simpson and J. G. McTavish had recently abandoned their country-born wives and brought new brides from Britain] — She has picked up sense enough to infer from their having changed partners, that the old ones were defficient in learning." As for Archy McDonald, his pride and affection stood out for all to witness.

All in all, that first summer was a time of contentment. Although, as feared, the floods destroyed much of the grain and potato crops and the kitchen garden was planted too late for really satisfactory results, the second seeding late in July provided enough produce to ensure a comfortable winter, and the salmon run exceeded all expectations — to the point where by late August they had to turn away dozens of Indian canoes laden with fresh fish because there were neither men nor facilities at the fort to preserve them.

On August 16 they traded and cured upwards of 1,000 salmon, and the next day 1,020 came in before eight in the morning and they were forced to refuse all who came later in the day. During the short season of barely two weeks' duration the handful of men at the fort preserved nearly eight thousand fish averaging six pounds each: five thousand were cured with salt brine and packed in makeshift barrels put together on the spot; three thousand were partially salted and then smoked in the curing house. McDonald calculated that these nearly twenty-three tons of salmon cost the Company only £13.19s.10d in trade goods, mostly tools such as knives, awls, chisels, files, hooks and scalpers, as well as rings, beads, buttons, looking glasses, combs, vermilion and a little tobacco (although the latter was not the favorite object with the Fraser River Indians that it had been at Kamloops).

McDonald could foresee a great future for the Fraser River salmon if a steady market could be found for them (perhaps as nearby as the Sandwich Islands) and a reliable method of preserving and packing developed. He suggested that a detached salting camp might be established near the fishing grounds up-river where hundreds of Cowichans and Nanaimos from the gulf encamped with their Kwantlen hosts during the annual run. With the fish so plentiful and so cheap, there was no need to worry about a fishery connected with the fort and they could concentrate on curing and packing.

Again he wrote begging McLoughlin to send an experienced cooper from headquarters so that next year he could have proper barrels made using staves cut from the fine stand of "Pin blanc" he had discovered in the woods not far off (near what is now known as the Stave River). His detailed report to the Governor and Northern Council repeated his pleas, pointing out that while the beaver trade had increased it was "in all probability still far short of expectations" due to the presence of American traders in the Gulf of Georgia, and suggesting several ways of increasing profits through the salmon harvest.

The following year, he was even more enthusiastic and continued his attempts to impress the faraway council with his hopes and plans.

In my last communication, I touched at some length on the prospect of curing salmon at this place, as an additional source of Returns, and I have now the satisfaction to inform you, that the experiment of last season completely proved the theory: the fish it is true arrived late . . . but from the 25th of August to the 15th of next month we were fortunate enough to procure upwards of 15,000, enough to make up more than 200 barrels, which in that very short space, we contrived to do into nearly that number of casks of our own making, with the means so imperfect however that I fear from the sample that remained with ourselves — the first cargo will not stand the test of a foreign market, and trust by the next season we shall be provided with a good cooper, that will know something of fish curing.

In spite of his doubts, McDonald learned that although the experimental shipment in 1830 "lost the brine," it was put to good use at Fort Vancouver and their proficiency in barrel-making so improved that the next year McLoughlin reported the salmon that arrived at headquarters to be of excellent quality. Langley's fishery continued to expand in succeeding years and from these beginnings grew British Columbia's thriving trade in Pacific coast salmon.

At the same time McDonald turned his hand to the lumber trade. In his earliest months at Langley he began clearing more land to extend the fields around the fort, but although burning was done to remove the underbrush, the timber itself was cut and squared by hand and made into shingles or planks. By mid-October that first year there were ten thousand cedar shingles "of excellent quality" in the woods, and a road was cut through to facilitate their transport to the fort. In addition, three hundred two-inch planks were cut and ready to ship to Fort Vancouver whenever a vessel came their way, and a large quantity of barrel staves prepared, to be hooped together by the cooper for next summer's salmon.

McDonald's only regret was that he was unable to find a suitable site on any of the shallow streams nearby to erect a mill, and all the work must be done by hand. It could not "by mere manual strength . . . be made a lucrative business, but I dare say few places are better adapted for shingles," he wrote to McLoughlin, noting in his journal that the wood around Langley seemed "uncommonly well adapted for all household purposes and it is a pity we are not in the way of securing a quantity of it for exportation." In this area, too, McDonald proved prophetic and his earliest attempts at lumbering, which continued and expanded during his four and a half years at Langley, foreshadowed the West Coast's booming lumber business.

It was no easy task to get his message through from Langley's isolation, however. The only word received from headquarters from the time of Simpson's departure in mid-October of 1828 to the same period of the following year was with the *Cadboro*'s brief visit in July. McLoughlin was not the best of correspondents, and all but one of the few messages he did send to Mc-

Donald failed to arrive. With the crops all in, the Indians returned to their winter homes, the salmon-curing well in hand and a period of fair weather following the fall rains, the chief trader decided to go himself to Fort Vancouver and confer with his superintendent, "conceiving that we are likely to be neglected here." He was determined not to be overlooked in the Columbia arrangements and prepared to put his case for expanding the Langley operations to his chief.

The journey, by way of the Gulf of Georgia, Puget Sound and the Cowlitz Portage, was a dangerous and difficult one, and McDonald decided that he, Annance and eight men would provide a safe enough party to hold off the Yukultas, chastened as they were by their last encounter with the Hudson's Bay men. Yale was to remain at the fort with seven men and all the women and children, who by now numbered thirty-one. It took nine days to reach their destination and they made their passage without interference, but the joy of being once again at the Columbia headquarters soon palled amid the general dissatisfaction of its inhabitants. Dr. McLoughlin himself was at odds with most of his officers and was "never half so much tormented in his life," McDonald wrote to Ned Ermatinger. "We are the same good friends as heretofore & I know he is harassed, but I also know that his temper is become much ruffled and that he is himself the cause of much of his trouble & unhappiness." Indeed, although McDonald made the most of the opportunity to urge upon the chief factor the extension of Langley's sphere of activity, he finally gave up waiting for the arrival of the York Factory Express which would bring mail from the East and instructions from the Governor and Council, and headed for home after just twelve days "heartily glad to be off."

He took time before leaving to put in writing his suggestions to McLoughlin, and on his return was gratified to receive a note from the doctor accompanying his personal correspondence which had arrived with the Express in early December, saying "you may depend upon your suggestions and Plans settled on while here being followed up." Not only had McLoughlin concurred with the idea of retaining an adequate number of men at Langley to expand their fishery and timber trade, he had agreed to send a trading vessel to work out from Langley along the coast in an attempt to drive away the American competition for furs, and there was talk of establishing a sawmill at Puget Sound Falls to be supervised from the Fraser River depot. In all, McDonald had reason to be satisfied with the results of his excursion.

Unfortunately once again their plans were thwarted. The tricky navigation at the Columbia River mouth claimed another victim that spring and for the second consecutive year a Hudson's Bay ship — the brig *Isabella* just recently put into service on the coast — went down, though this time with no loss of life. McLoughlin sent all available hands from Fort Vancouver to rescue what they could of the cargo, but hope of having their own vessel to get to the Indians up and down the coast and in Puget Sound before the Americans carried off most of the furs was gone. And at the same time, the Langley Outfit — the annual allotment of supplies and trading goods — was delayed.

McDonald heard nothing of this mishap until July 28. When no word was received from headquarters from December until June, he had sent Yale to the Columbia in hopes of learning what had occurred to cut off all communication, and the clerk returned on board the brig *Eagle*, sailing in convoy with the Company's two schooners *Vancouver* and *Cadboro*, leaving the ships at the Fraser River mouth to make haste for home with McLoughlin's long-awaited letters. He was to learn then, too, that Fort Vancouver had been attacked by a virulent epidemic of "intermittent fever." In 1830 nearly three-quarters of the Indians in the vicinity succumbed, and McLoughlin reported fifty-two of his own men on the sick list.

McDonald, with eight men, left Langley immediately to meet "the squadron" to hear first-hand news of the latest events at headquarters and to expedite the movement of his own Outfit. The three ships were due to go north where it was proposed to establish a new post on the Nass River next year, but McDonald could see that there was not enough time for all to make the trip and return to Vancouver that season. He had the Langley supplies transferred from the brig to the *Vancouver*, leaving the latter to make her way up the Fraser to the fort, while the other two vessels continued on their way northward.

Summer was well along and the Indians were already on their way up to the salmon grounds in great numbers. Yale was dispatched with two canoes to take on enough of the trade goods to keep the supply of salmon coming in during the days it took the schooner to make it up to Langley. Captain Ryan would follow with the *Vancouver* bringing the rest of the shipment, including an extra quantity of salt and two additional men sent by McLoughlin to assist with the salmon, and a number of pigs and horned cattle to add to Langley's growing livestock population.

Ryan put in at the wharf on August 15 and stayed several days enjoying Langley's hospitality while the fort was abustle with unloading the schooner and preparations for the coming of the salmon. The plan was that he would tour the shores of the sound with Annance on board to gather what furs they could from the Indians in that region and return in a few weeks to take on as much fish as they then had ready at the fort to ship to the Columbia.

On the 18th McDonald took Jane and the children on board the *Vancouver* to bid bon voyage to Ryan and his crew. The beach was crowded with onlookers — men, women and children from the fort and dozens of idle Indians who were still waiting for the salmon run to begin — all excitedly observing the rituals of the schooner's departure. When McDonald and his family stepped back on shore, the captain accompanied them as far as the gate of the palisade and then reboarded the ship and ordered his man to fire the parting salvo. In an instant all was confusion. The shot, intended merely as a farewell salute, found its mark in poor Pierre Therien, one of the stalwarts of McDonald's staff, and although Ryan quickly dropped anchor and returned to shore, their ministrations were unsuccessful and the victim survived only a few hours. Ryan set sail again with a heavy heart.

There was little time to mourn. Within days of the *Vancouver*'s departure the salmon made their appearance in the river, and in a matter of hours hundreds of the fishermen were busy with their nets along the banks. Between August 25 and September 15 more than fifteen thousand salmon were traded at the fort. So plentiful was the harvest that when Ryan returned with his vessel he was unable to make room on board for all that they had to ship.

Meanwhile, anxiety was mounting for another of McDonald's men. Maniso, one of the many Sandwich Islanders employed by the Hudson's Bay Company throughout the Columbia District, had mysteriously disappeared at the end of August. Some of his Owhyhee friends volunteered that he was subject to fits and that he had been known in his own country to wander about for days in a state of "mental derangement." A search was undertaken and the river dragged without results, and in no time at all stories began coming into the fort indicating that he had been murdered by a group of Nanaimos or perhaps by the Cowichans themselves. Hundreds of Indians were still gathered in the river for the salmon fishery and rumors flew thick and fast.

Nearly two weeks passed and on the very day that one of Kwantlens came in saying that "they found our dead man on the beach below the Nanaimo village all naked his head split in two several arrow wounds on his body and his right side rippt open with the knife," the absentee made a dramatic reappearance. "What . . . must have been our joy mingled with awe & amazement when we saw this same dead man walk in the Fort . . . a perfect skeleton!!!"

To McDonald the whole incident was a "remarkable instance" of the unreliability of "circumstantial evidence," and he acknowledged in his journal that perhaps he had discussed the affair "with greater prolixity than the case deserved" but, he protested, "the whole is just a perfect sketch of the daily occurrence" he had to deal with.

Throughout all this uneasy time the Indians themselves were gathering together a war party to punish the Yukultas for a number of their recent barbarities. Decked with war paint — "hideous looking rascals they are" — five hundred of them set off in their big canoes on the morning of September 21, leaving their families behind at their village near the fort, and it was not until October 2 that they began to reappear — in retreat, as it turned out, from their enemies.

"Day after day the canoes continued to arrive up to the 10th when it was found that no less than 8 with over 100 men [had remained] behind. It would appear that in the first inst. they were very successful against a small detached village which they ransacked & destroyed without mercy." The Yukultas returned, however, and caught their attackers by surprise, putting most of them to flight without a shot being fired.

"The remaining canoe being better provided with arms & ammunition made a stand, but only to become subject to . . . disaster. . . . The Yukeltas drove them ashore on a large Island, forced them to abandon their canoes — & in this desperate plight kept those that survived for about 20 days — Three of our principal Chiefs & 45 men were either killed or starved to death, & the remainder of these wretches at length found means to cross to the mainland by swimming or on frail rafts & in a distressing condition contrived to gain this neighbourhood in straggled parties the first week of Novr."

So went life at Langley, bloody murder and savagery drawing a marked contrast to McDonald's attempts to establish a little oasis of civilization in the wilderness. Jane and the children kept at their studies and a new baby brother, Alexander, was added to the scene in October. Prayers were read regularly on Sundays and holy days to the whole population of the fort. Births, deaths and marriages were all duly recorded in the daily journal, and rare celebrations helped to relieve the monotony and drudgery of life at the remote outpost. "The new year was ushered in with the usual complements. After a salute from all the Guns of the garrison, the men were ushered into the Hall and treated with just enough of the *wo be joyful* . . . one half of the pint generally allowed on such occasions — that they might be perfectly sober to lead their fair ones thro' the merry reel in the evening. . . . one fine fellow of our savage neighbours on hearing the report of our big Guns, contrived to find his way to us thro' the woods with a handsome Beaver *tout rond* for Dinner," McDonald recorded, and next morning "Our amusement of last night went off well, without much indecent frolick, but today the fellows are at it tooth & nail." The "debauch" went on for three days, after which "we tried the people's disposition to renew their contracts for this place in which I am happy to say we have succeeded to our full expectation — as many as we require are engaged for two & some for three years, and several of them at reduced wages. . . ."

The farm grew gradually in size and productivity. Floods in the spring had soaked the newly planted fields, and when the potatoes did come to maturity they were attacked by grubs and almost the whole crop destroyed. "What the flood left us is on the eve of being destroyed by caterpillars — the whole of the field planted 10th, 11th and 12th June is reduced bare to the ground . . . those vermin also got into our vegetable garden & are in a fair way of destroying everything." There would be little to salvage for the winter stores that year, but increasing numbers of cattle, pigs and chickens would provide a change from the plentiful salmon and there was enough grain to keep the larder well stocked.

When McDonald sat down at his desk that winter to compose his reports to the Columbia superintendent and the Governor and Council, along with all his personal correspondence he had much to discuss. Success in the salmon and timber trade helped make up for disappointments in furs and fields. He had had no word from headquarters since summer, but early in February a large packet of mail arrived, including thirty-two private letters, after "a march of 11 weeks thro the different tribes between Vancouver and this [Langley] . . . ."

McLoughlin wrote to express his approval of McDonald's handling of his many problems with the Indians and to explain again the difficulties at Fort Vancouver which prevented him from keeping in closer communication. The malarial fever which had raged through the preceding year around the Columbia River continued to take its toll and he had had seventy-six men at the fort stricken at one time, including the doctor, John Kennedy, and Chief Trader Peter Skene Ogden, who was to have established the new post at Nass in 1830.

Hundreds of the native people had died and "we were obliged to drive the Indians away instead of affording them the assistance they implored of us by our having as many of our people on the sick list as we could possibly attend to. This unfortunate sickness weakened our establishment so much that we had not the men to establish Nass . . . [nor] a sufficient number of sailors in health to man the three vessels which are all signed to establish that place." McDonald received a letter from Ogden, too, convalescing after his bout of fever and looking forward to the Nass expedition that summer.

It was a relief to be in touch with Fort Vancouver once again, but the real joy of the coming of the mail was contained in the private letters — from Edward Ermatinger, John McLeod, Duncan Finlayson, Alexander Stewart and other old fur trade friends in the East, and news from home, including a letter from John Halkett, acknowledging receipt of the "curiosities" that McDonald had shipped to him from Kamloops and reporting on young Daer, the sixth earl of Selkirk, now up at Oxford, and

Lady Isabella who was staying with the Halketts in London awaiting a visit from her mother and young sister.

This annual mail was always a highlight of the long, lonely winters, and that McDonald gave full measure in return to his far-flung correspondents is proved by the hundreds of his letters preserved in libraries and archives on both sides of the Atlantic. Edward Ermatinger saved all of the annual epistles McDonald wrote to him — a record of more than fifteen years from the time Ermatinger resigned from the Company until McDonald himself retired to the East.* That Ermatinger's letters were equally valued by his friend in the wilds is certain. "Few letters ever came into my hands that afforded me more pleasure & information than yours. . . . It not only communicated all the ordinary occurrences met with, in which you thought I might feel an interest, but gives me a faithful & feeling account of yourself & all that is dear to you. . . . I trust that long ere now you have my letter of last year, which will . . . convince you that I do not wish to fall into arrears with a friend & correspondent I so highly value."

Langley continued to prosper. By 1832, when the fever epidemic had abated at Fort Vancouver and Fort Simpson had been safely established up on the Nass River, affairs along the coast assumed a more orderly pattern. "Here we got rid of our opposition," wrote McDonald, and although there were still American coasters plying the waters, most of them concentrated their efforts to the north. At Langley, in spite of a return to the old tariff (twenty skins for a gun, two for a blanket), the returns increased to 2,500 — up from 1,400 during his first year on the Fraser. The cooper finally arrived to put the fishery on a more professional basis, and the fields and gardens were lush and bountiful. "Our gardens increase in comfort. . . . with country resources in abundance you will own [it] ought to keep a little establishment like mine in perfect affluence," he wrote to John McLeod, and the same correspondent heard from James Douglas, "Your friend Archy is doing wonders at Fort Langley."

The family was thriving too. Ranald and his three half-brothers (a fourth, Allan, arrived in May 1832) continued to

---

* This collection was deposited in the British Columbia Archives by Ermatinger's descendants more than half a century later.

work at their studies, "Tool"* sharing the head of the class with his stepmother. "I keep them at it, mother & all — my Chinook [Ranald] now reads pretty well & has commenced cyphering," he wrote in January 1832, acknowledging that it was "an agreeable & interesting pastime," and the fond father was already talking of sending the little boys to the Red River School as soon as he thought them ready for the move. "What I regret most is the condition of the boys, for there is nothing like early education."

The annual trips to Fort Vancouver in the fall became part of the pattern too. In 1832 he took passage on the *Eagle* with Captain Graves — "a good jovial fellow" — and after several days sailing pleasantly down the coast arrived at the mouth of the Columbia where Chief Factor Duncan Finlayson, recently assigned to the district, had just arrived, conducting the brig *Lama* which he had purchased for the Company from Americans trading in Hawaii. "Who was on board also but our old friend David [Douglas] after two years perambulation over the Californias." Douglas, who was on his second scientific foray in the Northwest, was on the way back to Vancouver too.

"The two nights we were outside the Cape, depend upon it there was no lack of news, but to the exploits of our friend & his man Johnson every other topic gave way — Bears, Bulls & Tigers had cause to rue the day they went there." Douglas the storyteller had sharpened his wit to entertain his old fur trade companions in fine style.

The whole company went on to Vancouver, and this time there was an air of conviviality around McLoughlin's table. Finlayson, the newly arrived chief factor, and James Douglas, the doctor's second-in-command, were both McDonald's good friends, and along with these two, David Douglas and the regular officers of headquarters, there were the ships' captains and mates to enliven the scene, and still another novelty — Bostonians Nathaniel Wyeth and John Ball who had come west with a party of American settlers to establish a colony in the Willamette Valley.

During that month at headquarters, McDonald and McLoughlin had plenty of time to discuss the future of Fort Langley. Although the farm and fishery both prospered there

* *Tool* (Ranald's nickname) is the Chinook name for a bird, so "Son of Raven."

163

[handwritten: Wyeth contributed news, views & conversation —]

were the continuing problems of shipping and the perpetual difficulty of communication at the inland fort. McDonald had for some time had in the back of his mind the idea that the area around Puget Sound, with its deep harbors, thick woods and good grazing lands, would be a suitable site for farming and lumbering on a larger scale. When he left for home in early December it was with orders from McLoughlin to explore the region en route and report back with his recommendations.

"For thirty miles along the coast and as many if not more towards the interior, it is fine prairie country interspersed with islands of oak and other wood." The soil, he said, was equal to that at Vancouver, and in the deep waters of Puget Sound vessels of any kind could come to within a few yards of shore. McLoughlin took quick action. He decided to establish immediately a new post, Nisqually (near what is now Tacoma, Washington), at the southern end of the sound. He thought it could in time replace Fort Langley, but McDonald and some of his fellow officers west of the mountains thought it more likely that it might replace Fort Vancouver, aware as they were of the increasing encroachment of the Americans on the Hudson's Bay Company preserves. "If he does not look sharp His Majesty will ere long be apt to lose his valuable domains on this side . . ." he warned prophetically.

McDonald soon received word from McLoughlin that he was to leave his comfortable berth on the Fraser and return to headquarters for another assignment. Reluctantly he prepared to move. Ranald he could take with him to Vancouver and enrol in the little school John Ball had established there for the children of the fort. Jane and the younger ones could remain at Langley or at Vancouver until the fall, but "they must all be moved on to Klyne." "Jenny" would be happier at Jasper House with her own family and if his plans worked out and the Company allowed him to go east on furlough in the spring of '34, he could see the boys settled at the new Red River "Academy" himself.

"I regret leaving Langley — it is a snug, comfortable place — but then I find it is high time for me to see & get my little boys to school. God bless them. I have now no less than five of them, all in a promising way."

CHAPTER ELEVEN

I Do Not Contemplate Remaining Much Longer in This Wilderness

1833 - 1835

There were general stirrings of dissatisfaction and restlessness among the old traders on the Pacific slope in the early thirties. The Russians to the north and the Americans all up and down the coast were a continuing threat to the orderly conduct of the business of the Hudson's Bay Company in the Columbia District, and it was obvious that a formal solution must be reached to the boundary question. As early as 1825 the Russians had reached agreements with the British and the United States governments that the Portland Canal, 54°40′ north latitude, should mark the southern limit of their claims. The Americans, represented by freetraders from the eastern seaboard, regarded the whole coast as open waters, and in the interior goodly numbers of "mountain men" still made their way through the lower passes of the Rockies from Missouri to compete with the Company for the Flathead furs.

Technically the British and Americans west of the mountains were still operating under the Treaty of Joint Occupancy agreed to in 1818; although it had not yet been renegotiated, it had been renewed with some alterations in 1827, and the independent Americans held firm in their continuing trade along the coast and in the mountain regions of what is now Montana and Utah. Bills were repeatedly brought before the Senate during this period by legislators who believed that the time had come for the United States government to establish some form of territorial rule beyond the mountains. It became more and more clear that whenever the boundary question was settled, one thing was certain: that the British would have no rights below the Columbia River.

In fact, the Americans almost universally had already made up their minds that the borderline should be drawn at least at the 49th parallel, and many went so far as to say 54°40'. The governors of the Hudson's Bay Company still clung to the view that the Columbia would be the divide, and the British Colonial Office chose to ignore the whole question in their preoccupation with events in other parts of the empire.

The establishment of Fort Nisqually was, in a way, an indication of the Hudson's Bay Company's acquiescence in American territorial claims. They well knew the charms and the value of the lovely Willamette Valley to the south of the Columbia River, and small numbers of retired Hudson's Bay men were already settling in that region. But they accepted — if only unofficially — the fact that the Willamette Basin would ultimately be under American control, and Simpson and the committee agreed that the Company should concentrate its efforts north of the river, in the Cowlitz Valley and the Puget Sound area. Here there were beautiful wide plains fit for grazing thousands of head of sheep and cattle, tall, deep forests for timbering and, in the Cowlitz, fertile prairie lands where gardens and rich crops of grain would flourish.

In 1832 McLoughlin had played a leading role in drawing up the prospectus for the "Oregon Beef and Tallow Company," a private venture involving officers of the Company in the Columbia District who proposed to invest their earnings in large-scale cattle farming both above and below the great river. McLoughlin could see no reason why fur traders should not turn their thoughts and their cash to extending their interests in the Columbia, instead of handing over their hard-earned profits to be invested far afield by Simpson and other legal and financial advisers in Montreal and London. He was quickly brought to heel and the Company itself took over the idea, although on the advice of their lawyers who suggested that the Hudson's Bay Company charter did not allow agricultural pursuits, in 1839 they established a subsidiary branch, the "Puget's Sound Agricultural Company," to take over this part of the business and gave officers and shareholders of the Company the opportunity to invest in relation to their interest in the firm. (For example, Archibald McDonald, as a chief trader, was allowed to purchase five shares at £100 each, John McLoughlin, a chief factor, got ten shares, clerks earning £100 annually were allowed to buy three shares, while junior clerks could take one or two shares according to their rate of pay.)

All this was in the negotiation stages when McDonald returned to Vancouver in March of 1833 with David Douglas, whom he had met at Puget Sound. He had stopped for twelve days on the way down from Langley at the site of the new Fort Nisqually to make a start on its first buildings, and left several men there to continue the work and prepare for a larger contingent to arrive in the summer. At that time McDonald was at one with McLoughlin in his optimism about the prospects of the private beef and tallow venture, and even though that spring, a few weeks after his arrival at headquarters, McLoughlin sent McDonald on an exploration trip down through the Willamette Valley, it had already been decided to develop the Puget Sound-Cowlitz region and McDonald himself was to return to Nisqually to supervise its beginnings.

McDonald came back from the Willamette on May 8 to find two interesting newcomers at Fort Vancouver. Dr. William Fraser Tolmie and Dr. Meredith Gairdner, naturalists and graduates in medicine of Glasgow University, sent out from Britain to serve both the Hudson's Bay Company and the Royal Horticultural Society in the Columbia, had arrived on board the *Ganymede* four days earlier.

McDonald, by now in his early forties and a senior member of the Columbia District management, took an immediate interest in the twenty-one-year-old Tolmie, a conscientious, studious youth, who was fascinated by all that the older man had to tell him: first of the natural beauties of the Willamette Valley whence McDonald had just come, and then, as they became bet-

Exile in the Wilderness

ter acquainted and took to going on long evening walks along the banks of the Columbia, extending the areas of discussion to include not only the affairs — past and present — of the Hudson's Bay Company, but also natural history, medicine, Scottish lore and even poetry.

An unusual pair — the ebullient, gregarious fur trader and the shy, dour, teetotal novice — but they became fast friends, and when McLoughlin decreed that they should both proceed north on the *Vancouver*, McDonald to trade along the coast and Tolmie to serve at Fort McLoughlin, the new post being established on Millbank Sound, McDonald suggested that he and Tolmie go overland via the Cowlitz to meet the schooner at Nisqually, thus giving the young doctor the opportunity to explore the country at close quarters and to gather birds and botanical specimens along the way.

Tolmie welcomed the proposal with enthusiasm, and when McLoughlin approved the scheme the two set off, with four Sandwich Islanders paddling their canoe along the "majestic Columbia rolling smoothly along . . . its wooded & winding banks rejoicing in the noonday sun." Tolmie had already been impressed by the beauties of the Columbia shores. With Gairdner he had gone exploring above the farm on foot "along the plateau by the border of wood . . . admiring the rich groves of lupin seen amidst the trees mixing with handsome columbines, sunflowers & a great variety of other herbaceous plants in flower," and as they proceeded downstream beside the "gigantic relics of the primeval forest, which form a broad belt of wood extending to the river's edge . . . the magnificence & grandeur of its colossal tenants was very impressive & the ground was beautifully carpeted with wild flowers & low creeping evergreen shrubs."

Tolmie's diary provides a vivid account of this fourteen-day journey, the first week spent exploring the small tributaries along the Columbia before proceeding up the Cowlitz River to its source. Just a few miles down from Fort Vancouver, the sight of an abandoned Indian village "which a few years ago contained two or three hundred inhabitants, but at present only its superior verdure distinguished the spot from the surrounding country" dramatically demonstrated the devastation wrought by the fever epidemic of 1830–31. It had "almost depopulated the Columbia R. of the aborigenes, committed its fullest ravages & nearly exterminated the villagers, the few survivors deserting a spot where the pestilence seemed most terribly to wreck its vengeance."

McDonald, while encouraging Tolmie in his scientific pursuits and occasionally gathering and pressing a few specimens himself, was preoccupied along the Cowlitz by his search for coal beds which he felt might be mined and put to good use by the Company and took samples from several locations which he left piled by the river to be taken back to Vancouver for testing when the canoemen returned.

The Cowlitz was a wide, strong stream, testing the mettle of the Kanaka boatmen all the way.

It was only by the most strenuous efforts that the canoe could be urged on — on one occasion were obliged to disembark and tow up with ropes & again the channel being obstructed with trunks and branches of trees, I disembarked. Mac. continued poling & the men were deep in the stream straining every nerve to get the canoe past the embarras, where there was imminent risk of its being swung round by the current & dashed to pieces broadside against the highest of the colossal trees which lay across the stream — their efforts being only sufficient to keep the canoe in its position. . . . Mac jumped out to assist and I [Tolmie] who as yet was a spectator from one of the trunks forming embarras, followed his example by leaping off the trunk nearest to stern of canoe, about 6 feet from it, but met with unexpected difficulty, being hurried down against embarras, unable to obtain footing in 3 or 4 feet of water, by swimming strongly, at length caught hold of canoe by stern & by its support planted feet firmly on the bottom & lent my strength to push canoe upward which by our united effort was effected & we got into comparatively smooth water. Being thoroughly soaked except head and shoulders, assist canoe men in poling and paddling to keep up the animal heat and comforted the inward man with a tass of aquavita.

On the seventh day McDonald decided it was time to start looking for transport to carry them across the portage when they could no longer navigate the river, and went off to one of the Indian villages scattered along the Cowlitz to try to engage some horses. Instead of horses, he drew only some unwelcome callers to their camp. They were "visited by several women who brought some kamass & then arranging themselves around the fire, squat-

ted on their hips, in indian file commenced a war of extermina-
tion against the creeking [*sic*] things in each other's heads, each
when she made a prize, adroitly placing it on the tip of her
tongue & then with the incisors giving the coup de grace. Ordered the filthy wretches to depart several times, but the luxury
of enjoying a good fire without the previous exertion of preparing
it was too great a temptation to be overcome by words."

This was not their only encounter with the blight that had
long been a characteristic of the Columbia Indians. Tolmie had
already on one occasion, after walking through one of the deserted Indian lodges they passed en route, found his "trousers
swarming with fleas, who were travelling rapidly upwards & required active measures to subdue their ambitious propensities."
McDonald had an even more unfortunate experience. Encamped near the Chehalis River with their destination just a day
and a half away, they were "visited in the evening by several
chiefs, the most important of which was dressed in a blanket, ca-
pot, blue vest & trowsers, a foot too long, english hat & Blucher
boots. He was a little old man, very forward & intrusive wishing
to invade the precincts of our tent, hitherto kept sacred from the
lousy disseminating presence . . . he succeeded however in favor-
ing Mac with a colony of fleas who kept him in purgatory all
night."

The last stages of the journey were covered on horseback, in
company with four oxen and an equal number of Company men
who had driven the animals up from Fort Vancouver to populate
the Nisqually farm, and accompanied by "a cavalcade of 4 indians, attired in large blue capots, leather tights & mocassins, bearing each his musket." Miles of rich level prairies that formed the
Cowlitz plains led them to the woody banks of Puget Sound,
where, on May 30, not far from the mouth of the Nisqually River, they sighted a forlorn group of unfinished wooden buildings,
the only visible proof that Fort Nisqually did exist. "The most
conspicuous object was a store half finished next a rude hut of cedar boards — lastly a number of indian lodges constructed of
mats hung on poles in the shape of a cartshed. Welcomed by a
motley group of Canadians, Owhyees & Indians, & parties of
the latter were squatted around the fire, roasting mussels."

There was certainly nothing in this to impress the newcomer, and McDonald at the first opportunity took Tolmie off to the

nearby prairie to expound on his vision of what the future held for the new fort. "Saw the proposed site of Fort & Farm. The fort is to be erected along the bank of a streamlet, which in its devious course through plain presents points well adapted for Millseats, & the most fertile spots in the comparatively barren prairie are to be ploughed for a crop of potatoes & pease, this season. . . ." There were plans for corn and sawmills, a thrashing mill, bridge and all the necessary outbuildings. "These are M's projects, but as he is to remove to another post this summer, he will not superintend their completion."

McDonald had expected to find the *Vancouver* lying at anchor offshore when they arrived at Nisqually, but after a week with no word of the vessel he and Tolmie set off with six men to paddle up the sound in hopes of meeting the ship or hearing some news of her whereabouts. Encamped the next night within sight of Vancouver Island, not far from the spot where McKenzie's party was murdered five years earlier, they "had pistols within reach" and prudence decreed that a watch be kept by the men in turns of two hours each.

In fact, they met friendly Indians. McDonald had been on the lookout for "Chihalucum the Soquamus chief" from whom he hoped to get information about the schooner, and when they came up with him the second day out from the new fort he accompanied them as far as Hood's Canal, along with his band of eighteen men, women and children. They encamped that afternoon within half a mile of the Indians' lodges and that evening went over to pay them a visit. Chihalucum's lodge "presented a greater appearance of plenty than any yet seen," according to Tolmie. "He is a chief of some note & well disposed towards the whites, displaying more hospitality than any other of the Indians met with on our journey, for he requested us to eat, on entering, while the others generally bargained for payment before giving what we asked."

The day after this encounter they sighted the swelling sails of the *Vancouver* as she came down the sound on the Pacific tide, and within hours they were on board and greeting Captain Ryan and his crew.

McDonald remained at Nisqually until June 21, long enough to see a small house constructed on the farm site and to mark out locations for mills and bridge and for new buildings and a stockade around the fort itself. Tolmie had been instructed to go on to Fort McLoughlin when the *Vancouver* had put down her cargo of trade goods and seed and supplies for the farm at Nisqually, but before the schooner set sail on her northward voyage Pierre Charles, one of the most able of the Company's servants in the whole Columbia District, had suffered a severe axe wound cutting his foot from ankle to toes, and McDonald decided that the doctor's services were more needed to bring this patient back to health than to minister to the ills at Millbank Sound. At the same time, he instructed the young medical man on the duties of Indian trader and farm overseer that he would undertake for the summer months.

In return, Tolmie, at McDonald's request, brushed up the older man's medical knowledge, giving him "a brief lecture on the Circulation of the Blood." Tolmie marvelled that a man "of his age" should show such a "laudable desire for self-improvement. " Together they whiled away the evenings, talking politics, reading aloud to each other from Belisair (and "contending about the pronunciation") and discussing with much amusement the question of the authenticity of James Macpherson's version of the poems of Ossian, a controversy that was much talked about in Scotland in the nineteenth century. They were a congenial twosome and there seemed to be no end to the topics of conversation that engaged their interest, whether sitting by the evening campfire or walking out on the plains to inspect the gardens or explore the nearby lands with an eye to the possibility of further expansion of the farm.

When McDonald headed back to Fort Vancouver with three men and three extra horses loaded with the 380 beaver skins he had traded during his brief stay at the sound, he took with him Tolmie's farewell gifts, an ivory-handled knife and fork and a horn dressing comb. Tolmie rode three miles out on the plains, accompanying his friend on the first leg of his journey, and reluctantly waved him on his way before returning to the company of his faithful dog, Nimrod, and the six men who would remain with him to carry on the work of erecting Fort Nisqually.

McDonald was back at Fort Vancouver by month's end, in time to go on to Kettle Falls with the brigade taking supplies to the interior. On the way down the Cowlitz he had met Chief Trader Francis Heron making his way up to take charge at

Nisqually, and learned from him that McLoughlin intended him to take over Heron's former post at Colvile. Heron was not happy about the change, but McDonald was well content. Colvile was generally regarded as the most comfortable post in the Columbia. As long as the appointment did not interfere with his furlough next year, all was well. McDonald had already made arrangements for Jane and her four boys to move to Michel Klyne's at Jasper House to spend the winter with her family and he wanted nothing to come in the way of his plans for his children's schooling in the East.

One of the responsibilities of the Colvile Bourgeois was the supervision of the Flathead trade southeast toward the mountains, which for the past two years had been carried on by Francis Ermatinger and his party of men who departed in the early spring to penetrate as far as they could into the territory where American traders from the East made great inroads on the Company's fur returns. Ermatinger was still away on this mission when McDonald arrived to take up his new charge, and as soon as his own affairs were put in order McDonald decided to go himself to the outpost on the Flathead River that served as the headquarters for the travellers, stopping first at the Kootenay post for an extra supply of trade goods for Ermatinger to distribute when he went back southward for the fall trade.

With his customary enthusiasm McDonald tackled this new problem. The Flathead trade had fallen off considerably in late years, but he felt that a more aggressive approach would justify itself in increased returns. By the time Ermatinger returned to Colvile just before Christmas, McDonald had already mapped out a plan of campaign and was preparing a long narrative covering the early history of American freetraders in the area between the Kootenay and Snake rivers, with comparative figures on cost of trade goods and payments for furs of the Missourians and the Hudson's Bay Company. His plan was to present his ideas to the Northern Council when he attended the annual meeting at York Factory on his way to Britain the following summer, suggesting that two parties be equipped, one to follow the usual route through the Coeur d'Alènes and Flathead country and the other to go up the Snake River from Walla Walla, the two to rendezvous at Trois Butes. When he dispatched Ermatinger in March he was still awaiting McLoughlin's approval for his scheme, which included the employment of two American freemen who had traded with the Company in the past, but he sent Ermatinger off with instructions to use his "usual activity & judgement to secure from Indians and freemen of whatever denomination & character all the Beaver you possibly can." He expressed his view that the Company should attempt to draw in freetraders who customarily sold their furs at little or no profit to entrepreneurs from the East by saying, "to good American trappers that may be disposed to hunt for us give any reasonable encouragement."

With Ermatinger's help he hoped to bring about a marked increase in the annual returns from Colvile, and at the same time discourage the Americans from encroaching further on what he regarded as Hudson's Bay territory. "We must not allow ourselves to run off with the idea that opposition will die away of itself," he warned, but rather should "commence with double energy . . . meeting them with men & goods in the heart of the Snake country."

At the same time Chief Factor Duncan Finlayson was on his way up the Columbia from headquarters with the east-bound Express. With him was Ranald, who had spent the winter at the little school at Fort Vancouver and was to join his father at Colvile and accompany the Express across the mountains. Their route, as usual for the Express, took them through the Athabasca Pass, and when they reached Boat Encampment on May 2 they found Michel Klyne waiting for them with the horses to carry them through the mountains to Jasper House. A few days with the family, a chance to admire the beautiful baby girl who had been born to Jane in February at her father's home, and McDonald was on his way again. Whether Jane and the youngsters accompanied them east to Norway House at this time is not recorded, but if not then, she made her way across the prairies sometime that summer and the family boarded with the Reverend William Cockran at the Red River settlement during McDonald's absence in Europe.

McDonald joined Simpson and the chief factors and chief traders at the council meeting in July, and on September 12, with John Tod and Robert Miles, he boarded the *Prince George* at York Factory and set sail for England. With him he carried David Douglas's letter of introduction to Sir William Jackson

Hooker, a prominent figure in the Royal Horticultural Society, who was a professor at Glasgow University and later keeper of Kew Gardens and editor of the *London Journal of Botany*.

Hooker had been instrumental in organizing Douglas's expeditions to North American and Douglas was anxious that he and McDonald should meet. "Mr. McDonald is . . . a great friend to all travelling botanists. . . . he is one of my best friends." It is likely, too, that Tolmie, who had been introduced to the Hudson's Bay Company by Hooker, had written about his new friend, for Tolmie noted in his diary on the same day that he mentioned writing to Hooker that he had sent McDonald "introductory Letters to my father & Uncle Alexr." McDonald was looking forward to visiting the eminent scientist when he went north to renew old ties with family and friends in Scotland.

He docked at Falmouth on October 9 and three days later was in London paying his respects at Hudson's Bay House. There were reports to be given and long conferences with the secretary, William Smith, and with Benjamin Harrison and others of the committee who welcomed the opportunity to get first-hand reports of their far-off outposts whenever officers appeared in England on furlough. On October 22 he and John Tod had a formal session with the governor and committee, along with Duncan Finlayson who had arrived from Montreal, and he then felt free to go on to Glasgow. There he met with a "kind & hospitable reception" from Hooker and his family and fellow botanists, before going up to the Highlands where his old Caledonian friends waited to entertain him. McDonald still had two older brothers and four sisters living in Argyll and Inverness, and a large circle of family and "auld acquaintance" were eager to gather around to hear his tales of life in the Indian country.

Back in Edinburgh in January, he was joined by Duncan Finlayson and the two compared notes on the joys of a fur trader on furlough. "Few Hudson's Bay men home on their rotation have enjoyed their time better than I have," McDonald wrote to Hooker.

He returned to London to meet again with friends at Hudson's Bay House, and it was there, after a few weeks' holiday in Paris, that he learned of David Douglas's strange death in Hawaii. Douglas, who had sailed from the Columbia for the Sandwich Islands in October 1833, had been trampled and gored to death in a bull pit in Hawaii on July 12, 1834, in mysterious circumstances which led to considerable controversy in the months that followed. "The manner in which that melancholy event was said to have taken place seemed to us all about Hudson's Bay House so very improbable . . . however, I am sorry to say it was but too true," McDonald wrote to Hooker.

While McDonald was making the most of his all too brief sojourn in Europe, Jane, with admirable determination, let no opportunity pass her by in her first brush with the "civilized" world at the Red River settlement. She and the children were all part of the Cockrans' large household, the older boys enrolled at the Red River Academy and Jane busy with Allan and the new baby. She had time, however, to think seriously about her faith, no doubt encouraged by the presence of religious observances all around her in the clergyman's home. McDonald himself was a staunch Episcopalian and he had always made sure that Bible study and religious discussion were part of the regular life of his household. It is not surprising that Jane decided to acknowledge her beliefs formally, and on November 2, 1834, she and all the children — Ranald, Angus, Archy, Alexander, Allan and Mary-Anne — were baptized by Mr. Cockran.

McDonald came home by way of New York and Montreal, and rejoined his family at Red River in time to attend the meeting of the Northern Council in June. The settlement he had known so well in its infant stages had grown to a population of nearly five thousand, two-fifths of them white, and it was obvious that Jane and the children had enjoyed their stay in the growing community. He was delighted with the progress they had all made in his absence, and after much soul-searching he and Jane agreed that the four older boys should remain there to continue their education, Ranald, Angus and Archibald at the Red River Academy, and Alexander, who was only six, with his grandparents the Klynes, who had retired to the settlement that summer. The Northern Council had confirmed McDonald's appointment to Fort Colvile and he would take his wife and the two little ones back across the mountains with the fall Express.

Another important decision was reached at the same time. Simpson and McTavish had seriously disturbed the old patterns of "custom of the country" marriages when they cast aside their native-born wives and brought new brides from Britain out to the fur country a few years earlier. McDonald was anxious, while a clergyman was at hand, to formalize his own family situation and on June 9 "after council broke up the whole cortege appeared at the parsonage House before the chaplin & assistant chapn. of the Honble. Company, where Archy & Jenny were joined in Holy wedlock & of course declared at full liberty to live together as man & wife & to increase & multiply as to them might seem fit," the bridegroom reported to Edward Ermatinger. The Reverend David Jones, Cockran's assistant, described in more sober terms the "laudable" affair. "Mr. Chief Trader M. was married to the Mother of his children at Mr. Cockran's house as I returned homewards," his journal records, and he admiringly remarked on the "sacrifice and self-denial" of the parents in parting from their children "in order to procure for them moral and religious improvement. . . . he is to embark immediately for the Western side of the Rocky Mountains taking with him his wife and two small children leaving four others with us whom he cannot expect to see in less than *five years time*!"

It was a heart-breaking move but McDonald had hopes that their separation might not be that long. He confided to friends that he was only awaiting his "second parchment," the sought-after chief factorship which brought with it the assurance of full pay for a year after retirement and half pay for six years thereafter (and that at double the income of a chief trader), before he would make plans to leave the service and establish himself on a comfortable property somewhere in the East. The recent reduction in the number of chief factors from twenty-five to sixteen had severely cut back on promotions but he had reason to hope that his own would come in the not too far distant future.

"I certainly do not contemplate the idea of remaining much longer in this wilderness," he wrote, observing that the only reason to stay on was to amass "a *handsome provision for our children*." He had had time to reflect on the future of his family and had no desire to "let [them] loose upon the wide world while young, without guide or protection. . . . Much better to dream of less — to set ourselves down with them in time, & to endeavour to bring them up in habits of industry — economy & morality, than aspire at all this visionary greatness for them."

However, that time had not yet come, and he and his Jenny must pack their trunks for the long journey west. They bade a sad farewell to the boys on July 14, and three days later arrived at Norway House to join James Douglas who was coming from York Factory in charge of the Columbia Express. Duncan Finlayson was included in the party too: six gentlemen, two families with their attendants, twenty-four servants and fifty-one horses (eleven for the passengers) made up the group. "Our inland voyage last summer was very agreeable," McDonald wrote to Edward Ermatinger, "at least the two Factors & I found it so." The big canoes carried them across via the Saskatchewan River. On September 21 they were at Edmonton, at mid-October arrived at Jasper House, and by the end of the month the McDonalds were settled at Fort Colvile where they were destined to remain for the next nine years.

CHAPTER TWELVE

A Considerable Sort of Canadian Farmer

1835 - 1841

Fort Colvile was a little Eden — a beautiful valley three or four miles in length with the wide Columbia River winding its way through and high hills embracing it on all sides. The fort itself nestled in an arm of the stream, its tall cedar fences enclosing fifteen or twenty log buildings, and all around on the plains horses and cattle grazed and large fields of wheat, barley and potatoes flourished.

Colvile was the supply depot for all the Hudson's Bay Company's interior posts — for the Flathead and Kootenay camps which were in its domain, and for the Thompson's River and New Caledonia districts to the North. It was on the regular Express route to the East, the final stop before crossing the mountains. There the furs were brought together from Fort Vancouver, the mountain regions and the northern posts, and the books made up for the committee in England. For travellers from the East it was the gateway to the Columbia District. After making their way along the rugged route through the Athabasca Pass they reached the bend of the Columbia River west of the mountains, and there they found boats and supplies waiting to take them the three hundred miles down the Upper Columbia to Colvile.

George Simpson had marked out the site on his way back east from his 1825 inspection trip, confident that "an excellent farm can be made at this place where as much Grain and potatoes may be raised as would feed all the Natives of the Columbia and a sufficient number of Cattle and Hogs to supply His Majesty's Navy with Beef and Pork." His idea was that the new post could provision the whole of the interior and at the same time gather in the furs from a wide radius.

A mile or so from the chosen site was a small Indian village overlooking the churning waters of Kettle Falls. It had about one hundred and fifty regular inhabitants, and in late summer several hundred Indians from neighboring tribes joined them to gather thousands of salmon into their huge baskets and spread them out to dry on the flat rocks at the river's edge.

These Quiarlpi — "Basket People" — were quiet, amiable neighbors. They had welcomed Simpson on his way through, helped him select a place to build the fort, and maintained a happy, comfortable relationship with their HBC friends. They were not particularly interested in furs — salmon were their mainstay and they lived in plenty, except in the years when the run was scant and they failed to put by enough to see them through the winter. Their chief in 1824 had turned over to Simpson "the land and the woods, because the whites would make better use of them than himself" but he had reserved Kettle Falls as "necessary to his own people, remarking that the strangers, being able to get food out of stones and sand, could manage to live very well without fish."

Like the Fraser, the Columbia carries torrents of water down from the Rocky Mountains, but the Columbia is wider all the way and its descent more gradual. From Colvile, just below the 49th parallel, 2,200 feet above sea level, it dropped at that time in easy stages over about 500 miles to the ocean, although its many treacherous falls and rapids had claimed numerous victims and continued to do so with disturbing frequency. It was generally agreed that the Upper Columbia, between Boat Encampment and Colvile, particularly around the aptly named Dalles des Morts, should not be attempted before late summer, and Kettle Falls was always impassable, a regular mile-long portage around the huge bubbling basin nearly 2,500 feet wide at the lowest point, which in three great rocky leaps fell a total of about 50 feet.*

When McDonald arrived at Colvile in the fall of 1835 more than two hundred acres were under cultivation. Back in April 1826 three young cows and three pigs had been brought to the new post from Fort Vancouver, and this stock increased over the years until in 1837 he was able to report that the "three calves are up to 55 . . . and three grunters would have swarmed the country if we did not make it a point to keep them down to 150." That year, too, with the acreage increased, more than five thousand bushels of grain were harvested, most of it ground into flour at the fort's own grist mill, and the substantial farm also produced quantities of potatoes and turnips, along with melons, cucumbers and garden vegetables. "In no part of the *pays de sauvage* could I be quartered more to resemble the condition of a considerable sort of Canadian farmer than where I am," McDonald told Edward Ermatinger.

It was a comfortable life, basking in the warmth and contentment of that sunny little valley, a welcome change from the uncertainties and constant turmoil of Langley and the bachelors' hall at Nisqually. With about twenty-five men to carry on the work of the farm, he was able to enjoy his family around him in the commodious Bourgeois's house, and plenty of stimulating company in the many visitors who made Fort Colvile a port of call: fellows of the fur trade, as well as newcomers to the scene, missionaries, scientific parties, even settlers who were beginning to trickle into the Oregon territory in the thirties. "You know my own propensity for talking when I have about me anyone decent to talk with," he admitted to Edward Ermatinger. McDonald was, for the time being, content.

The very domesticity of Colvile was a symbol of the beginning of the end of the old ways. Not only were the fur returns diminishing. The coming of the silk hat to replace the beaver in Europe created the need for the Company to find new markets if

* The multitude of dams and diversions built along the Columbia during this century have altered the course and character of the river since McDonald's time. Fort Colvile itself is now completely submerged by Lake Roosevelt, man-made by the building of Grand Coulee Dam in 1941.

it was to continue to show the substantial profits of old, even if it were possible to continue to bring in the furs. McLoughlin had developed a large, successful farming operation at Fort Vancouver, and McDonald at Colvile helped to prove that the future of the region was in agricultural pursuits, that the days of the fur trade on the Pacific slope were numbered.

"The Beaver itself is rapidly disappearing," McDonald wrote to the Governor and Council in April 1838, and in the same dispatch he pointed out that the farm produce was so abundant that it had cleared a profit of more than £1,200 the preceding year. The fur trade no longer had its old allure for young "gentlemen" in Britain, partly because the relatively few commissions that were available were firmly held by aging "senators" — "worse still than the Family Compact," according to McDonald — who stayed on in the Company and left little room for advancement, and partly because the novelty of the exotic life in the Indian country had now worn off and little of a romantic cast could be ascribed to it. McDonald repeatedly wrote to McLoughlin both from Langley and from Colvile complaining that his "clerks," who were supposed to keep the fort journal and look after the routine bookwork, were inadequate. "I am not assisted with the scrape of a pen by the Clerks . . . I may almost say there is not a man in the district that can sign his own name," he wrote in January 1837. And to make matters worse, following the example of some of the old Company men who had retired to farms in the Willamette Valley in the early thirties, increasing numbers of McDonald's French-Canadian servants were showing reluctance to renew their contracts, wishing to attach themselves to the Roman Catholic missions that were springing up in the neighborhood.

Father Modeste Demers and Father Francis N. Blanchet, who had come from Quebec and arrived in the Columbia in 1838, were settled in the Cowlitz and Willamette areas but included Okanagan, Walla Walla and Colvile on their rounds. In 1841 Father Pierre-Jean deSmet established himself near the Flathead post and drew not only the Company's servants to his mission, but also the freemen from the mountains, further interfering with the gathering of the furs. Everything was "deranged by the presence of so many new faces," McDonald wrote to Simpson.

While McLoughlin and the French-Canadian employees of the Company favored the Roman Catholic priests, another group of missionaries, Protestants sent out by the American Board of Commissioners for Foreign Missions whose headquarters were in Boston, had come to minister to the Indians on the Pacific coast as well. Marcus Whitman and Henry Harmon Spalding crossed the continent via Missouri in 1836, bringing with them their wives, the first white women to cross the Rocky Mountains. The Whitmans established their mission station at Waiilatpu, near Fort Walla Walla, and the Spaldings among the Nez Percés Indians at Lapwai some distance to the east on the Clearwater River. Two years later Elkanah Walker and Cushing Eells arrived, also with their wives, to build the Tshimakain Mission sixty miles south of Fort Colvile. These two parties with their companions heralded the first real wave of settlement in old Oregon and marked the end of an era in the fur trade.

To the Hudson's Bay men, these developments did not at first pose a serious threat to their position on the west coast, and they encouraged and assisted the newcomers in every possible way. With the founding of the Puget's Sound Agricultural Company in 1839 the Company itself bowed to the changing scene and decided to establish a farming community in the Cowlitz Valley. "The harvest is far more promising than the Beaver trade & will no doubt ere long become the grand consideration everywhere west side the R. mountains . . ." McDonald noted. To carry on these new agricultural pursuits for the Company, in the summer of 1841 James Sinclair brought a group of one hundred and twenty men, women and children across the mountains, mostly Métis descendants of old fur traders, recruited at Red River.

A year later the Americans began to arrive in larger numbers. Dr. Elijah White led a party of one hundred settlers to the Willamette by a southern route, bringing with him a commission from the United States government to act as Indian agent west of the mountains, although at that time possession of the lands had not yet been determined. And in 1843 came the first big migration; two hundred wagons bearing one thousand new settlers crossed the Blue Mountains, a direct result of Marcus Whitman's visit to Washington to discuss the future development of Oregon with American government officials. There had still been no agreement between Britain and the United States on the boundary question, but the Americans had suddenly taken the initiative and with a sizeable settlement established in the Willamette Valley formally set up a provisional government for their citizens there.

The great wave of wagon trains had begun; "Oregon fever" struck the frontier towns east of the mountains, and in a few short years the whole district was transformed. In effect, Great Britain forfeited her claims to the lower regions of the Pacific slope by failing to counter these American moves.

What the Indians thought about all this can only be conjectured. Initially they were both curious and friendly, although as the years passed they became more and more uneasy and distrustful of their new neighbours. The missionaries, both Protestant and Roman Catholic, served mainly to confuse the issue. The priests who within a few years were "thick as blackberries" in the region made great strides. As McDonald remarked to Elkanah Walker, there were few among the native people who were not "much captivated by the showey ceremony of the R.C. divine." The Indian love of formality and pageantry responded to the Latin chants and long ritualistic masses, while the Protestant clerics to whom "nothing seems so detestable as papacy" did their unassuming best to compete for the Indians' attention while struggling to keep food on the table and a roof over the heads of their wives and growing families.

The Roman Catholics lost no time in baptizing as many converts as they could. In less than a week on their first visit to Colvile in November 1838 Blanchet and Demers "conducted 19 baptisms and celebrated holy mass many times in the presence of native chiefs, who attended with as great a respect as if they had been fervent Christians. . . ." In the summer of 1839 they again visited the district and on that occasion baptized thirty-six children. The priests "gave them what instruction it was possible to give in that short space of time . . . and were thus able to scatter abroad a few seeds of the divine sowing . . . among such well-disposed nations."

At the same time they cast their disapproving eyes on their Protestant brethren. "They have fabricated an imitation of our historic ladder, and have not hesitated to place a mark on it at the sixteenth century to indicate the rise of their religion. . . . I took occasion to relate to the natives the fifteen centuries prior to that epoch of terror. . . . I made them see the enormous distance separating the religion of modern fabrication from the Catholic religion," said Father Blanchet.

One cannot doubt that McDonald was right when he remarked that all they succeeded in doing was throwing the Indians into a state of puzzlement, however attentive they might appear to be. "The poor Indians get bewildered and they do not know which religion is best," he reported to John Rowand, and to Hooker he complained of the "sectarian doctors" causing "confusion worse confused."

When Paul Kane, the artist, visited the Walkers a few years later, he observed that the Spokanes at Tshimakain "all seem to treat the missionaries with great affection and respect: but as to their success in making converts, I must speak with great diffidence. . . . I have no doubt that a great number have been baptised, but I am also aware that almost all Indians will take a name from a man whom they esteem, and give him one in return, and the more ceremony there is about the transaction, the more importance will be attached to it, and the greater inducement to others to be equally honoured."

The missionaries from the American Board of Foreign Missions had other problems besides the competition from the priests. Rivalries and criticism amongst themselves created tensions that interfered with their work and they were unable to agree even on such points as whether wine ought to be used in the communion service or whether women ought to "pray aloud." Far from accepting the Indians' docile and "well-disposed" attitude as sufficient indication of their willingness to be "saved," the Protestants struggled to improve them. They condemned their laziness and their great love of gambling, and even Chief Big Head who was their friend and mentor failed to please Mary Walker: "He does not manifest the proper spirit," she said, "and we think none of the people do."

It would have been impossible for the simple, easy-going Indians of the Columbia to meet the hard Calvinist standards these single-minded men and women set. The missionaries found it difficult to measure up themselves. Fond as she was of the McDonald family, Mary Walker heartily disapproved of the wine decanter on their dinner table, and when one of her husband's many visits to Colvile extended over a Sunday she worried in her diary that he might "be tempted to engage in conversation not proper for the Sabbath day." Elkanah, for his part, frowned on poor Mary when she, after struggling with laundry and cooking and child care in indescribably primitive conditions six days of the week, indulged herself by reading old newspapers instead of religious tracts or sermons on the seventh. It was not as if she needed to be reminded. "Think I have been rather off my guard, quite too cheerful," she once noted in her diary. "Have not been as careful as I ought to maintain a prayerful spirit. Try to do better tomorrow."

These eastern missionaries with their inexperienced young brides had crossed the mountains totally unprepared for the primitive conditions that awaited them, ill-equipped to provide themselves with their most basic needs. When Walker and Eells appeared at Colvile in September 1838, leaving their wives with the Whitmans at Waiilatpu while they staked out a site for their mission station, they relied entirely on McDonald's good will to introduce them to the neighboring Indians, to assist them in choosing a suitable place to build, and to provide them with supplies and with a carpenter, tools and hardware for their houses.

When they brought their wives back with them the following spring, expecting the women, one of them with a small infant, to set up housekeeping in what, in effect, were merely log pens with neither roofs nor floors, McDonald insisted that Myra Eells and Mary Walker, with six-months-old Cyrus, move in with his own family until their dwellings were habitable. That the New Englanders were naive and improvident is in no doubt, and although their board, like the Catholic missions, was charged by the Hudson's Bay Company for goods purchased, there was much more to the practical assistance and moral support given than money could buy.

McDonald looked on from his comfortable vantage point at Colvile observing "the various characters from all nations now strolling to the far west. . . ." In his heart he confessed that he was still "influenced by a kind of inherent love for everything that tends to the glory of Great Britain & the prosperity of its descendents" and he saw no good in "Brother Jonathan making rapid strides towards us for the formation of a New State."

"Despite all you hear of the charms of Oregon I am by no

means disposed to become a citizen of that . . . new section of the great American Republic," he wrote to a friend, explaining later to Edward Ermatinger, "They are a great & enterprising nation certainly, but with equal correctness may it not be said that the moral & social virtues are lost sight of in the monstrous growth of the Confederation."

Of his future he said, "I am not for perpetuating my own ex-ile in the wilderness from a mere romantick notion of founding Colonies for future generations." To Ermatinger he wrote: "Do not . . . my friend suppose that I am myself smitten with this col-onization mania of ours. That a large population may in course of time spring up all over that country I do not at all doubt, but with one eye one can see the motley crew of which it must neces-sarily be composed: it will be of every cast & hue into which the naturalist has subdivided the three primary branches that first peopled mother earth, — and God's mercy be upon the executive ruler that will have to keep them all good peaceable subjects."

He was aware that few of his fellow fur traders agreed with him. McLoughlin showed every indication that his intention was to stay in the West when he retired, and many of the other Co-lumbia District partners knew that their Indian wives and fami-lies would be happier to remain with the pioneers of the Pacific coast than to go east to try to establish themselves among strang-ers at Red River or in the Canadas. On the old traders who abandoned their native-born wives and families when they left the Indian country McDonald was firm in his views. His quick-witted young wife could easily adapt to a new environment. "Mrs. McDonald would not feel herself much at a loss even in St. Thomas," John Tod reported to Edward Ermatinger after visit-ing the family at Colvile, and McDonald was already paving the way for the boys to be moved to schools in England or in Lower Canada, with the idea of moving east himself. "I do sincerely trust many years will not pass over my head 'till I am free of this blessed country."

As it happened, years did pass at Colvile before his dreams could be realized. Many the winter evenings planning that com-fortable retirement in the East; many the hours spent before a crackling fire in "happy imagination" with Frank Ermatinger, before it could be achieved. There was still much to be done on his expanding establishment at Kettle Falls. Hopes for the future must be pushed to the back of his mind while he attended to the growing demands of the present.

In February 1839 the Hudson's Bay Company signed an agreement with the Russian American Company securing a ten-year lease on a narrow strip of land about three hundred and fifty miles along the coast from the Portland Canal north to Mount Fairweather. In return for this concession, the Company was to provision the Russian posts, and a fair share of those supplies must come from Colvile, although the formation of the Puget's Sound Agricultural Company that same year was to play an important role as well.

During his first year at Colvile, McDonald had begun a program of improving and expanding the already well-established farm. In 1836 new stores and outbuildings went up, and a larger mill to take care of the increasing crops of grains he planned as he sent the men and horses out to plough the virgin plains, gradually increasing the acreage year by year. By the time Elkanah Walker arrived there in September 1838, the missionary could write to his wife a glowing description of the situation she would soon find herself in:

> We passed through a small park of pine timber & came to the brow of a high hill . . . behold Colvile broke upon our view like a city under a hill. You may depend upon it, it was a rich sight . . . after being so long without seeing anything that indicated that the hand of industry had been there. To see fields well fenced, large stacks of all kinds of grain, cattle & hogs in large droves in a country so far removed from the civilized world was a feast to my eyes. . . .
>
> Mr. M. raises great crops. He estimates his wheat this year at 1,500 bushels and his potatoes at 7,000. He employs about 20 men on his farm. Colvile, the fort, is . . . twice as large as any I have seen this side of the Mountains. It is built of timber set up on end. In and about the fort are quite a number of dwelling houses, also three or four large stables and store houses for grain. He is well provided with farming tools, carts and sleds, a sleigh and a gig. In the latter he promised to give me a ride.

The following March, when Mary Walker arrived to live with the McDonald family until her mission home was ready, she echoed her husband's glowing impression. After passing through the "most magnificent mountain scenery" along the sixty-mile route from Tshimakain to Colvile she came to the "pleasing and romantic" site of the "elegantly constructed" fort. "Majestic craggy mountains of granite covered with yellow pine & at this season of the year capped with snow present themselves on either hand. . . . It is on a fertile little plain on the Columbia encircled by mountains. I never was in a place I like the looks of better. . . ."

It was not long before spring broke through and, if anything, the setting became even more beautiful. "The deep snow soon melts," a travelling botanist observed, "and all at once the whole country is ornamented by flowers, which exhibit a brighter degree of colouring than could be expected from the first rays of the spring sun. . . . the flowering of the *clarkia pulchella*, clothing the whole region, far & wide in its purple."

For the McDonalds, the missionaries were a welcome addition to the scene. They had always been limited to the companionship of other fur trade families, and the prospect of conversation with educated men and women so recently arrived from the outside world was exhilarating. Although Jane had had little contact with white women, the newcomers were quick to observe that she was "a jewel . . . of rare excellence," and that her children bore comparison to any they had known in New England. "The deportment of her numerous children was living testimony to her maternal efficiency," wrote Cushing Eells, and Mary Walker noted in her diary that Jane was "nearly white & speaks good English. Their children appear as well I think as any I ever saw in N.E. [New England]. Their mother attends to their instruction having been herself educated by her husband."

The missionary women remained with the McDonalds nearly six weeks and in spite of their many differences the visit marked the beginning of a warm friendship between these oddly assorted couples. The men of the mission, of necessity, made frequent trips to Colvile for supplies, and as time went on, the women too began to exchange visits, taking their children along to spend a few days at each other's homes.

Jane was invited to become a member of the Columbia Maternal Association, the first women's organization west of the Rocky Mountains, which was formed by Narcissa Whitman and Eliza Spalding at Waiilatpu in September 1838 and included the women of all the ABCFM mission stations. They seldom all met together, but in their widely separated homes they set aside the second and last Wednesday of every month for "conversation, reading & prayer" with their children, choosing "suitable literature dealing with motherhood and the care of children." These lonely women were "sensitive of the evils that beset the young mind especially in a Heathen land" and agreed "to form ourselves into an Association . . . to assist us in the right performance of our Maternal duties."

It was a novel experience for Jane McDonald, when she visited with the children at Tshimakain or when Myra Eells or Mary Walker came to stay at Colvile, to join with her devout new friends for the regular "maternal" meeting, and later to chat companionably over their stitchery while the children played about them. A subscription to *Mother's Magazine* was added to the regular periodical fare — the *Albion*, the *Patriot*, the *Quebec Gazette*, the *Montreal Herald*, *Blackwood's Magazine* and others — that circulated from hand to hand around the region, and Jane further broadened her range in preparation for the day of departure for the East.

The family "school" continued to be a busy and interesting place. Amongst all her duties of supervising the kitchens and the dairy as well as her own household — "Her Butter, Cheese, Ham & Bacon would shine in any ordinary market" her husband boasted — Jane made time for regular sessions in the classroom. "Although I have more attendants than you have, still they leave me quite enough to do," she wrote to Mary Walker.

In July 1839 twin boys, Donald and James, were added to the household, who with a son, John, born in May 1837, brought the number of children at home to five, with three older boys still at school at Red River, and Ranald sent east to St. Thomas (now in Ontario) that spring to learn the banking business from Edward Ermatinger. The twins soon became a great joy to all around them. The idea of two babies at once was a new one to the Indians, and the natural affection they felt for all children was multiplied by such a phenomenon. The son of the Indian woman who was brought into the household to help nurse the infants became something of a curiosity himself and for the rest of his life bore the name "Le Lait" because he had been fed on cow's milk.

In the summer of 1840, within days of Jane's return to Colvile from a visit with the whole family to Tshimakain, the pair began to run about the fort in all directions, and the proud father reported to the Walkers that "one half her occupation now is in keeping in her two little boys . . . a task that gives her great delight." They were apparently identical in every way. "Our two young chaps are thriving . . . keeping up with each other in everything to a tee — their first, second and third teeth appeared with each the very same day."

As time went on they became "very fine little fellows, now that they begin to speak becoming exceedingly interesting. In features, voice, height & colour of hair they are so alike as scarcely to know the difference; & to mend the matter the mother, to a thread, keeps them in the same kind of garb." Old Big Head, the Kettle Falls Chief, was so taken with them that as soon as they were old enough to ride he presented them with a horse of their own.

McDonald apologized to Edward Ermatinger for his nursery talk. "Did I not know that I was addressing himself an indulgent Father, I would not presume to dwell quite so long on the subject.

"Were you at this moment to see them, assisted by an elder brother going five years, who thinks himself amazingly wise with tables, chairs, sofas, cushions, tonges, broomsticks, cats, dogs, & all other imaginable things they can lay their hands on strewed around me, you would say 'twas a delightful confusion, & then exclaim 'McDonald, how the deuce can you write with such a racket about you.'"

In September 1841 another son, Samuel, was born, and a few months later McDonald was writing to Walker with a "strange request." The records of the Columbia Maternal Association included the names and birthdates of all its members' children and he had need to consult them to put his own family tree back in order. "The fact is, the two little chaps when their mother was indisposed last season, took a wonderful liking to Books & pictures & behold, the leaf with the names in the prayer Book disappeared."

While the younger members of the family were enchanting their doting parents at home, the older boys at Red River, though far away, were not forgotten. Angus, Jane's eldest, had been taken ill, and finally, in the summer of 1841, was sent home to Colvile with little hope of recovery. The following year young Archy, fourteen, went to England to a school near Clairmont in Surrey. And Ranald, whose sojourn in St. Thomas had proved disastrous, ran away in the spring of 1841 to a life of adventure on the high seas, while his father worried about what the future would hold for his eldest son.

As early as 1836 McDonald was making plans for Ranald to go to the bank in St. Thomas where Edward Ermatinger could "take him in hand" and initiate him into the business world. "Bear in mind he is of a particular race, & who knows but a kinsman of King Comcomlie [*sic*] is ordained to make a great figure in the new world," he wrote. It was not until 1839, however, that the young "Chinook," then fifteen, actually made the move. "Having seen nothing of him myself for the last four years, I am much at a loss how to speak of him to you now —," McDonald wrote to Ermatinger. "All say he is a promising, good natured lad. Before he went to Red River in '34, I had him myself pretty well advanced in Arithmetic, so that one would suppose he is now something of a scholar: yet, I am aware boys of his age leaving school, not unfrequently are very defficient, & that a little practical learning about that time brushes them up amazingly." Mr. Cockran had reported that Ranald had "*certain indescribable qualities* which leads me to imagine that he will make the man that is best adapted for the world —" but McDonald himself confessed to his friend that he could not "divest myself of *certain indescribable fears* which you can conceive as well as I can. . . . You know the Rock on which split all the hopes & fortunes of almost all the youth of the Indian Country — Ranald I hope will have none of those fatal notions. — His success in the world must solely depend on his own good conduct & exertions."

Ranald was apprenticed to Ermatinger in the fall of 1839 but he soon discovered that banking was not his chosen vocation, and when Ermatinger wrote to McDonald that Ranald had even suggested the army as a career, the impatient father replied, "What in the universe could have put the 'Army' in the head of the baby — does he forsooth think I am going to buy a commission for him? please have the goodness to tell him I am exceedingly displeased at his notions & that the sooner he drops them the better." Without waiting for further communication, Mc-

Donald made application on his son's behalf to the Hudson's Bay Company to take him on as an apprentice clerk, but before anything could come of it the boy had bolted and the first McDonald knew of it was "from Master Ranald himself . . . a few lines dated in March [1842] from London." It was a great disappointment: "My wife too, is much concerned to hear of the little satisfaction he is likely to afford us," but McDonald reassured Ermatinger, "Never mind my friend, we have done our duty, & things must now be allowed to take their course."

The joys of the family man with the enchanting little ones who surrounded him at his remote outpost in the foothills of the mountains were tempered by his concern for the older boys, scattered so far from his own influence and their mother's love and protection. He was determined to make every effort to move East as soon as he possibly could.

CHAPTER THIRTEEN

Various Characters from All Nations Strolling to the Far West

1841 - 1844

Throughout the years in "exile" McDonald's annual letters to Edward Ermatinger reflected the changing man and the changing scene. In the early days a trip to Fort Vancouver and a "delightful cruise . . . round the mouth of the Wallamatte" on the newly arrived Hudson's Bay Company steamer, the *Beaver*, was a highlight of the year (1836), and the comradeship of an evening with Frank Ermatinger was worthy of a complete description:

> After 11 months' separation occupied on both sides in all the scenes & vicissitudes of fortune peculiar to this blessed country, I need scarcely say time did not lack [*sic*] on our hands the first night. — Were I not afraid some of your temperance friends might overhear you read this letter I would say good Strong Beer, Port, Madeira & excellent Cogniac gave increased Stimulous to the conversation. . . . We acknowledged in Suitable terms the honor you did us in a drop of Brandy & water while concocking the Colvile letters, by drinking yours in a *bumper* with something like three times three . . . your wife & two little ones were thought of also. — & perhaps even then the good

things were not immediately stored away. — To guard against the possibility of a false impression going abroad however I must assure you that this kind of manifestation of good fellowship does not often occur with us. . . . In the first place what I in days gone bye conceived a glorious merrymaking I now look upon as beastly, & in the next place were I unfortunately even so much inclined my constitutional frame would not endure it — when I do venture in a very moderate allowance, the system is painfully affected by it. — So much for temperance. . . .

But as the years passed life at Colvile became increasingly eventful and the correspondence encompassed a broader range of topics. Columbia happenings continued to predominate, but Ned Ermatinger was the one knowledgeable old friend in Upper Canada with whom McDonald could discuss the political affairs that concerned him most, those of Upper and Lower Canada where he expected to take up his new life in the near future.

So anxious was he to improve his knowledge of the scene that one quiet day in 1843 he sat down at his desk to test his knowledge.

I took my sheet of Cartridge paper, rule & compasses & in a trice sketched off what I call a very good picture, that would not disgrace the mathematical talents of the Honble Surveyor General Parke himself, of every county from Essex to Grenville with their cities & privileged boroughs, & gave each its member or members according to circumstances. — Kent & one of the Ridings of York I then found unoccupied, but since see them confirmed in favor of Wood & the defeated candidate from Terrebonne [Louis Lafontaine], the nominee of the celebrated Dr. Baldwin & the old McKenzie clique — My next effort in the fine Art was to colour out my new map with your municipal districts, seats of the country, the Wardens, clerks, counsellors & all. . . . With this my beautiful panorama I suppose I must now endeavour to tutor myself into the best knowledge I can of the workings of your new constitution, & follow the progress for good or evil of your new men. . . .

Ermatinger, who was himself actively involved in local politics in Middlesex (in 1844 he was elected to represent the riding in the legislative assembly of the United Provinces), was happy to oblige his comrade in the fur country with first-hand news from the hustings, and to see that he received the copies of eastern newspapers he begged for. It was merely an annual diversion, though, and the letters took months to reach their destination and their replies as long to return. Of more pressing interest were the fast-moving developments at his own backdoor. By 1841, with missionaries, settlers and scientific parties all making their way west of the mountains, even the ceremonial inspection tour of the newly knighted Sir George Simpson, spanning the continent on his way to Russia on a round-the-world journey, was just one of many events in Colvile's crowded calendar.

The New Year celebrations were scarcely over in January of 1841 when word reached Colvile that fire had destroyed the Eellses' log house at Tshimakain. Myra Eells, several months along in a difficult pregnancy, had moved with her husband into the Walkers' tiny home, and with the temperature at ten degrees below zero, they had little hope of making much progress in getting another roof over their heads. As soon as he heard the news McDonald gathered together a work party, his carpenter, Goudie, and three of the men, to take provisions and tools to the victims and to set to work then and there to rebuild their home. Two of the young "gentlemen" at Colvile volunteered their services too, and the missionaries were soon again housed in a snug dwelling of their own. It was one of the many occasions when McDonald rescued his friends at the mission from their various difficulties.

A month later another messenger brought news of a worse disaster — this time from Kamloops where Samuel Black had been murdered in his own home by a vengeful Indian. "Late last night we received most calamitous news from Thompson River," McDonald wrote to Walker, asking him to forward a letter to Pierre Pambrun at Walla Walla since the party he was preparing to send to Kamloops would leave him short-handed. "Nothing short of the death of poor Mr. Black at the hands of a murderous Indian. . . . To this melancholy affair no direct cause can be assigned, unless it could be traced to their superstition & the villainous practices of their man of medicine — One of their Chiefs [Tranquille] died very suddenly, & the Conjurors made out that the medium of the whites was too powerful for them to avert, & hence took this frightful revenge. — It was done by a solitary Indian in the house, while the unfortunate man was in the act of stepping into his own room from the Hall — The Ball together with a good deal of shot entered the small of the back & came out below the chest!! — Our lamented friend never spoke a word after."

Black's murder required a different kind of action. Again the two young clerks, Donald McLean and John McPherson, were dispatched with ten men to provide the upper fort with the strength required to calm the restless Indians and protect the Company's property at the establishment. Chief Trader John Tod was expected to go down from New Caledonia to take temporary charge of the post, and then the Colvile men could return, bringing with them Black's widow and three small children to remain with the McDonalds until other arrangements could be made for them. But at the same time Company policy would not allow the murderer to go unpunished, and although it took months to find him, McDonald reported to Simpson in October that a war party had been sent out and "the murderer is now annihilated."

Within weeks of Black's murder there was another sudden death in the ranks of the Company's senior officials. Pierre Pambrun, who had charge of the post at Walla Walla at the bend in the Columbia about two-thirds of the way from Colvile to Fort Vancouver, was seriously injured in a fall from his horse and survived the accident only a few days.

Then came a summer of intense activity. In June an American government exploring party, under the direction of Captain Charles Wilkes of the United States Navy, made its appearance in the Columbia, and "a place so famed as Colvile for its beautiful sceneries, & as some say for its domestic Comforts to a man in need, you may be sure was not a dead blank on their *Carte de route*," McDonald reported, remarking wryly, "Their object 'tis said is entirely scientific." It was clear that the American government had decided to stake its claim and this "Squadron of 5 ships & countless number of Scientific men exploring the country far & wide in their respective departments" were gathering information to be used as ammunition in the boundary discussions, while at the same time they made use of the facilities of the Hudson's Bay Company to secure horses, guides, supplies and hospitality along the way. "They of course stood in want of our assistance which they received & acknowledged with apparent gratitude, besides the tender of good bills on the government."

Another important visitor was expected that summer. Throughout the early months of the year the Colvile correspondence files were filled with plans for the arrival of Sir George Simpson and his entourage. Orders came from all directions. Rowand sent messages from Edmonton; McLoughlin had his own ideas of how the governor should proceed through the Columbia; McDonald had other suggestions; and Simpson kept them all guessing about which route he would follow after making his way through the mountains. It was McDonald's job to see that there were men and boats at Boat Encampment, as well as men and horses at the Bow River traverse in the Kootenay District, to meet the governor whichever way he chose to come, a considerable strain on the Colvile forces at the farm's busiest season in the year that saw its most extensive crops ever.

In the end all went well and Sir George described his overland descent on Colvile in vivid style: Within fifty miles of the fort "we resolved, in reliance on fresh horses and tolerable roads, to wind up with a gallop. We accordingly raced along, raising from the parched prairie such a cloud of dust as concealed everything from our view. In about five hours we reached a small stream, on the banks of which four or five hundred of the Company's horses were grazing. Not to lose so fine an opportunity of changing our sweating steeds, we allowed our cavalcade to proceed, while each of us caught the animal that pleased him best; and then, dashing off at full speed, we quickly overtook our party."

Word had been sent ahead to Colvile that the governor was about to make his appearance. Jane had been busy in the kitchen for days making preparations for the event and when McDonald rode out to meet his guests — a good hour's ride from the fort — he took with him "such materials for a feast as we had not seen since leaving Red River," according to Simpson. "Just fancy, at the base of the Rocky Mountains, a roasted turkey, a sucking pig, new bread, fresh butter, eggs, ale, etc; and then contrast all these dainties with short allowance of pemmican and water. No wonder that some of our party ate more than was good for them."

The whole party, which included John Rowand from Edmonton, and his son, a young physician, along with Simpson's secretary, Edward Hopkins, and a Russian count on his way to

Sitka, decided to bathe in the quick-flowing river to freshen up before continuing on to the fort. "After our hard and dusty ride, we were so much more impatient than usual, that Mr. Rowand [junior], after splashing about for some time and discanting on the pleasures of swimming, struck against his watch. Handing ashore the luckless chronometer, he cast off his inexpressibles on the bank, but, as misfortunes never come alone, he found, on attempting to dress, that that soaked garment had drifted away of its own accord to complete its bathe. In order to supply Mr. Rowand's indispensable wants, a quarter of an hour elapsed in searching for a superfluous pair of trousers, — the enthusiastic swimmer enjoying all this additional time in the water."

They were obviously in high spirits, and in spite of their "tattered garments and crownless hats" rode into the fort in triumph after their "long and laborious journey of nearly two thousand miles on horseback, across plains, mountains, rivers, and forests" during which "on an average" they had been in the saddle eleven and a half hours a day. "During seven weeks, we had not had one entire day's rain; and we had been blessed with genial days, light winds, and cool nights." About eighty men, "whites and savages, all ready, in their Sunday best," were waiting to greet them at the gate.

The governor was pleased with Colvile. "On reaching the summit of a hill, we obtained a fine view of the pretty little valley in which Colvile is situated. In a prairie of three or four miles in length, with the Columbia River at one end, and a small lake in the centre, we descried the now novel scene of a large farm, barns, stables, etc., fields of wheat under the hand of the reaper, maize, potatoes, &c. &c. and herds of cattle grazing at will beyond the fences." That afternoon he rode out with McDonald to inspect the farm and he freely acknowledged that Colvile had fulfilled the promise he had foreseen when he marked out its site sixteen years earlier. More than that, "the whole place bears a cleaner and more comfortable aspect than any establishment between itself and Red River" and "the bread that we ate, was decidedly the best that we had seen in the whole country." McDonald had reason to be proud of his accomplishment and he basked in the governor's approbation.

The Indians of the neighborhood had not forgotten George Simpson's earlier visit and the day after his arrival they gathered in large numbers to greet him, recalling the terms of their old agreement with him "with perfect accuracy." Simpson had always had a way with the Indians. He understood their love of ceremony — indeed, he shared it — and he was happy to contribute to the speech-making, taking turn about with an old chief "whose whole wardrobe was the hide of a buffalo."

"At the close of half an hour, the old fellow . . . was sent away as happy as a king, with a capote, a shirt, a knife, and a small stock of ammunition and tobacco. Finding that speeches were so well paid, the chief's heir apparent and several others came to have their talk out, taking care, of course, to continue the palaver till the equivalents were forthcoming."

Simpson and his party remained at Colvile only three days, but within hours of his departure McDonald was preparing for the arrival of an even larger company. James Sinclair and his hundred and twenty settlers, bound for the Cowlitz Valley, were expected momentarily to make their way through the mountains from Red River. McDonald anticipated that they would come down the Columbia by boat and was somewhat chagrined when one of their number, young Joseph Klyne, arrived at Colvile with a message from Sinclair saying that they had come via the Bow River route. "It is with no small surprise & some disappointment I heard that after all you were coming on *by land*," he told Sinclair. McDonald had already dispatched five boats and a guide to meet the party at Boat Encampment, and he knew that with the Columbia's history of tragedies they would fear the worst when they found no sign of the Red River party. It meant now that he would have to round up a sufficient number of horses to speed them overland on their way westward.

Klyne was sent back to Sinclair with two Colvile men and twenty-two horses and McDonald wrote to Archibald McKinley at Walla Walla asking him to provide an additional twenty or thirty which "would be a great relief to them, & in no small degree tend to pass them thro upon less expenditure of provisions than slower marching would necessarily require." To Sinclair he said, "to make this place in the existing state of things would be a perfect waste of time & labour, as, at Colvile, a single boat is not at my disposal," and he sent along "a thumb sketch of the country" showing him the best route to take via old Spokane House to Fort Vancouver. About a week later Sinclair himself appeared on the scene, having left his charges to make their own way to Spokane where he planned to rejoin them. More provisions were gathered together to send along with him to his rendezvous. "I have been quite on the run here," McDonald wrote to his neighbors at Tshimakain, "goers & comers almost every hour of the 24."

Not the least interesting of these to the missionaries were their fellow "reapers," the Spaldings, who that same week had been driven from the Lapwai mission by the Nez Percés and had taken refuge at Colvile. "In one half hour [they] poisoned his two choice milch cows and manifested much ill feelings in other respects," McDonald reported to Simpson, and to Walker he voiced his concern for the couple "in the hands of those uncouth raskals they have to do with." A few months later he was worrying over the "pranks" of the Cayuse Indians around the Whitman mission at Waiilatpu. "Assuredly I do not feel easy on their account all over," he wrote to Walker, describing the sense of foreboding that overcame him "the moment I see a letter from that quarter." As it turned out his unease was justified. Some years later the Cayuse murdered Marcus and Narcissa Whitman along with eleven others at the Waiilatpu Mission.

But the year 1841 was not over yet and there were still noteworthy events to come. In September, the month of the Sinclair and Spalding visits, Jane gave birth to her ninth son, Samuel, apparently an easy confinement because two weeks later her proud husband noted that the youngsters were all "blessed with perfect health" and that their mother was "now thank God again as active as a girl of 18. . . ." It was not for long that they could rejoice in such universal well-being. Fifteen-year-old Angus had returned home that fall suffering from what his father described as the "Columbia leprosy" and with no hope held out for recovery, although McDonald did send him down to the doctor at Fort Vancouver for advice and briefly clung to the view that perhaps his case was not as serious as they had at first feared. Jane, however, kept the boy for the most part close by her, a gentle, intelligent lad, much loved by the little ones and a favorite with his elders as well. "His mother desires me to say she could not well spare Angus as Fort hunters are rather scarce at present," McDonald wrote jokingly in reply to an invitation from Walker some months after the boy's return, but to Sir George he confessed with a heavy heart, "I am sure I need not say how much we have been distressed by his case & the afflicting circumstances attending it." Angus died the following April.

November saw the arrival of Father Pierre deSmet, coming to Colvile from his newly established mission to the Flatheads in the Bitter Root Valley with requests for supplies and provisions to see him through the winter, and field seed for his spring planting. McPherson, at the Flathead camp, had already supplied him with more provisions than McDonald thought he should have, particularly of grease which was in very short supply everywhere in the district, but he kept his guest for three days — in deSmet's view he received "a warm hospitable reception" — and sent him off with a bag of flour and some garden supplies.

McDonald thought very little of the Flathead mission. He felt it interfered with the fur trade, was a drain on his own establishment, and in fact that the priests accomplished very little in their chosen field.

However docile the red man west of the R. Mountains may seem to the philanthropists at first sight, I am much mistaken or there are greater difficulties in converting him to the habits of civilised life than is generally supposed. . . . Mr. deSmet found them apparently well disposed & most tractable beings upon such cursory visits, did . . . [he] . . . expect to find them otherwise? The Indian is too good a politician to say no, you must not come here, but when we have you, if you don't come up to our expectations in liberality we know how to serve you. With the Indian traders it is the very same. They are fond of them because they obtain their wants from them & cannot do without them; but he that gives the most Blankets is the favorite, & the Priest that gives most tobacco will be the favorite too.

Disillusionment was setting in, and as the old year gave way to the new, with one of the coldest winters in memory imprisoning them all at the fort, McDonald had time to reflect on the future. Word had come through that at last the sought-after "second parchment" was his. The Northern Council authorized his promotion to chief factor late that year, and at the same time Frank Ermatinger was named chief trader. "Your Brother & I owe our promotions to two singularly rare chances: a Savage Indian & a vicious horse," he wrote to Edward acknowledging that the two vacant commissions were created by the untimely deaths of Black and Pambrun the preceding year. At the same time he confessed that he hoped the change would speed his retirement, trusting that the day was not far off when he would be tendering his greetings in person in St. Thomas.

More and more of the Company's men of all ranks were leaving the service, some "with the intention of returning free & independent by some defile of the R. Mountains" to settle in the new West, others to retire to the East. Colvile's two young clerks were among their number. "It is not a fickle or a casual comer & goer I ought to have," McDonald protested to Simpson, asking for a new clerk, "but a rising man fixed to the Service . . . a smart European apprentice of two or three years standing would be the man for our plain business at present." Little did he know that the young "gentleman" he would be assigned that year would cause him more grief and heartache than he could have imagined from his past experience with the insouciant young men he complained of.

William Thew soon appeared at the fort and although in mid-June McDonald told McLoughlin he wanted no part of this young clerk at Colvile — "Perhaps it is intended to pawn Mr. Thew on us. I beg to be excused for anything is better than him," — the young man stayed on and an unhappy summer was made more miserable by the presence of this arrogant and demanding ne'er-do-well whose laziness was only exceeded by his insolence.

Thew had already made his mark in the Indian country. After several years in the Saskatchewan territory he had been sent to New Caledonia at the request of John Rowand, who explained to Simpson that he was "exceedingly negligent and inefficient" and had neither "the will nor the wish to make himself useful." By this time his salary had been reduced from £75 to £60 and both years he was attached to Fraser's Lake in New Caledonia the Company's servants under his charge deserted. "No cause assigned but I presume it will not be difficult to discern," Peter Skene Ogden remarked.

"Really, with the general character throughout the country which this youngster bears, I cannot look upon his being quartered with me, merely to suit his own idle & unambitious disposition, for four long months, as at all a compliment," McDonald raged to McLoughlin. Shortly after his arrival at Colvile, Thew had taken a fancy to Charlotte Ferris, the young girl who helped Jane with the children — "a member of my own household!" said McDonald indignantly — and the situation became so uncomfortable and the young man's presence so unwelcome that his host "was obliged to forbid him my house & discontinue all further intercourse with him. . . . He is however still provided for three times a day at a separate mess by my wife & family, on whom I believe it is well known, necessarily devolves the kitchen duties at Colvile during the summer months."

Unfortunately the matter was not to be settled so easily. Early in August McDonald returned to the fort from Okanagan where he had gone to supervise the movement of Colvile's annual Outfit from Vancouver to find that Thew had taken on "incredible airs" in his absence. The young clerk attacked McDonald in the yard "with exceeding violence" and only McDonald's determination to avoid an open rupture prevented him from retaliating. The next afternoon, however, "the scoundrel followed me to the fields with a table knife in his pocket, [and] provoked me with the most insufferable language till we reached the Fort Gate when I was irresistibly compelled to knock him down." In spite of his "age and corpulence," McDonald had tired of turning the other cheek.

Thew, it seems, did not know when to stop. He pursued McDonald to the door of his own house and when Jane appeared and admonished him to leave, he brandished his knife and threatened "to put it into your husband's heart." With that McDonald ordered him "to be off my Fort before the next sun rose," and sent off an account of the proceedings to all the chief factors and chief traders in the district. "It would be well," said McLoughlin, "you send a narrative of this affair across the Mts. with him so as Gentlemen might know how to act towards him," and James Douglas wrote that Thew's "conduct is a matter . . . without precedent . . . & most disgraceful to himself." To McDonald, it was "most unaccountable how such a useless character could be so long tolerated in the country." Another of the old traders blandly remarked, "That Gentleman appears determined to immortalize his name in some shape or other, if not by good actions, by going to the other extreme." Thew left the Company's service the following spring.

But that summer was marred by a more serious calamity

than the mere misbehavior of a clerk. The treacherous Columbia — "fertile in disasters as it ever has been" — reached out yet again to claim its quota of victims. In its long record of casualties hardly a year passed when one or two, or more, of the Company's boatmen did not disappear in its turbulent waters, and many the dramatic rescues when lives were saved though often whole cargoes lost, as the great river boats were flung recklessly about in the swirling cascades.

In 1838 McDonald had been on the scene at Colvile to receive the survivors of one of the worst catastrophes ever recorded on the Columbia, when twelve lives were lost in a boat attempting to pass through the Dalles des Morts on the way down from Boat Encampment. John Tod had charge of the overland party from the East that season, and along with new recruits for the Company's service and the usual number of voyageurs to man the boats and carry over the portages, he had care of a number of passengers: Fathers Blanchet and Demers, the two Roman Catholic priests from Quebec, Robert Wallace and Peter Banks, two visiting English botanists, and their wives, and the families of two of the Company's men. There were not enough boats waiting at the encampment to transport so large a group and Tod arranged to leave some of the party behind to wait for a boat to return for them. In spite of his precautions, the craft that went down was overloaded, and the inexperience of one of his passengers was no doubt partly responsible for the tragedy.

"Another melancholy event on the Columbia river!" McDonald reported to James Douglas, who was that year filling in at Fort Vancouver while John McLoughlin was in Europe on furlough. "No fewer than 12 souls perished below the Dalles aux Morts." The boat was laden down with twenty-six persons aboard — André Chalifoux, the pilot, and another Company servant, Pierre Leblanc, each with a wife and three children, the two naturalists and their wives, and twelve other men all with their private baggage, and twenty-two "pieces" (each weighing ninety pounds) belonging to the Company. According to the missionaries' account, after damaging their boat at the head of the rapid, the "bouts" experienced further difficulty as they neared the end of the run, and when the boat filled with water Wallace "stands up, removes his coat, puts his foot on the side of the bateau, and hurls himself into the water with his wife, shouting 'courage, my friends!' The bateau loses its equilibrium, over-turns, and all are precipitated into the midst of the waves!"

In the struggle that followed, Chalifoux and his wife with one of their children managed to make the shore, along with Mrs. Leblanc and a number of the old hands. The other five children were all consumed by the churning waters, as were Leblanc, Banks, Mr. and Mrs. Wallace and three of the Company's servants.

The memory of that calamity was still green in the early summer of 1842 when McDonald suffered a more personal loss to the river. Over the years Colvile had become a close-knit, companionable little community. The offspring of the Hudson's Bay men grew up together almost as brothers and sisters, sharing the run of the fort and fields through their childhood, and frequently as they came into their late teens marrying the sons or daughters of their fathers' friends and comrades. By the forties, Colvile's population included a number of families that spanned three generations.

Canote Umphreville, "a good faithful servant of 31 years standing in the Columbia," the most experienced of all the Columbia River guides, was steering the boats from Colvile down to Fort Vancouver as he had done six times a year for as long as anyone could remember. His son, young Canote, his son-in-law Pierre Martineau, David Flett, McDonald's personal servant, and the usual number of paddlers were with him when the "overwhelming whirlpools" of the OK Dalles near Fort Okanagan seized Canote's boat, and the old guide, his son-in-law, Flett and two other hands were drowned.

"These mighty vortexes are of such a nature that one boat is swallowed down when others a few minutes after pass in perfect safety," McDonald explained, describing the incident to Hooker. To McKinley, his neighbor at Walla Walla, he wrote, "Excuse me if I don't write more . . . the lamentable tale you will have heard of has thrown me into a painful state of mind — My Guide, My Miller & My own servant all gone!!!"

He was unable to maintain the calm with which he observed on another occasion, "Their day was come, and whether in the whirlpool or parlour must be fulfilled to a second." Fifty years later, Ranald recalled his father's mourning. "My father retired some distance to give vent to his grief and sorrow, for [Canote] &

Flett were favorites with him." According to Ranald, "Flett was an excellent cook & baker & in fact was on his way to Fort Vancouver to teach them the art of baking good bread. With him my father lost his [travelling] kitchen (a great basket containing the service of the table)."

McDonald was not the only one to feel the loss. His heart went out to Mrs. Martineau, who at the very time that word was received of the accident at the Dalles had just buried her six-year-old son. "What a sad blow poor Martineau's wife has sustained within the short space of the same three days — on the 3rd of this month, three days after she lost her father, her husband & nearly her brother, her only boy of six years old was killed here on the spot by the rolling down upon him of one of our fence Boullins while in the act of climbing over it."

McLoughlin, too, was having troubles that year. George Simpson's stay at Fort Vancouver during the winter of 1841–42 brought out into the open the many long-standing conflicts and disagreements between the two men, and McLoughlin, who for years had held full sway over the Columbia, resented the governor's interference in his affairs. Simpson had for some time wanted to consolidate the coastal business, which he thought was far too expensive for its returns, and to close down all the posts to the north except Fort Simpson, using the steamer *Beaver* to conduct the trade. McLoughlin argued vehemently against this, as he did against Sir George's suggestion, made with the agreement of the London committee, that the Columbia headquarters be moved from Fort Vancouver to Vancouver Island. The Hudson's Bay governors were by now well aware that the lands around Fort Vancouver were bound soon to come under American rule, and they were anxious to see the headquarters re-established in British territory.

McLoughlin had other ideas, and his objections may have been partly on personal grounds. He already had interests of his own in the Willamette Valley and there was no doubt that he had firm plans for retiring to that district and developing a business of his own in the midst of the hundreds of settlers who were pouring in. Nothing was really settled, but the open correspondence that moved from fort to fort about the Columbia allowed no secrets, and it was known far and wide that the rift was growing wider between the irascible Dr. McLoughlin and the governor.

When Simpson left for the North to proceed up the coast, visiting the Company's establishments on his way to the Russian phase of his round-the-world tour, the two parted on anything but amicable terms. The tragic events of the succeeding weeks ensured that never again would they be able to resume the old easy friendship of the early days in the Columbia.

Unknown to his father and friends in the South, young John McLoughlin was having trouble with his men at Stikine, the Columbia's northernmost post located up the coast on land leased from the Russians. When word spread through the district that he had been murdered by his own servants after what was said to have been a drunken brawl at the remote outpost, the horror and consternation were universal. George Simpson arrived on the scene just four days after the murder, examined some, though not all, of the witnesses, and to McLoughlin's everlasting wrath accepted their word that young John had been a harsh and brutal taskmaster and, what was more, "a man lost to Liquor."

Simpson took the murderer on to Sitka with him, to be dealt with by the Russian authorities, cautioning McLoughlin, senior, to say as little as possible about the whole matter. To the grieving father this was a supreme insult, and he became obsessed with the need to clear his son's name, writing volumes of words describing the tragedy and the events that followed to all his friends and associates far and near.

"The pile upon pile of papers the unhappy father has laboured to fill up upon this harassing question to prove his son to have been what in my opinion he was not is truly astonishing," McDonald wrote to Simpson, and he confessed that "I cannot disguise my dread of the attack that will be made upon me this summer if I go down [to Fort Vancouver] to bring me into his own way of thinking as I believe it is his habitual practice with everyone with whom he comes in contact."

John McLoughlin, junior, son of McLoughlin's native-born wife Marguerite Wadin McKay, had had a chequered career. Resisting his father's efforts to educate him abroad and equip him for the life of a gentleman in the "civilized" world, he had only recently joined the Company's service and in short order been assigned to the charge at Stikine, an appointment that McDonald and others among the old traders regarded as less than judicious.

But it was Simpson who bore the brunt of McLoughlin's anger and resentment. McLoughlin actually accused the governor of being "the cause, though unintentionally, of the murder of my son," and he never forgave him for the way in which he handled the situation. That the Company, in an official dispatch more than a year later, attempted to smooth things over by asserting publicly that they believed the murder to be the result of a "preconcerted plot" and that there was "no just foundation for the charges of drunkenness and of excessive severity in punishing the men under his command" did not lessen the poor father's efforts to bring "justice" to the offenders.

It was a downhill road for McLoughlin from then until he left the Company's service and retired to the Willamette Valley in 1845. Affairs in the Columbia District bore a gloomy aspect for the remaining years of McDonald's stay west of the mountains.

There was one saving grace, however. Through the years since McDonald's meeting with Sir William Hooker in Glasgow in 1834 he had kept up a sporadic correspondence with the eminent horticulturist, and when Hooker took charge of the recently established Kew Gardens at Richmond in Surrey, he wrote to his old fur trade friend asking his assistance in collecting specimens and seeds from the Rocky Mountain regions. Many of McDonald's seed samples thrived in the experimental gardens at Kew, and through Hooker's recommendation his services were rewarded with an honorary membership in the Royal Horticultural Society. It was an absorbing interest, and one that brought with it a pleasing distraction from the more immediate problems and concerns of his everyday life.

Few of the fur traders shared his enthusiasm: "I am extremely sorry to have to report that, with the single exception of our mutual friend Mr. Tolmie, the Gents, of the west side are very reluctant to dab in anything connected with the vegetable or animal kingdom," he reported to Hooker, but A. C. Anderson, a young clerk in the New Caledonia, he hoped he might "enrol into our service."

McDonald told Hooker that he had sent a copy of the "printed instructions from the Directors of the Royal Botanical Gardens, Kew" off to New Caledonia in hopes of arousing some interest there, and suggested that "it would be worthwhile if Mr.

Tolmie had at his disposal a little brown paper to hand about to those Gentlemen at distant parts. If they did nothing the loss of the paper would not be great; & the having a few sheets would be a stimulus for them to fill them up." McDonald himself sent off a selection of bulbs and tubers and some "Bitter-root or spad-lum I made some exertion to get . . . it is a very pretty vernal flower rising but little above the ground, generally found on sandy hillocks & volcanic rocks slightly covered with earth," consulting his few botanical textbooks to assist in his description of the plant.

"I fear . . . I shall fall far short of reaching your high expectations from my botanical researches in the Columbia — I however flatter myself I at least have the *wish* to be useful; and shall continue of that disposition to serve you . . . while it is my lot to sojourn west side of the Rocky Mountains."

Tolmie was by this time in charge of the Puget's Sound Agricultural Company at Nisqually, and he and McDonald continued to exchange letters along with newspapers and books from their meagre libraries, frequently discussing details of the packets they sent back to their botanical friends in England. At the same time, through Hudson's Bay House in London, McDonald sent a number of boxes of animals collected in the Colvile region to the zoologists at the British Museum.

Dr. J. E. Gray, who was with the museum from 1824 to 1875 and was responsible for building the definitive mammal collection gathered during the mid-nineteenth century when interest in natural history was at its peak in Britain, catalogued many of the specimens sent by McDonald from the Columbia, and a number of these remain today in the teaching collection at the British Museum of Natural History.

Gray's list of specimens received on November 28, 1843 — a very large box one assumes — included two rare pronghorn, or "jumping" deer, with horns spanning fifteen to seventeen and a half inches, a small buffalo skin six feet by four feet, a reindeer, wolverine, black bear, eagle and a number of smaller mammals. The following year he received twenty-five specimens, including six reindeer, along with a wolverine, bear, porcupine, otters, hares, squirrels and other rodents. In the summer of 1845 another box arrived in poor condition, many of its sixteen creatures with decayed skins and only their skulls salvageable. Amongst them all was another deer from the Columbia River valley, a buffalo, hares, foxes, lynx, mink and skunk. The usual method of rubbing the skins with arsenic as a preservative had apparently been ineffective.

The whole world of natural history captured McDonald's attention and he must have been one of North America's first conservationists in his expressions of concern for the damage done by the encroachment of man on his wilderness home. As early as January 1841 he suggested to James Douglas at headquarters that the Company establish a nature preserve. "The moment the freehold grant is obtained [in the Puget Sound region] I move that the Clalum district in a line from Hood's Canal to the Pacific be barred up & appropriated to the preservation of the poor expiring Beaver race, still, leaving country enough for the ostensible objects of the Agricultural Company. . . ."

But the hard years — "three campaigns of four & twenty years of it on west side" — were taking their toll. His accomplishments were great. McDonald's record of long-term achievement in the solitude that characterizes the life of a fur trader is rare. "In no other circumstances does so much depend on the personal qualities of the man," wrote one fur trade historian and McDonald had given ample proof that he had cultivated that "manliness, straightforwardness and decision of character" required of a man left to his own devices and desires in isolation on remote outposts in the wilderness. He had kept his standards high through all those long, lonely years in all aspects of his active life, never giving in to the temptation to take the easier course, to let up a little in his devotion to duty or in the style of living he had set for himself and his family. It had not been easy, and as the years passed his constitution began to show the effects of the strain.

In the fall of 1843 Jane, with a new baby, Joseph, born in March of that year, Samuel, the twins and John, all within six years of him in age, and still mourning the recent loss of Angus, was in "a very precarious state of health." McDonald himself before that winter was out took to his bed with what he originally diagnosed as "rheumatic Pains" but which developed as the months went on into a more serious back problem that kept him confined to his room and brought Dr. Whitman up from Waiilatpu to try to minister to his ills.

It was time to make plans for the move East. "At all events, my services for another year cannot be depended upon," he wrote to Simpson, "my mind is made up to see if I cannot manage to recross the Mountains this fall." He resolved "with the little vigor I have" to lose no time "in setting about the formation of some sort of a home that hereafter may become a kind of rallying point for the numerous progeny depending on my support. . . ."

That it would be an expensive proposition he did not doubt, but since his health would not allow him to continue to draw his chief factor's active shares for as long as he had hoped, "one may as well lay himself on the shelf with eight 85ths in the hope of a retired interest while it is worth having." A chief factor received 2/85ths, a chief trader 1/85th, of the shares of the profits assigned to the officers annually, and according to Company policy he would continue at full pay for a year, and half pay for the six succeeding years after his retirement.

McDonald had no illusions about the state of the fur trade, and although during his last few years at Colvile he repeatedly reported his district returns only slightly down from earlier years and asserted that "we might still make something of it in this region were we perfectly quiet, & the natives left undisturbed," to one of his friends back east he wrote, "the H.B. gold dust is gone forever" and suggested that they must put their minds to finding "substitutes for Beaver."

At any rate, he would have a competency. Through all his twenty-four years with the Company the everyday expenses of living had been provided for and the greatest portion of his annual salary went back into Hudson's Bay stock, which yielded a good steady income. Of his other occasional ventures in the business world he did not expect much.

Like most of the Hudson's Bay officers remote from the centres of commerce, McDonald entrusted his investments to Simpson, though for a time Samuel Gale, his friend of Selkirk days, in Montreal, acted for him as well. While some of his railway stock, a popular speculation in the early forties, brought him good returns, one disastrous venture promoted by the governor along with Sir John Pelly, another member of the Hudson's Bay Committee in London, caused heavy losses, and McDonald was not quick to forgive Pelly for his part in the fiasco.

At Simpson's suggestion, in 1839 McDonald invested £500 in a lumber venture that "Pelly, Pelly & Simpson" had established in Norway, but in the two succeeding years no annual reports were proffered, but rather only hints of the "unfavorable state of the wood markets" and the suggestion that there was no "prospect of early improvement," which made for general unease on the part of the investors. That Pelly's son, who had been sent to Norway to manage the business, in short order decided to marry and return to England to live did not increase their confidence. When the firm was dissolved McDonald found that in two years, instead of gaining interest in the transaction, he had actually lost 20 per cent of his investment. He found he was not alone.

Chief Factor Duncan Finlayson, writing from Fort Garry in June 1843 to James Hargrave who had himself lost £1,000, complained about the "gloomy" Norway venture: "Public men and men of business, may gloss over their actions, as they choose, but in this case, I do not think we have been fairly dealt with. — we knew nothing of the business in which we were strongly advised to embark & to become shareholders — We came forward with our money, with confidence in the parties to whom it was entrusted, and under such circumstances, they were, if not legally at least in equity honor bound to refund every shilling of it, but instead of this, we are, it appears, to be losers of about one fifth of the principal."

McDonald wrote directly to Sir John Pelly in the same vein. "It is now however, I suppose, needless, on the part of so many of us in this country, by our own simplicity so fearfully involved in this unhappy affair, to cavil on the subject at the 11th hour. The deed is done, & seemingly there is no alternative. . . . True, we Indian traders unfortunately have but a very limited idea of the general commerce, but somehow or other we cannot very well bring ourselves to reconcile to each other the two facts . . . a profit of from 8 to 10 per cent accruing annually . . . up to the hour our interest in it commenced, & that . . . on a more enlarged & improved scale . . . it should not yield one shilling."

He could ill afford the loss but, more than that, he and his fellow fur traders felt they had been taken advantage of. "If others of my fellow sufferers do not make their sentiments known with equal candour assuredly it is not because they feel their unexpected loss with less chagrin & disappointment," he wrote, ". . . in this instance it is in the *manner* in which we were induced, as if even blindfolded, to stake some of us our all in a speculation we knew nothing at all about."

Fortunately he still had his railway shares, along with a considerable quantity of Hudson's Bay stock, and with his retired interest in the Company he would be able to live in some comfort on a country establishment somewhere in the East.

He was still concerned about the expense of such an undertaking. For one thing, "the unavoidable expense of servants is what I dread myself," he confessed to Edward Ermatinger. "Without outdoor & indoor servants too, I foresee one cannot promise himself a very comfortable & a very productive establishment in the Canadas. Northwesters from their constant habit of commanding others, & that at times in great numbers, will not readily accomodate themselves to the uphill work of the indefatigable and thriving backwoods-man."

It was time to pull up all the old roots, to say the final farewells. McDonald made one last journey down the Columbia to Fort Vancouver that summer, and Jane and the children went to Tshimakain early in July for a brief last visit. Early in September Myra and Cushing Eells and their two boys appeared at the fort to bid bon voyage to the travellers.

After their departure Charles Geyer took leave of his host. A German botanist who had made his headquarters at Colvile since arriving the preceding winter "ill-provided for the work he has undertaken in this remote corner of the world," Geyer had been outfitted by McDonald "with little trifles of my own" to carry on his scientific explorations in the neighborhood and was effusively grateful for the generosity with which he had been received.

As soon as the Eells family returned to the mission station, the Walkers' caravan wended its way up to the fort. The last remaining days were not long enough to reminisce over their five years of fellowship and mutual help in the remoteness of the western wilderness. The missionaries were reluctant to part from their friends. They recalled the many kindnesses: the warmth of their first reception at Colvile when Jane made them all welcome in her own quarters and found a young girl to help Mary with her baby son so she could explore the countryside with her new companions; the first Christmas at Tshimakain when McDonald had sent Walker home from Colvile "loaded with good things" for the family festivities — "port, beef, buffalo tongues, cheese, etc." They recalled the Maternal Association meetings and Sunday services when they had worshipped together; the wintry day when Elkanah ran out of chewing tobacco and "felt it necessary to make the 140-mile round trip to Colvile to replenish his supply"; McDonald's words of encouragement for Walker's Flathead primer, and the pleasure of Elkanah's "dandy new suit" ordered from London by his Colvile mentor — "I am exceedingly happy to hear that the fit & everything about it has given such ample satisfaction — my correspondent in London is afraid I made a mistake in the measurement," McDonald wrote to his six-foot-four friend. All these were remembered, along with the many other elements embraced by their friendship. It was not easy to say good-bye.

Nearly a quarter of a century had passed since McDonald had first arrived in the Columbia. He had known the beautiful Pacific slope as virgin land, had travelled rivers never before viewed by a white man's eyes. He had early envisioned the day when its vast plains would fall into orderly patterns of waving grain fields; when its teeming salmon would feed uncounted mouths beyond the reaches of the Nass, the Skeena, the Fraser and the Columbia; when its forest timbers would provide lumber for markets around the world; when its minerals would yield wealth yet unknown.

From the days long ago when he had brought those earliest pioneers to Red River to form the first colony in Canada's West, he had known the inevitability of the progress of settlement into the Indian country. The fur trade might slow the wave, but the tide had now turned, and the growing communities in the Willamette and Cowlitz valleys, with their mills and shops and churches and schools, were just forerunners of the numbers of villages that would spring up west of the mountains in the near future, both north and south of whatever line the British and American governments agreed on in their boundary negotiations. He had played his part. Red River, Kamloops, Langley, Nisqually, Colvile — all bore his mark. His early experiments in agriculture and fisheries and lumbering would lead the way for his successors. He was ready to move on.

CHAPTER FOURTEEN

His Life Was One of Much Usefulness

1844 - 1853

September 21, 1844 — departure day. All the families of the fort and most of the neighboring Indians gathered at the river's edge to wave them on their way. The big Columbia River boat was well filled, the boatmen nudging the children into their places, and Jane trying to keep track of Joseph, who was only eighteen months old. She was pregnant again, the new baby due within weeks, but there was no time to wait if they were to make it through the mountains and on to Red River before winter set in. When the moment came, they would halt their progress until she was able to continue, but this baby would be born far from the comforts and conveniences of any commodious fort, under frosty open skies in the midst of the majestic mountains. A "young relative" of Jane (presumably Charlotte Ferris), would be her only female companion, and ten-year-old MaryAnne would share much of the care of her little brothers.

The Columbia was running hard — unusually "boisterous" for so late in the season — and almost impossible to pass with their well-laden craft. As they neared Lake Kootenay McDonald decided to make camp and let the high water run its course. Some years before he had made some interesting geological observations in the region and while the others rested he could go off in a small Indian canoe to take some samples of the ore that he suspected might have a high silver content, and send them off to be tested in the Company's laboratories in London. "I am very much mistaken or they are indeed indications of a very rich mineral country," said the note accompanying the packet he sent back to James Douglas at Fort Vancouver. (A year and a half later the chemists' report on the sample proved it to have a large proportion of silver content.)*

McDonald took time then, too, for a touch of nostalgia. Alone in the stormy night by the shores of the beautiful lake, he reflected on his own mortality. "By the light of a blazing fire which warmed myself and my two naked companions for the night, I cut my initials on a large tree along side of us, to commemorate my own dear name, as no nook or corner could be spared me on the recently explored Hyperborian shore."

When the party arrived at Boat Encampment on October 10 the westbound Express had not yet arrived, but McDonald was not alarmed by the delay. "Upon the whole had an agreeable trip of it," was the message sent back to Walker to assure him of their safe journey up the river. "The weather was charming & the Indians kept us in fresh grub with Bears, Mountain Sheep, Chevreaux & Rein Deer." Jane may have felt differently about it, but she had crossed these mountains before and she knew that there was worse to come before the new baby was due to arrive. She could only hope that they would not have too long to wait for the horses that would carry their baggage back through the rugged Athabasca Pass to Jasper, and they could set off on this next arduous lap of their journey.

"The mountains around us are covered with snow, but at the altitude usually assigned it is perpetual: over a very small portion of that elevation we shall have to pass . . . & of course on old snow about as hard as ice — upon that there is usually two feet of new snow end of Octob. to encounter which we are prepared," McDonald wrote.

* By the end of the century mining operations were being carried on at this site, later to be taken over by Cominco and developed as their well-known Bluebell Mine at Riondel.

Prepared no doubt they were — "accoutered *à la façon du nord*, with snowshoes, guns, axes, blankets . . . [and] provisions" — but the most stalwart of men found the beauties of the mountain scenery small recompense for the hardships of the tortuous crossing through the rugged, snow-clad summits of the Rockies. That late in the season fresh snow had already begun to fall and the horses, when they were not tripping in mud holes or stumbling over the upturned roots and gigantic tree trunks that lay across their path, struggled through drifts which frequently engulfed them up to their haunches or slithered on icy patches that flung them, packs and all, back down the precipitous inclines that reached to the height of land over which they must cross.

As far as the eye could see there seemed to be no end to that vast, endless ocean of mountain peaks. More often than not, choosing the least of the evils, the miseries of struggling over the uneven terrain on snowshoes seemed preferable to the pitfalls of riding on horseback, however sure-footed the animals might be on a normal trail.

"The scenery [is] Wild & Majestic beyond description," wrote George Simpson of the Athabasca route, but he added, "the track is in many places nearly impassable, and it appears extraordinary how any human being should have stumbled on a pass through such a formidable barrier . . . which nature seems to have placed here for the purpose of interditing all communication between East and West sides of the Continent."

When Paul Kane followed the same path east in the fall of 1847 he described it as the worst he had ever encountered. On the first day out from Boat Encampment his horse got stuck in a mud hole and sank up to its neck. As the days passed and they reached higher and higher altitudes, the snow grew thicker with every step — often as deep as twenty or thirty feet — and the cold was so intense that Kane's campfire scorched his face when he attempted to get near enough to thaw the solid mass of ice that formed on his hair and beard. As they were forced to cross and recross the rivers, the waters they forded almost covered the backs of their horses and a heavy snowstorm blew into their faces, blinding them to the view of the banks on the opposite side.

It was difficult enough for the strong, able-bodied voyageurs. That it should be attempted at all by a woman in the final stages of pregnancy seems incredible. There can be no doubt that Mc-

Donald and all the men assisting them in their passage helped carry the little boys — five of them under the age of seven — but Jane McDonald, indomitable and uncomplaining, had to make her own way through the snow and the ice and the tangled underbrush. When, at last, they reached Jasper House they were able to transfer to canoes and enjoy what was, in comparison, a degree of comfort as they proceeded along the Athabasca River.

It was not until November 23, still some distance west of Fort Assiniboine, that the inevitable symptoms signalled the imminent arrival of the new baby, and another son, Benjamin, made his appearance. Ice was forming in the river and as they paused for Jane to gather strength it became evident that they could not continue on to Red River as planned. McDonald sent a messenger south to Edmonton House appealing for help, and within days a party of "men, Indians & 25 horses" came to the rescue, providing transport for them all down to the fort.

On December 9, seventy-nine days after leaving Colvile, they climbed the long hill that led up to the gates of the palisade, and beyond them John Rowand's warm, hospitable fireside was a welcome haven. Their host was concerned about the heavy demands so many unexpected guests would make on his winter's provisions, but he made the best of it and the McDonalds gratefully settled in to spend the winter at Edmonton.

Rowand's post, set high on a promontory above the North Saskatchewan River, had a regular population of nearly one hundred and thirty, and like Colvile it frequently played host to "comers and goers" on the main east-west route. When the McDonald family moved into their temporary quarters there, they found at least one other family billeted at Edmonton for the winter, along with two of Simpson's part-Indian sons who had been placed in Rowand's care.

The big fort, centre of the whole Saskatchewan District and supplier of York boats, horses and pemmican for all the travellers up and down the great river, was, as always, a hive of activity. Within its three-hundred-by-two-hundred-foot palisade Chief Factor Rowand, famed for his influence over the dreaded Blackfoot, as well as the less warlike Assiniboines, Crees, Sarcees, Piegans and Bloods who traditionally traded at the fort, ruled with an iron hand. He liked to have firm control of all that went on in his broad domain, but that winter events transpired that were beyond his power to command.

The damp, penetrating cold of the river's edge brought fever and ague into the camp, and MaryAnne, her father and his personal servant were among the many who were soon tossing feverishly in their beds with the burning, aching debilities of the disease. Scarcely were they on the mend when several of the children on the establishment came down with scarlet fever, mild in form at first. In early May it attacked the little McDonald boys "in a more malignant shape," and within a week, between May 13 and May 20, Donald, James and Joseph died.

McDonald's "dear little interesting twins" and their two-year-old brother were committed to a common grave at Fort Edmonton, and their brothers remained in perilous condition when the eastbound boats departed from the fort a few days later leaving McDonald and his wife behind, battered by this sudden fearful change in their fortunes.

It was not until June 5 that the remaining children were well enough to travel. Three homeward-bound European servants of the Company had stayed behind when the Brigade set off to assist the sorrowing family when they were able to make the move, and it was with heavy hearts that they bade farewell to their old friend Rowand. At Carlton House they were further delayed when one of the boys suffered a relapse, but in a few days they were again sailing along the Saskatchewan toward Cumberland House. At the Pas "the fatal contagion" struck again. "Already sufficiently borne down with sorrow & fatigue," Jane McDonald fell ill, and her husband quickly decided to make for Red River where she might be in the comforting circle of her family with her own mother to care for her. It meant missing the annual meeting of the Northern Council to which Simpson had summoned him, but the situation was desperate.

Throughout the trip the weather was wild and turbulent, and as they entered Lake Winnipeg they "all nearly perished" in a particularly violent storm which pelted hailstones "the size of turkey eggs" on their heavily laden craft and sent them running for cover to the shelter of the nearest post, Fort Alexander, on the lake's eastern shore.

At Norway House Chief Factor Donald Ross was making arrangements to send the regular fall boats to Montreal. It was impossible to fit McDonald and his entourage in with the eighteen other passengers he already had waiting for places in the three big canoes being readied to make the journey. In the end without detouring to Red River, they travelled from Fort Alexander via Fort Frances, Fort William and the Sault in what turned out to be the uncongenial company of George Gladman and his wife and family.

It was anything but a pleasant voyage, entailing "many hairbreadth escapes from drowning, and the endurance of a vast amount of vexation and misery, that, with a better defined arrangement and more agreeable Companions could well have been avoided." Remembering all the times he had facilitated the travel arrangements of his fellow traders, McDonald rather resented his many difficulties, but when he wrote to Ross some months later he had recovered some of his old buoyancy and aplomb. "On this once to me exceedingly unpleasant subject I at one time intended to have reported to you some of the facts & occurrences; but I believe 'tis now scarcely worth while — I may get over it."

By that time he had begun to realize some of his old dreams of moving about in the civilized society of old Canada. En route east the family took passage from Windsor on the *London* and travelled along Lake Erie to Port Stanley, just a few miles from St. Thomas where the Ermatingers waited to welcome them. Not only did the two friends find their warm fellowship as they had so long remembered it, there were other old acquaintances to greet there too. Angus and Jean McKay, two of the "Churchill pilgrims," were settled on a neighboring farm, and Ermatinger brought them along to reminisce with their former leader. John, the little boy who had very nearly been lost before birth on that long trek across the ice-encrusted trail from Churchill to York Factory, had grown to manhood now, and McDonald happily greeted McKay, "decidedly . . . the most correct & efficient man in my squad in '13 & '14." What memories they called to mind.

From St. Thomas the family went on to Buffalo, and from there along the Lake Ontario front to Cobourg and a few days' visit with John Dugald Cameron, who had built an imposing retirement home at nearby Grafton. It was Cameron with whom McDonald had first travelled across the mountains in 1821, and who had been in charge of the Columbia District in those early days. As they made their way eastward on this last journey, their route was punctuated by a series of flashbacks summing up McDonald's long career in the Indian country. The "genial Gael" greeted all his old friends along the way with pleasure and delight, and in Montreal that winter there were dozens of fur trade companions to reminisce with over well-appointed dining tables, to help him catch up on the local political scene, and to provide proof that he had been right in his decision to abandon his wilderness life.

The family lived temporarily in a comfortable little cottage at Chambly, not far from Montreal. Alexander and Allan had come east with Peter Skene Ogden the preceding year and were boarding at the Chambly rectory while attending school there. Jane and the younger children were happy to be settled next door where they could all be together whenever the older boys were free. Archy junior was to come home from England at the end of his school term, and McDonald was making arrangements for MaryAnne to attend school for the first time in her twelve years at the Sacred Heart Convent in Montreal.

His plan still was to acquire a sizeable farm somewhere in the vicinity but it might take some time to find a desirable property. Meantime he concentrated on searching for a suitable dwelling in the city, where he could have the children all around him and see them enrolled in the good schools he had brought them east to attend. At the same time he himself could enjoy the congenial companionship of the many fur trade comrades who made their homes along the St. Lawrence and Ottawa rivers.

J. G. McTavish he saw often in Montreal, and John Clarke, John McBean and others were there too. George Simpson and Duncan Finlayson were both at nearby Lachine, married to two sisters, cousins of the governor. John McLeod and George Barnston lived not far off and came to the city frequently, and Edward Ermatinger lived in Montreal during the sittings of the legislature. Even Frank Ermatinger turned up on furlough in the spring of 1846 and reported that "Archy is my constant companion" on a "round of N.W. dinners."

The Oregon question had suddenly captured the attention of the politicians in the East, and McDonald was wined and dined and consulted on all sides. Governor-General Cathcart called him in for two long interviews and found his company so agreeable — perhaps their mutual interest in geology distracted their minds from the more serious subject of the moment — that he invited him to dine at Government House and tell Lady Cathcart of his adventures in the West.

"My very lap dog from Oregon was hailed here as a perfect wonder," he wrote to a friend, amused that the territory so long neglected should have become the centre of attention. The Democrats had won the United States presidential election in 1844 on their slogan of "Fifty-four forty or fight" and the Americans were pushing to extend their rule. The time had come to end the Treaty of Joint Occupancy that had been in effect since 1818 while the British could still retain the lands north of the 49th parallel. In 1846 the boundary line was agreed upon and the Canadian government in Lower Canada became aware of the presence of this British territory they had until now regarded as wilderness Indian country.

The McDonalds spent two years in Montreal, in the "good house with small garden" on St. Urbain Street to which they moved in the spring of 1846. In June 1847 they purchased a large farm on Carillon Bay, forty-two miles from Montreal and three miles below St. Andrews East, where the Ottawa River widens into the Lake of Two Mountains. But it was nearly a year before improvements on the existing house were completed and the family made the move to the country. Then McDonald officially retired from the active rolls of the Hudson's Bay Company.

By this time the older boys were becoming established in their professions: Archy "bound" to a civil engineer in Montreal, and Alexander apprenticed to a land surveyor farther up the Ottawa River. The others, except for Benjamin and Angus Michel who was born in November 1846, were all at school. MaryAnne came home on holidays from the Sacred Heart Convent and delighted them all with her newly acquired proficiency at the piano, particularly her father who years earlier had so longed for music in his home at Fort Colvile that he had come close to importing an organ from England to satisfy his desires.

McDonald himself had been bonded as a surveyor of lands in the districts of Quebec and Montreal, and made justice of the peace for the parish of Argenteuil. His political instincts quickly made him a leader in the little community, and in 1849 he led a delegation representing fourteen hundred citizens of Argenteuil

County that appeared before the new governor-general, Lord Elgin, to protest the Rebellion Losses Bill which had been introduced to the legislative assembly that February by the Baldwin-
Lafontaine government. Feelings ran high on the issue and led to
ugly riots in Montreal, the burning of the Parliament Buildings
and the stoning of the governor-general. Little had the old fur
trader expected such behavior from the Tories, however great his
reservations over the rise of republicanism and the capabilities of
his fellow colonials for responsible government. It was difficult to
tell "who is Whig or who is Tory," he observed, "who is for doing
good from who is bent on doing evil."

To a friend back in the Columbia he wrote in wonder about
the great rush for gold in California, torn between the two
worlds. "Can we believe 1/10th of what we hear of the richness
& abundance of the Gold? . . . the great city of Montreal will ere
long be visibly diminished in population by the Swarms of adventurers taking flight to the gold region. Are you aware that at
one time I & a few other choice spirits on west side were within
an ace of possessing that locality in free & common sockage?
What nuncopups [sic] we were that we did not forthwith close a
bargain with the . . . California governt."

But he did not hanker after wealth or fame. His old friends
found him mellowed with the years, his ambition tempered, "age
having . . . transfused good & kind feelings into his wit."

The farm, now christened "Glencoe Cottage," was prosper-
ous and comfortable, situated on one of the most beautiful sites
on the Ottawa River, the view from its wide verandas taking in
the broad sweep of the island-dotted Lake of Two Mountains.
Even with the two older boys away, the household was always
full of young people, with MaryAnne and her brothers as they
grew into their late teens becoming the centre of a gay social
scene. Within a few years a wing was added to the house, and an
adjoining seventy-five acres of land purchased to enhance the
property.

Jane took to life in their new community with her customary
dignity and poise. She was something of a curiosity to her neighbors. They knew of her exotic origins and accepted them, while
learning to love and respect her for her great spirit of warmth
and charity. As the wife of one of the county's most substantial
citizens, this remarkable woman who had known no life but that

of the wilderness Indian country took her place unaffectedly in the local society, quietly performing "little acts of kindness" that were remembered long after her death.

With the rest of the family she became an active and devout member of the little Anglican congregation of Christ Church in Saint Andrews East. She had two young maids to assist with the housework, leaving her free to engage in her other interests. In spring she loved to get back to the land, out into the sugar bush where she directed the maple syrup harvest, a convivial annual event with all the children and their friends gathering the pails in the woods and the horse-drawn sleds hauling the huge barrels of clear, sweet sap into the boiling booth "not 120 yards" from her kitchen door.

Life was good; the reward well earned. The last years passed busily and happily, the less rigorous pace bringing improved health to them both. McDonald divided his time between his magisterial duties and directing the farm, which he managed with the assistance of Allan, the eldest of his sons at home, a hired man and a boy.

In May of 1852, while in the process of purchasing the adjoining piece of land to add to his property, McDonald decided to put his other affairs in order as well and drew up a new will. Ranald he believed to have been lost at sea, but for the other two older boys, Archy junior and Alexander, and for MaryAnne he provided financial bequests, leaving the farm to Allan on condition that he allow Jane "enjoyment" of the house and property to the end of her days.

"My beloved wife Jane Klyne, in whose maternal solicitude for my dear children I place implicit confidence" was named "tutrix" of all the minor children, still four in number, and portions of railway stock were to be set aside in their names. He had little thought that his testament would be called into use so soon.

The end came swiftly and unexpectedly on a crisp, cold day the following winter. On January 15, 1853, after only a few days' illness, Archibald McDonald died, his loving family all around him at Glencoe Cottage. His death was "deeply and widely lamented" reported the Montreal *Gazette*, eulogizing this "pioneer of civilization" in the West as a "kind-hearted good man . . . always active, intelligent, and upright, esteemed for the impartiality of his conduct, and the kindness of his manners . . . . his courage, skill, and physical prowess as a young man were extraordinary, and to these were united mental qualifications of no mean order. . . . His life was one of much usefulness."

Postscript

Jane Klyne McDonald lived on at Glencoe Cottage for twenty-six years after her husband's death, running the farm with the assistance of her sons, in turn, until all had moved on to other careers. She remained an active, independent woman all her days. According to her son Benjamin, in 1855 she made the long journey alone from St. Andrews to Red River, travelling west over the waterways to be with her mother at her home on Euclid Avenue, Point Douglas, during her last illness. Jane Klyne's brothers, George and Adam, were politically active at the Red River Settlement in 1869–70, both being among the Métis who opposed Louis Riel at that time. George, a supporter of Dr. John Schultz and the English faction, was one of forty taken prisoner by Riel at the time of the disturbance, and later was one of twenty elected to the French side of the "Convention of 40." In December 1870 he was elected to represent the electoral division of Ste. Agathe in the first legislature of Manitoba. Jane McDonald continued an active parishioner at Christ Church, St. Andrews East, and in 1877 presented to the church in her husband's memory a large two-panel stained glass window depicting the Good Shepherd and Saint Stephen, with the names of all the members of the McDonald family forming a border around it. She died on December 15, 1879.

Ranald MacDonald (all the sons of this generation changed the spelling of the family name to MacDonald), who was reported in American newspapers to have drowned in the South Seas when he was set adrift from a merchant vessel off the coast of Japan in 1848, reappeared at St. Andrews to visit his family several years after his father's death, recounting an incredible tale of his adventures in the hermit kingdom (see Lewis & Murakami, *Ranald MacDonald 1824-1894*). Ranald had been imprisoned in Japan for nearly a year, and was enlisted to teach English to a group of government officials, two of whom later served as interpreters when Commodore Matthew Perry made his first foray into the forbidden country. He had returned home after a stopover in Australia's gold fields, near Melbourne, and after a time spent with his stepmother, drawn by the discovery of gold on the Fraser River, he returned to the West. He engaged in various mining and business ventures in and near the gold fields, and was later joined by two of his half-brothers, Allan and Benjamin. Ranald lived out his last years near the site of his parents' old home at Fort Colvile, and died at Boundary Creek, Washington, on August 24, 1894. Although his father made no mention of him in his last will, believing his first-born to be dead, Jane McDonald made him a bequest of $400, the same sum she left to the widow of Archy junior.

Archibald MacDonald junior continued in his career as a civil engineer in the Ottawa-Montreal area, residing in the village of St. Andrews East until he drowned when his sleigh went through the ice on the Ottawa River in February 1868. He married Kate Antrobus of Three Rivers in 1858, and their only son, Archibald III, died at the age of five.

Alexander MacDonald joined the service of the Hudson's Bay Company as a young man, serving in various parts of the Northwest. He was chief factor at Moose Factory at the time of his death in July 1875, in his forty-fifth year.

Allan MacDonald, with his half-brother Ranald and younger brother Benjamin, was engaged in ranching and running pack trains to the gold mines near the Bonaparte River in British Columbia in the early 1860s. He sold his share in the Cameron claim, later proved to be one of the richest in the whole region, to return home to St. Andrews where he married Harriet Robertson, daughter of Dr. William Robertson and sister of Dr. Patrick Robertson, long-time family friends from St. Andrews. They had one son and three daughters, and the family later moved west, where Colonel MacDonald served as Indian agent in the Northwest territories and, finally, in Winnipeg, where he died in 1901. With his brothers John and Samuel, he served as an officer in the 11th Battalion, Argenteuil Rangers, formed by the Honorable J. J. C. Abbott, another family friend from St. Andrews. The regiment saw scattered action at the time of the Fenian raids in 1866, and he was a captain in Colonel Garnet Wolseley's Red River expedition when it went west in 1870.

MaryAnne, the McDonalds' only daughter, who was born at Rocky Mountain House in February 1834, remained at home until her marriage to Dr. James Barnston, son of her father's old friend Chief Trader George Barnston, in 1857. Dr. Barnston was both a medical practitioner and a professor of botany at McGill University. He, his wife and their infant daughter and only child died within eighteen months of each other in the late fifties. MaryAnne was known around St. Andrews as the heroine of a near-drowning in the bay near her home when she was only sixteen. According to local records, "on the day of her adventure she was alone with a lady friend and the servants. While sitting on the verandah and watching some small boats which looked like stationary black specks on the sunlit water of the bay, a sudden obscurity swept over the lovely landscape and the birds and all the living creatures around the cottage suddenly became silent and anxious-looking. Before the boats reached the islands, a storm, as we seldom witness in this part of Canada, burst in all its fury. A little skiff containing two boys further from safety than the others was soon capsized. When Miss McDonald, who had anxiously watched it through her glass from the first, perceived that the two boys were clinging to the boat, in spite of the buffeting of the waves . . . she rushed to her skiff (a good one), slipped the painter from the port, and rowed out to their rescue. The journey, nearly a mile in length, was a perilous one, but being an expert skuller and very strong for a girl of her age, she managed to reach them just as their strength was becoming exhausted. The storm having abated to some extent, the return was soon accomplished." MaryAnne was awarded the Royal Humane Society medal for bravery on July 26, 1850, and was presented with a silver tea service in recognition of her heroism.

John MacDonald, in 1857, his twentieth year, left St. Andrews East to work in Edward Ermatinger's bank in St. Thomas, Ontario. Ill health interrupted this career after a few years and he went to British Columbia, where he died at Fort Shepherd at the age of twenty-seven. His brother Benjamin travelled north to bring his body back down the Columbia River by boat to Colvile, Washington, his birthplace, for burial.

Samuel MacDonald, who was eleven at the time of his father's death, became a notary and divided his time between Montreal and St. Andrews East, where he lived. In 1871 he married Emily Elizabeth Roberts, of Fredericton, New Brunswick (an aunt of Sir Charles G. D. Roberts), and they had two sons and two daughters. Samuel died in Montreal in the spring of 1891.

Benjamin MacDonald, the son who was born in the Rocky Mountains as Archibald and Jane Klyne McDonald journeyed east to their retirement in 1844, married Elizabeth, the daughter of the Reverend James Pyke of Hudson Heights, Quebec, and granddaughter of Chief Factor J. G. McTavish, in 1872. In 1862, when he was only eighteen, Benjamin left St. Andrews for the Fraser River gold fields, travelling by way of Montreal and New York and by steamer down the coast of North America to the Isthmus of Panama which he crossed on the narrow-gauge railway. He then boarded another steamer which took him to San Francisco and Victoria, where he visited with his parents' old friends the Douglases. Sir James Douglas was then Governor of British Columbia, and his wife, a daughter of Chief Factor William Connolly and his Cree wife Susanne, was described by Benjamin in an unpublished memoir as "a distant relative" of his mother. Benjamin spent several years in business with his half-brother Ranald and his brother Allan, assisting them with their ranch and running pack trains into the Cariboo gold country near the Bonaparte River. In the succeeding years he engaged in various business ventures in the fast-developing area around Kootenay Lake and northern Idaho, Washington and Oregon, and for some time he made his headquarters at Colvile, where he had an interest in the first steamer on the Columbia River, *The Forty-Nine*. He later moved to Montana and thence to Los Angeles, California. He died in 1918.

Angus Michel MacDonald, born in Montreal after the family moved east, was only six years old when his father died. He remained on the farm with his mother and died there in August 1867, aged twenty years.

Appendix

List of Selkirk settlers who walked with Archibald McDonald
150 miles from Churchill Creek to York Factory in early April
1814 and made their way by boat and on foot up the Hayes
River to Lake Winnipeg and the Red River colony by early
summer:
Angus McKay, *20.*
Jean, his wife, *20.*
George Sutherland, junior, *17.*
Donald Sutherland, *his brother, 19.*
Jannet Sutherland, *his sister, 13.*
Alexander Gunn, *49.*
William Gunn, *his son, 21.*
George Bannerman, *23.*
Hector MacLeod, *17.*
Elizabeth McKay, *24.*
John Matheson, *acting overseer, 22.*
Hamen Sutherland, *20.*
Barbara Sutherland, *his sister, 22.*

Robert Gunn, *piper, 22.*
Mary Gunn, *his sister, 20.*
Alexander Bannerman, *21.*
Mary Bannerman, *his sister, 24.*
Christian Bannerman, *his sister, 19.*
George Sutherland, senior, *18.*
Adam Sutherland, *his brother, 16.*
John Murray, *21.*
Alexander Murray, *his brother, 19.*
Alexander Sutherland, *24.*
Katherine Sutherland, *his sister, 22.*
Neil Smith, *17.*
Jean Smith, *his sister, 14.*
Andrew McBeath, *19.*
Jannet McBeath, *his wife, 17.*
Charles McBeath, *his brother, 15.*
Henry McBeath, *his brother, 16.*
Hugh Bannerman, *19.*
Elizabeth Bannerman, *his sister, 21.*
Isabella Bannerman, *his niece, 20.*
William Bannerman, *20.*
Christian Bannerman, *his sister, 16.*
John McPherson, *20.*
Katherine McPherson, *his sister, 24.*
James McKay, *Angus's brother, 19.*
Ann McKay, *his sister, 22.*
John Matheson, senior, *23.*
Betty Gray (McKay?), *19.*
William Sutherland, senior, *24.*
Margaret Sutherland, *his sister, 16.*
Robert Sutherland, *his brother, 19.*
Elizabeth Fraser, *30.*
George Gunn, *14.*
Esther Gunn, *his sister, 24.*
Alexander Matheson, *22.*
John MacIntyre, *23.*
James McDonald, *blacksmith, 21.*
Samuel Lamont, *millwright, 22.*

Acknowledgments

I would like to express thanks to the Hudson's Bay Company for permission to publish extracts from its records, and to the Yale University Library for extracts from the Coe Collection, Walker-Whitman Papers. I am particularly grateful to the many librarians and archivists in Canada, the United States and Great Britain who have assisted me in the research, to the Canada Council for two research grants, to Governor General Edward Schreyer, who when Premier of Manitoba made possible a memorable flight over the route between Churchill and Winnipeg followed by the Red River settlers in 1814, and to Professor W. L. Morton for his generous encouragement and advice. To my husband, both editor and historian, and my children, all of whom helped in their different ways, my thanks are also due.

J.M.C.

Manuscript Sources

Most of the material for this biography has been taken from primary sources, among them the following:

— *Hudson's Bay Company Archives* (microfilm copy), Public Archives of Canada, Ottawa.

— *Walker-Whitman Papers*, Coe Collection, Beinecke Rare Book and Manuscript Library, Yale University Library.

— *Selkirk Papers* (copies), Public Archives of Canada, Ottawa.

— *Ermatinger Family Papers, John McLeod Papers, Miles Macdonell Papers, Hargrave Papers, Red River Census, James Douglas Express Journal 1835*, and others in the Public Archives of Canada, Ottawa.

— *Fort Langley Journal*, typescript of the British Columbia Provincial Archives copy in the possession of Hugh MacMillan, Toronto.

— *The Archibald McDonald Papers, the Ranald MacDonald Papers,*

Appendix

John Work Journals, Abel Edwards Journal and others in the British Columbia Provincial Archives, Victoria, B.C.

— *The American Board of Commissioners for Foreign Missions Papers,* Harvard University Houghton Library.

— *The E. E. Dye Papers, the W. L. Lewis Papers,* and the *Frank Ermatinger Letters* in the Oregon Historical Society Library, Portland.

— *The McDonald of Dalilia Papers* in the University of Edinburgh Library.

— *The Yester Papers* in the National Library of Scotland.

— *McDonald, Geyer and Douglas Correspondence* in the Kew Gardens Library.

— *Register of Accessions for 1843, 1844 and 1845,* British Museum (Natural History), London, England.

— Various miscellaneous papers in the Public Record Office, London, England; Scottish Records Office and Register House, Edinburgh; the Glencoe and NorthLorn Folk Museum; Manitoba Provincial Archives; Kamloops Museum and Library; Fort Langley National Historic Park; Vancouver Public Library; Toronto Public Library; Ontario Legislative Library; Whitman College Archives, Walla Walla, Washington; Washington State College, Pullman, Washington; Spokane Public Library, Washington; Tacoma Public Library, Washington; and the Bancroft Library, University of California, Berkeley. The author gratefully acknowledges the assistance of all these institutions, as well as the help of the Peterborough Public Library and the Trent University Library, Peterborough.

Bibliography

Barker, Burt Brown, ed. *Letters of Dr. John McLoughlin written at Fort Vancouver, 1829-1832.* Portland, Oregon: Pub. by Binfords & Mort for the Oregon Historical Society, 1948.

Barron, Frank Laurie. *The York Trials of 1818: Lord Selkirk and John Strachan.* Unpublished M. Phil. thesis, Waterloo University, 1970.

Bethune, A. N. *Memoir of the Rt. Rev. John Strachan D.D., LL.D., first Bishop of Toronto.* Toronto: H. Rowsell, 1870.

Bowes, G. E., ed. *Peace River Chronicles.* Vancouver: Prescott Pub. Co., 1963.

Bryce, George. *The Romantic Settlement of Lord Selkirk's Colonists.* Toronto: Musson, 1909.

———. *Mackenzie, Selkirk, Simpson.* The Makers of Canada, vol. 8. Toronto: Morang, 1911.

Campbell, M. W. *McGillivray Lord of the Northwest.* Toronto: Clarke, Irwin, 1962.

———. *The Saskatchewan.* New York: Rinehart, 1950.

238

Bibliography

Cole, Jean Murray. "Exile in the Wilderness, Archibald McDonald's Ten Years at Fort Colvile." *The Beaver,* Summer 1971.

Cox, Ross. *Adventures on the Columbia River.* 2 vols. London: H. Colburn & R. Bentley, 1831.

DeSmet, Father Pierre-Jean. *Life, Letters and Travels. vol. 2.* New York: F. P. Harper, 1904.

DeVoto, Bernard, ed. *The Journals of Lewis and Clark.* London: Eyre & Spottiswoode, 1954.

Douglas, David. "David Douglas' Second Journey to N.W. parts of N. America 1829-33." *Companion to the Botanical Magazine,* vol. 2 (1836).

————. *Journal Kept by David Douglas . . . in North America, 1823-27.* Reprint. New York: Antiquarian Press, 1959.

————. "Sketch of a journey to the north-western parts of the continent of North America during the years 1824, 5, 6, & 7." *Companion to the Botanical Magazine,* vols. 2 and 3 (1836-37).

————. "Sketch of a Journey to Northwestern Parts of the Continent of North America during the years 1824, 1825, 1826 and 1827." *Oregon Historical Quarterly,* vols. 5 and 6 (1904-1905).

Drury, C. M. "Botanist in Oregon in 1843-44 for Kew Gardens, London." *Oregon Historical Quarterly,* vol. 41 (1940).

————. "The Columbia Maternal Association." *Oregon Historical Quarterly,* vol. 39 (1938).

————. *Elkanah and Mary Walker.* Caldwell, Idaho: The Caxton Printers, 1940.

————, ed. *First White Women over the Rockies.* 3 vols. Glendale, California: A. H. Clark Co., vols. 1, 2, 1963; vol 3, 1966.

Dye, E. E. *McDonald of Oregon.* Chicago: A. C. McClurg, 1907.

Elliott, T. C. "Peter Skene Ogden, Fur Trader." *Oregon Historical Quarterly,* vol. 11 (1910).

Ermatinger, Edward. *Life of Colonel Talbot and the Talbot Settlement.* Reprint. Belleville, Ont.: Mika Publishing, 1972.

————. "York Factory Express Journal." *Royal Society of Canada Proceedings and Transactions.* 3rd series, vol. 6 (1912).

Fiennes, Ranulph. *The Headless Valley.* London: Hodder & Stoughton, 1973.

Fleming, R. H., ed. *Minutes of Council Northern Department of Rupert*

Land, 1821-31. General editor E. E. Rich. Toronto: Champlain Society, 1940.

Franchere, Gabriel. *A Voyage to the Northwest Coast of America.* Reprint. Chicago: Lakeside Press, 1954.

Galbraith, J. S. "Early History of the Puget Sound Agricultural Company." *Oregon Historical Quarterly,* vol. 55 (1954).

Geyer, Charles. "Journals 1845, 1846 and 1847." *London Journal of Botany,* vols. 4, 5 and 6 (1845, 1846 and 1847).

Gibbon, J. M. *The Romance of the Canadian Canoe.* Toronto: Ryerson Press, 1951.

Glazebrook, G. P. de T., ed. *The Hargrave Correspondence 1821-1843.* Toronto: Champlain Society, 1938.

Gray, J. M. *Lord Selkirk of Red River.* Toronto: Macmillan, 1963.

Halkett, John. *Statement respecting the Earl of Selkirk's settlement of Kildonan upon the Red River, in North America; its destruction in the years 1815 and 1816; and the massacre of Governor Semple and his party* (London, 1817).

Harper, J. R., ed. *Paul Kane's Frontier.* Toronto: University of Toronto Press, 1971.

Harvey, A. G. *Douglas of the Fir.* Cambridge, Mass.: Harvard University Press, 1947.

Howay, F. W.; Sage, W. M.; and Angus, H. F. *British Columbia and the United States.* Toronto: Ryerson Press, 1942.

Innis, H. A. *The Fur Trade in Canada.* Toronto: University of Toronto Press, 1956.

Irving, Washington. *Astoria.* Reprint. 2 vols. Philadelphia and New York: Lippincott, 1961.

Jessett, T. E., ed. *Herbert Beaver's Reports and Letters.* Portland, Ore.: Champoeg, 1959.

Johansen, D. O., and Gates, C. M. *Empire of the Columbia: A History of the Pacific North West.* New York: Harper, 1967.

Johnson, F. H. "Fur-Trading Days at Kamloops." *British Columbia Historical Quarterly,* 1937.

Johnson, W. R. *Legend of Langley.* Vancouver: Langley Centennial Committee, 1958.

Kane, Paul. *Wanderings of an Artist.* Reprint. Edmonton: Hurtig, 1968.

Knox, Olive. "Chief Factor Archibald McDonald." *The Beaver,* March 1944.

Lamb, W. Kaye, ed. *The Letters of John McLoughlin from Fort Van-*

Bibliography

couver to the Governor and Committee. General editor E. E. Rich. 3 vols. First series, 1825-38; second series, 1839-44; third series, 1844-46. Toronto: Champlain Society, 1941, 1943, 1944.

Landerholm, Carl, ed. *Notices and Voyages of the Famed Quebec Mission to the Pacific Northwest 1838-1847.* Portland, Ore.: Champoeg Press for the Oregon Historical Society, 1956.

Laut, A. C. *Pathfinders of the West.* New York: Macmillan, 1904.

Lent, D. G. *West of the Mountains.* Seattle: University of Washington Press, 1963.

Lewis, W. L. "Archibald McDonald, Biography and Genealogy." *Washington Historical Quarterly,* vol. 9 (1918).

————, and Murakami, N. *Ranald MacDonald 1824-1894.* Spokane, Wash.: The Eastern Washington State Historical Society, 1923.

MacGregor, J. G. *Peter Fidler, Canada's Forgotten Surveyor.* Toronto: McClelland & Stewart, 1966.

MacKay, Douglas. *The Honourable Company.* Reprint. Toronto: McClelland & Stewart, 1966.

MacLennan, Hugh. *Seven Rivers of Canada.* Toronto: Macmillan, 1961.

MacLeod, Margaret Arnett, ed. *The Letters of Letitia Hargrave.* Toronto: Champlain Society, 1947.

————, and Morton, W. L. *Cuthbert Grant of Granttown.* Toronto: McClelland & Stewart, 1963.

Martin, Chester, ed. *Journal of Occurrences in the Athabasca Department by George Simpson, 1820 and 1821, and Report.* General editor E. E. Rich. Toronto: Champlain Society, 1938.

————. *Lord Selkirk's Work in Canada.* Oxford: Humphrey Milford, 1916.

May, E. G. *A Hundred Years of Christ Church, St. Andrews, P.Q.* St. Johns, Que., 1919.

McAdam, Adam. [pseud.] *Communications from Adam McAdam, originally published in the Montreal Herald, in reply to letters inserted under the signature of Archibald Macdonald, respecting Lord Selkirk's Red River Colony.* Montreal, 1816.

McDonald, Archibald. *Narrative respecting the destruction of the Earl of Selkirk's settlement upon Red River, in the year 1815.* London, 1816.

————. *Reply to the letter, lately addressed to the Earl of Selkirk, by the*

Hon. and Rev. John Strachan, D.D., &c. Being four letters (reprinted from the Montreal Herald), containing a statement of facts, concerning the settlement on Red River, in the district of Ossiniboia, territory of the Hudson's Bay Company, properly called Rupert's Land. Montreal, 1816.

McKee, Ruth Karr, ed. *Mary Richardson Walker, Her Book.* Caldwell, Idaho: The Caxton Printers, 1945.

McKelvie, B. A. *Fort Langley, Outpost of Empire.* Toronto: Nelson, 1957.

————. *Pageant of B.C.* Toronto: Nelson, 1955.

McKelvey, S. D. *Botanical Explorations of the Trans Mississippi West 1790-1850.* Cambridge, Mass.: Harvard University Press, 1955.

McLeod, Malcolm, ed. *Peace River. A Canoe Voyage from Hudson's Bay to Pacific, by the late Sir George Simpson, (Governor, Hon. Hudson's Bay Company) in 1828. Journal of the late Chief Factor, Archibald McDonald, (Hon. Hudson's Bay Company), who accompanied him.* Ottawa: J. Durie, 1872.

Merk, Frederick, ed. *Fur Trade and Empire, George Simpson's Journal 1824-25.* Cambridge, Mass.: Harvard University Press, 1931.

Morgan, Dale, and Harris, E. T., eds. *The Rocky Mountain Journals of William Marshall Anderson. The West in 1834.* San Marino, Cal.: Huntington Library, 1967.

Morse, Eric W. *Fur Trade Canoe Routes of Canada Then and Now.* Ottawa: Queen's Printer, 1969.

Morton, A. S. *A History of the Canadian West.* Toronto: Nelson, 1937.

————. *Sir George Simpson.* Toronto: Dent, 1944.

————. *Under Western Skies.* Toronto: Nelson, 1936.

Morton, W. L., ed. *Alexander Begg's Red River Journal and the Papers relative to the Red River Resistance of 1869-1870.* Toronto: Champlain Society, 1956.

————. *Manitoba: A History.* Toronto: University of Toronto Press, 1957.

Mowry, W. A. *Marcus Whitman.* New York: Silver Burdett & Co., 1901.

Nichols, M. L. *Ranald MacDonald Adventurer.* Caldwell, Idaho: The Caxton Printers, 1940.

Niven, F., and Phelps, W. J. *Colour in the Canadian Rockies.* Toronto: Nelson, 1962.

Bibliography

Nixon, O. W. *How Marcus Whitman saved Oregon.* Chicago: Star Publishing Co., 1895.

Nute, Grace Lee. "Botanist at Fort Colvile." *The Beaver,* September 1946.

———. *The Voyageur.* St. Paul, Minn.: Minnesota Historical Society, 1955.

———. *The Voyageur's Highway.* St. Paul, Minn.: Minnesota Historical Society, 1965.

Oliphant, J. O. "Angus MacDonald; A Few Items out of the Old West." *Washington Historical Quarterly,* vol. 8 (1917).

———. "Old Fort Colvile." *Washington Historical Quarterly,* vol. 16 (1925).

Oliver, E. H., ed. *The Canadian Northwest.* 2 vols. Government Printing Bureau, Ottawa: 1914, 1915.

Ormsby, Margaret. *British Columbia: A History.* Toronto: Macmillan, 1958.

Prebble, John. *Culloden.* Harmondsworth, England: Penguin Books, 1967.

———. *Glencoe.* Harmondsworth, England: Penguin Books, 1968.

———. *The Highland Clearances.* Harmondsworth, England: Penguin Books, 1969.

Pritchett, J. P. *The Red River Valley.* Toronto and New Haven: Yale University Press, 1942.

Prosser, W. F. *A History of the Puget Sound Country.* Chicago: 1903.

Reid, R. L. "Early Days at Old Fort Langley." *British Columbia Historical Quarterly,* 1937.

Rich, E. E., ed. *Colin Robertson's Correspondence Book, September 1817 to September 1822.* Toronto: Champlain Society, 1939.

Ross, Alexander. *Adventures of the First Settlers on the Oregon.* Reprint. New York: Citadel Press, 1969.

———. *The Fur Hunters of the Far West.* London: Smith, Elder, 1855.

———. *The Red River Settlement.* Reprint. Minneapolis: Ross & Haines, 1957.

Ross, Eric. *Beyond the River and the Bay.* Toronto: University of Toronto Press, 1970.

Sage, Walter N. "Life at a Fur Trading Post in British Columbia a Century Ago." *Washington Historical Quarterly,* vol. 25 (1934).

———. *Sir James Douglas and British Columbia.* Toronto: 1930.

Selkirk, Thomas Douglas, 5th Earl of. *A letter to the Earl of Liverpool from the Earl of Selkirk, accompanied by a correspondence with the colonial department (in the years 1817, 1818, 1819), on the subject of the Red River settlement in North America.* London, 1819.

―――. *Sketch of the British fur-trade in North America, with observations relative to the North-West Company of Montreal.* London, 1816.

Shipley, Nan. *The James Evans Story.* Toronto: Ryerson Press, 1966.

Simpson, George. *Narrative of a Journey Round the World during the Years 1841 and 1842.* London: Henry Colburn, 1847.

Sinclair, Sir John, ed. *The Statistical Account of Scotland.* 21 vols. vol. 7. Edinburgh, 1791-99.

Spragge, G. W., ed. *John Strachan's Letter Book 1812-1834.* Toronto: Ontario Historical Society, 1946.

Strachan, John. *A Letter to the Right Hon. the Earl of Selkirk, on his settlement at the Red River, near Hudson's Bay.* London, 1816.

Strong, T. N. *Cathlamet on the Columbia.* Portland, Ore.: Binfords & Mort, 1906.

Thomas, C. *History of the Counties of Argenteuil, Que., and Prescott, Ont., from the Earliest Settlement to the Present.* Montreal: 1896.

Tolmie, William Fraser. *Physician and Fur Trader. The Journals of William Fraser Tolmie.* Vancouver, B.C.: Mitchell Press, 1963.

Van Kirk, Sylvia. "Women and the Fur Trade." *The Beaver,* Summer 1971.

Vaughan, Thomas, ed. *Paul Kane, The Columbia Wanderer, 1846-47.* Portland, Oregon: Oregon Historical Society, 1971.

Wallace, W. S., ed. *Part of a Dispatch from George Simpson Esq. to the Governor & Committee of the Hudson's Bay Company London . . . 1829.* General editor, E. E. Rich. Toronto: Champlain Society, 1947.

―――. "The Literature Relating to the Selkirk Controversy." *Canadian Historical Review,* March 1932.

Wilkes, Charles. *Narrative of the United States Exploring Expedition, 1841.* vol. 4. Philadelphia: C. Shuman, 1844.

Williams, Glyndwr, ed. *Andrew Graham's Observations on Hudson Bay 1767-91.* London: Hudson's Bay Record Society, 1969.

Wood, L. A. *The Red River Colony.* Toronto: Brook, 1915.

Notes

Key

PAC   *Public Archives of Canada, Ottawa*
SP   *Selkirk Papers*
HBCA   *Hudson's Bay Company Archives*
BCPA   *British Columbia Provincial Archives*

Chapter 1

A Gentleman of Respectable Character (1811-1814)

Page
5   University of Edinburgh, Dalilia Papers, Selkirk to Dalilia, August 14, 1811.
6   SP, vol. 79, Selkirk to Dalilia, January 9, 1812.
6   McDonald Family Papers.
6   John Prebble, *Glencoe*, p. 211.
8   SP, vol. 1, Selkirk to Dalilia, July 9, 1812.
8   Ibid., August 4, 1812.
9   Ibid.
10   Dalilia Papers, Selkirk to Dalilia, May 8, 1813, and January 6, 1813.
11   *Montreal Herald*, May 25, 1816; McDonald to the Rev. John Strachan (pamphlet reprint, 4 letters, June 1816).

12   Dalilia Papers, McDonald to Dalilia, June 23, 1813.
12   Ibid., Selkirk to Dalilia, May 8, 1813.
13   HBCA, C.1/778, *Prince of Wales* ship's log.
14   SP, vol. 4, McDonald to Selkirk, May 1814, and July 24, 1814.
14   Ibid., p. 3037, Colin Robertson to Selkirk, January 1, 1817.
14   Ibid., vol. 1, p. 183, Miles Macdonell to Selkirk, July 24, 1814.
15   Ibid., William Auld to Andrew Wedderburn Colvile, September 16, 1813.
15 on   The account of the winter of 1813-14 at Churchill Creek is taken from Archibald McDonald's Journal, SP, vol. 68, augmented by the Journal and Correspondence of Dr. Abel Edwards relating to Fort Churchill and Churchill Creek, 1813-14, in the BCPA.

Chapter 2
The Long Walk: They Found It Somewhat Laborious (1814)

22 on   SP, vol. 68, McDonald Journal, 1813-14.
23   BCPA, Journal and Correspondence of Dr. Abel Edwards, William Auld to Edwards, February 7, 1814.
23   Ibid., Copy of Instructions to Mr. McDonald, February 25, 1814.

Chapter 3
He Must Be Driven to Abandon the Project (1814-1815)

34   McDonald Journal, 1813-14.
35   Ibid., vol. 4, McDonald to Selkirk, July 24, 1814.
36   *Montreal Herald*, June 6, 1816, Archibald McDonald to the Rev. John Strachan.
41   SP, vol. 4, McDonald to Selkirk, July 24, 1814.
44   Ibid., vol. 1, Coltman's Report.
44   *Montreal Herald*, May-June 1816, McDonald Letters to the Rev. John Strachan.
44   McDonald Journal, 1814-15.
45   Archibald McDonald, *Narrative respecting the destruction of the Earl of Selkirk's settlement upon Red River, in the Year 1815*, p. 6.
45   *Montreal Herald*, May-June 1816, McDonald to Strachan.
45   McDonald, *Narrative*, p. 10.
46   John Strachan, *A letter to the Right Hon. the Earl of Selkirk, on his settlement at the Red River near Hudson's Bay*.
46   McDonald Journal, 1815.
46   McDonald, *Narrative*, p. 7.
47   McDonald Journal, 1815.
48   Ibid.
48   McDonald, *Narrative*, p. 8.
48   *Montreal Herald*, June 1816, McDonald to Strachan.
48   McDonald Journal, 1815.
49   Ibid.
50   *Montreal Herald*, June 1815, McDonald to Strachan.
50   McDonald Journal, 1815.
51   Ibid.

Notes

52   Ibid.
52   SP, vol. 63, Miles Macdonell Journal, June 16, 1815.
53   McDonald Journal, 1815.
53 on   Ibid.
53 on   HBCA, B.235/a/3, fos.28,28d, Peter Fidler Journal.

Chapter 4

The Outrages Have All Been on One Side (1815-1816)

59   *Montreal Herald,* June 1816, McDonald to Strachan.
59   Earl of Selkirk, *Letter to the Earl of Liverpool,* p. 6.
59   McDonald Journal, 1815.
60   HBCA, E.10/2, Colin Robertson Correspondence and Miscellane-
        ous, Robertson to Selkirk, August 25, 1815.
60   McDonald Journal, 1815.
60   SP., Colin Robertson's Journal, vol. 65, p. 17353.
60   Ibid., vol. 77, Robert Semple to Selkirk, September 11, 1815.
61   Ibid.
61-2   Ibid., vol. 5.
62   Ibid., Papers from St. Mary's Isle, vols. 1-8, Selkirk to Colvile, Oc-
        tober 25, 1815, etc.
63   G. W. Spragge, ed., *The John Strachan Letter Book.*
63   W. S. Wallace, "The Literature Relating to the Selkirk
        Controversy," *Canadian Historical Review* (March 1932), pp. 45-50.
64   Spragge, *The John Strachan Letter Book.*
64   Strachan, *A Letter to the Right Hon. the Earl of Selkirk.*
65   Archibald McDonald, *Reply to the Letter, lately Addressed to the Right
        Honorable the Earl of Selkirk, by the Hon. and Rev. John Strachan, D.D.,* p.
        9.
65   E.E. Rich, ed., *Colin Robertson's Correspondence Book.*
65   McDonald, *Reply,* pp. 44 and 20.
66   Ibid., p. 10.
67   John Gray, *Lord Selkirk of Red River,* p. 135.
68   John Halkett, *Statement respecting the Earl of Selkirk's settlement of Kildo-
        nan, upon the Red River,* deposition of John Bourke, appendix, pp.
        xlix-liv.
69   Ibid., also deposition of Michael Heden, appendix, pp. lv-lx.
70   SP, Coltman's Report, deposition of Dr. John Allan.
70 on   Gray, *Lord Selkirk of Red River,* p. 160 on.
71   Halkett, *Statement respecting the Earl of Selkirk's settlement.*
72   SP, vol. 8, McDonald to Selkirk, September 1, 1816.

Chapter 5

They Cannot Take From Us Our Good Conscience (1817-1819)

76   SP, vol. 3, Lady Selkirk to Colvile, May 19, 1817.
77   Ibid., vol. 2, Samuel Gale to Lady Selkirk, June 3, 1817.
77 on   PAC, Colonial Office Records, M.G.11, Q.150 (1818, Part 2), Ar-
        chibald McDonald deposition, September 23, 1817.

78   SP, vol. 2, Samuel Gale to Lady Selkirk, July 8, 1817.
81   Ibid., June 13, 1817.
81   Ibid., vol. 4, Lady Selkirk to Colvile, September 12, 1817.
81   Ibid., vols. 65 and 66, Colin Robertson's Journals, 1815 and 1817.
82   Ibid., vol. 16, McDonald to Lady Selkirk, August 20, 1818.
82   Rich, *Colin Robertson's Correspondence Book*.
82 on See Gray, *Lord Selkirk of Red River*, Chapters 10, 11, 12, re trials.
83   SP, vol 1., Coltman's Report.
83   Ibid., vol. 16, McDonald to Selkirk, August 31, 1818.
84   *Dumfries & Galloway Courier*, November 10, 1818.
84   British Museum, Liverpool Papers, 38368.f.237b; Samuel Hull Wil-
      cocke, ed., *Report of the Proceedings connected with the disputes between the
      Earl of Selkirk and the North West Company, at the assizes, held in York in
      Upper Canada, October 1818*.
85   SP, vol. 17, McDonald to Selkirk, January 9, 1819.
87   Ibid., vol. 19, McDonald to Selkirk, September 8, 1819; Dalilia Pa-
      pers, Dalilia to Selkirk, March 26, 1819.

Chapter 6
Two Novices in the Fur Trade (1820-1821)

91 on See Chester Martin, ed., *Journal of Occurrences in the Athabasca Depart-
      ment by George Simpson.*
96   HBCA, B.89/b.1 & 2, Île-à-la-Crosse Correspondence Book, 1820-
      21.
97   Rich, *Colin Robertson's Correspondence Book*, Robertson to Irving, June
      1821.
98   Frederick Merk, ed., *Fur Trade and Empire*, p. xxxviii.
98   W. S. Wallace, ed., *Part of a Dispatch from George Simpson Esq. to the
      Governor & Committee of the Hudson's Bay Company, London*.
98   R. Harvey Fleming, ed., *Minutes of Council Northern Department of Ru-
      pert Land*, George Simpson to Colvile, September 8, 1821.

Chapter 7
A Sense of Separation (1821-1825)

100   HBCA, D.4/116, McDonald to Governor and Council Northern
      District, April 6, 1822.
100   Merk, *Fur Trade and Empire*, p. 47.
100   HBCA, D.4/116, J. D. Cameron to Governor and Committee,
      April 3, 1822.
101   Paul Kane, *Wanderings of an Artist*, p. 27.
101   Merk, *Fur Trade and Empire*, p. 96.
101   HBCA, D.4/116, J. L. Lewes to Simpson, April 2, 1822.
102   W. L. Lewis and N. Murakami, *Ranald MacDonald 1824-1894*; Merk,
      Fur Trade and Empire, p. 98.
103   Ibid., p. 170.
104   Unpublished memoir of Benjamin MacDonald.
104   HBCA, D.3/1, Simpson's Journal, 1824-25.

Notes

105   Merk, *Fur Trade and Empire*, p. 65.
105   Ibid., p. 87.
106   Ibid., pp. 51, 137.
107   HBCA, D.4/5,fo.29d., Simpson to John McLoughlin, April 10, 1825. Merk, *Fur Trade and Empire*, p. 145.
107   HBCA, D.4/5,fo.29d, Simpson to John McLoughlin, July 11, 1825.
108   L. R. Masson, ed., *Les Bourgeois de la Compagnie du Nord-Ouest.*
109   BCPA, John McLeod Papers, McLoughlin to McLeod, November 9, 1825.

Chapter 8

Along the Skirts of the Mountains (1826-1828)

113 on   HBCA, D.4/119, McDonald to William Connolly, March 14, 1826.
113 on   Ibid., B.97/a/2, Journal of Occurrences at Thompson's River 1826-27; Wallace, *Part of a Dispatch*, Thompson River District Report 1827, Appendix A (iii), McDonald to Governor and Council Northern Department, April 5, 1827.
115   HBCA, D.4/120, McDonald to Simpson, July 30, 1826.
115   BCPA, John Work Journal, 4A.
116   David Douglas, "Sketch of a journey to the northwestern parts of the continent of North America during the years 1824,5,6 & 7," *Companion to the Botanical Magazine*, ed. W. J. Hooker, vol.2 (August 1836–July 1837), p. 269.
116   David Douglas, "Sketch of a Journey to Northwestern Parts of the Continent of North America during the years 1824, 1825, 1826 and 1827," p. 358.
117   Ibid., pp. 359-60.
118   HBCA, B.97/a/2, Journal of Occurrences at Thompson's River 1826-27.
119   Wallace, *Part of a Dispatch*, Thompson River District Report 1827, McDonald to Governor and Council.
120   HBCA, B.97/a/2.fo.28, Kamloops Correspondence 1826, McDonald to McLoughlin, September 30, 1826.
120   Archibald McDonald, *Peace River, A Canoe Voyage from Hudson's Bay to the Pacific by the late Sir George Simpson*, ed. Malcolm McLeod, p. 35.
120   Wallace, *Part of a Dispatch*, p. 34.
121   HBCA, B.97/a/2, Kamloops Correspondence 1826, McDonald to McLoughlin, September 30, 1826.
121   HBCA, B.97/a/2.fo.29, Journal of Occurrences at Thompson's River 1826-27.
122   A. L. Farley, *Historical Cartography of British Columbia* (BCPA).
122   SP, p. 8432 (299), McDonald to Colvile, April 15, 1826.
122   Wallace, *Part of a Dispatch*, Thompson River District Report 1827, McDonald to Governor and Council.
123   Ibid.
124-7   HBCA, B97/a/2, fos.12,13,13d,14,14d,15, Journal of Occurrences at Thompson's River 1826-27, November 28, 1826, to March 28, 1827.

127   David Douglas, *Journal Kept by David Douglas . . . in North America,*
        1823-27, p. 244.
128   Ibid., p. 246.
129   Ibid., p. 256.
129   Edward Ermatinger, "York Factory Express Journal," *Royal Society*
        of Canada Proceedings and Transactions, vol. 6 (1912).

Chapter 9

Certain Death in Nine Attempts out of Ten (1828)

130   Fleming, Minutes of Council Northern Department, p. 203.
131   Ibid., p. 216.
132   McDonald, *Peace River*, p. 1 on.
132   Wallace, *Part of a Dispatch.*
132   Grace Lee Nute, *The Voyageur*, opposite preface.
133   Merk, *Fur Trade and Empire*, Appendix B, III, p. 348.
134   BCPA, John McLeod Papers.
135   HBCA, B.239/c/1, Simpson to J. G. McTavish, August 4, August
        26, and September 22, 1828.
136   See Eric Morse, *Fur Trade Canoe Routes of Canada Then and Now.*
137   PAC, Ermatinger Family Papers, John Tod to Edward Ermatinger,
        February 14, 1829.
137 on McDonald, *Peace River*, p. 17 on.
141   Wallace, *Part of a Dispatch.*
141   McDonald, *Peace River*, p. 37.
142   Ibid.
143   Fort Langley Journal, October 11, 1828.

Chapter 10

New Harvests in a Mild, Lush Land (1828-1833)

144 on Fort Langley Journal, June 27, 1827, to July 30, 1830.
148   HBCA, D.4/123, McDonald to Governor and Council, February
        25, 1830.
149   Fort Langley Journal, March 21, 1829.
150   Ibid., April 24, 1829.
151   Ibid., July 1829.
151   Ibid., April 19, 1829.
152   Ibid., July 7, 1829.
152   BCPA, A B 40 M142A, Archibald McDonald Papers, McDonald
        to Edward Ermatinger, March 5, 1830.
153   Ibid., March 5, 1830, and February 20, 1831.
153   Fort Langley Journal, August 17, 1829.
154   HBCA, D.4/123, McDonald to Governor and Council, February
        25, 1830.
154   HBCA, D.4/125, fos.62, 62d, McDonald to Governor and Council,
        February 10, 1831.
154   Burt Brown Barker, ed., *Letters of Dr. John McLoughlin written at Fort*
        Vancouver 1829-32, p. 266.

Notes

155 HBCA, D.4/123, McDonald to McLoughlin, September 14, 1829. Fort Langley Journal, September 26, 1829.
155 Ibid., October 23, 1829.
156 Archibald McDonald Papers, McDonald to Edward Ermatinger, March 5, 1830.
156 HBCA, D.4/123, McDonald to McLoughlin, November 14, 1829.
156 Barker, *Letters of Dr. John McLoughlin*, pp. 70-1.
157 HBCA, B.113/b/1, McDonald to James M. Yale, June 21, 1830.
157 Barker, *Letters of Dr. John McLoughlin*, p. 140.
157 Fort Langley Journal, July 30, 1830.
157 HBCA, B.113/b/1, McDonald to McLoughlin, August 18, 1830.
158 Ibid.
158 Ibid., McDonald to Captain Ryan, September 13-14, 1830.
158 Ibid., McDonald to McLoughlin, September 20, 1830; ibid., Extracts from Journal, August 31 to September 16, 1830.
159 Ibid., Extracts from Journal, September 21, 1830, and later note on war party.
160 Fort Langley Journal, January 1, 1830.
160 HBCA, B.113/b/1, Fort Langley Correspondence 1830-31, McDonald to McLoughlin, August 18, 1830.
161 PAC, MG19A23, John McLeod Papers, McDonald to McLeod, February 20, 1831.
161 Barker, *Letters of Dr. John McLoughlin*, pp. 174-6.
161 PAC, John McLeod Papers, McDonald to McLeod, February 20, 1831.
162 Archibald McDonald Papers, McDonald to Edward Ermatinger, February 20, 1831.
162 BCPA, John McLeod Papers, McDonald to McLeod, January 15, 1832.
162 Walter N. Sage, *Sir James Douglas and British Columbia*, p. 68.
163 Archibald McDonald Papers, McDonald to Edward Ermatinger, February 20, 1833.
164 HBCA, D.5/4, McLoughlin to Simpson, March 20, 1833.
164 PAC, MG19A23, John McLeod Papers, McDonald to McLeod, February 20, 1833.
164 Archibald McDonald Papers, McDonald to Edward Ermatinger, February 20, 1833.

Chapter 11

I Do Not Contemplate Remaining Much Longer in This Wilderness (1833-1835)

166 W. Kaye Lamb, ed., *The Letters of John McLoughlin from Fort Vancouver to the Governor and Committee*, First Series, pp. 137-8.
167 Clarence B. Bagley, "Journal of Occurrences at Nisqually House 1833," *Washington Historical Quarterly*, 55, no. 3 (July 1915): 179-88.
167 on W. F. Tolmie, *Physician and Fur Trader*, p. 175 on.
173 BCPA, A B 20 C72M, McDonald Papers, Fort Colvile Narrative.
174 Ibid., Colvile Correspondence, McDonald to Francis Ermatinger, March 1, 1834.

251

Exile in the Wilderness

174   BCPA, Fort Colvile Narrative.
174   Lewis and Murakami, *Ranald MacDonald*, pp. 107-8.
174   Wallace, *Part of a Dispatch*, p. 253.
175   Kew Gardens Library, Hooker Correspondence, David Douglas to Hooker, September 28, 1833.
175   Ibid., McDonald to Hooker, January 20, 1835.
175   *London Morning Herald*, February 26, 1835.
176   A. G. Harvey, *Douglas of the Fir*, p. 233.
176   Hooker Correspondence, McDonald to Hooker, April 15, 1836.
176   HBCA, E.4/1a, fo.115d.
176   Wallace, *Part of a Dispatch*, pp. 257-8.
176   Ibid.
176   Archibald McDonald Papers, McDonald to Edward Ermatinger, April 1, 1836.
177   Church Missionary Society, London, England, Journals of the Rev. David Jones, June 9 and July 14, 1835.
177   Archibald McDonald Papers, McDonald to Edward Ermatinger, April 1, 1836.
178   PAC, MG24 A35, James Douglas Journal.

Chapter 12
A Considerable Sort of Canadian Farmer (1835-1841)

180   George Simpson, *Narrative of a Journey Round the World during the Years 1841 and 1842*, August 1841.
181   PAC, John McLeod Papers, McDonald to McLeod, January 25, 1837.
181   Archibald McDonald Papers, McDonald to Edward Ermatinger, February 2, 1838, and January 25, 1837.
182   McDonald Papers, Correspondence of Archibald McDonald relating to Fort Colvile, McDonald to Governor and Council, April 20, 1838.
182   Archibald McDonald Papers, McDonald to Edward Ermatinger, March 5, 1841.
182   PAC, John McLeod Papers, McDonald to McLeod. January 25, 1837.
182   HBCA, D.5/7, McDonald to Simpson, April 23, 1842.
184   Hooker Correspondence, McDonald to Hooker, April 2, 1843.
184   Yale University Library, Coe Collection, Walker-Whitman Papers, McDonald to the Rev. Elkanah Walker, August 12, 1839.
184   C. M. Drury, ed., *First White Women over the Rockies*, vol. 2.
184   Carl Landerholm, ed., *Notices and Voyages of the Famed Quebec Mission to the Pacific Northwest 1838-1847*, p. 9.
185   Ibid., pp. 33, 17, 45.
185   G. P. de T. Glazebrook, ed., *James Hargrave Correspondence*, John Rowand to Hargrave, December 29, 1840.
185   Hooker Correspondence, McDonald to Hooker, April 2, 1843.
185   Kane, *Wanderings of an Artist*.

Notes

185   Drury, *First White Women*, vol. 2, p. 239.
186   Ibid., pp. 181, 51.
186   Archibald McDonald Papers, McDonald to Edward Ermatinger, March 22, 1844, February 2, 1838, February 1, 1839, March 30, 1842, and April 2, 1840.
186   Hooker Correspondence, McDonald to Hooker, April 2, 1843.
187   HBCA, Reel C75, Hargrave Papers Series 1, McDonald to Hargrave, March 22, 1844.
187   PAC, MG19 A22(2), Ermatinger Family Papers, John Tod to Edward Ermatinger, February 28, 1928.
187   Archibald McDonald Papers, McDonald to Edward Ermatinger, April 2, 1840.
187   Ibid., McDonald to Edward Ermatinger, January 25, 1837.
188   Lamb, *The Letters of John McLoughlin*, Second Series, pp. xi-xii.
188   C. M. Drury, *Elkanah and Mary Walker*, pp. 104-5.
189   Ibid., p. 256.
189   W. J. Hooker, ed. *London Journal of Botany*, vol. 5, 1846, pp. 198-285.
189   Drury, *Elkanah and Mary Walker*, pp. 104-5, 256.
190   Drury, *First White Women*, vol. 1, p. 209.
190   Archibald McDonald Papers, McDonald to Edward Ermatinger, January 25, 1837.
190   Walker-Whitman Papers, Jane McDonald to Mary Walker, January 5, 1840.
190   Spokane, Washington, Public Library, typescript of interview of W. S. Lewis with Christina McDonald McKenzie Williams, May 28, 1921.
191   Walker-Whitman Papers, McDonald to the Rev. Elkanah Walker, August 17, 1840, March 25, 1840.
191   Archibald McDonald Papers, McDonald to Edward Ermatinger, March 30, 1842.
191   State College of Washington, Pullman, Wash., McDonald to the Rev. Elkanah Walker, March 14, 1842.
192   Archibald McDonald Papers, McDonald to Edward Ermatinger, April 1, 1836, and March 10, 1839.
193   Ibid., McDonald to Edward Ermatinger, March 5, 1841, and March 15, 1843.

Chapter 13

Various Characters from All Nations Strolling to the Far West (1841-1844)

194   Archibald McDonald Papers, McDonald to Edward Ermatinger, January 25, 1837, and February 2, 1838.
195   Ibid., February 2, 1838.
195   Ibid., March 15, 1843.
196   Walker-Whitman Papers, McDonald to the Rev. Cushing Eells, January 15, 1841.
196   Ibid., McDonald to the Rev. Elkanah Walker, February 18, 1841.
197   HBCA, D.5/6, McDonald to Simpson, October 21, 1841.

197	Archibald McDonald Papers, McDonald to Edward Ermatinger, March 30, 1842.
197	HBCA, D.5/6, McDonald to Simpson, June 20, 1841.
198 on	Simpson, *Narrative of a Journey Round the World*, vol. 1.
200	Colvile Correspondence, McDonald to James Sinclair, September 10, 1841.
201	Walker-Whitman Papers, McDonald to the Rev. Elkanah Walker, August 25, 1841.
201	HBCA, D.5/6, McDonald to Simpson, September 19, 1841.
201	Walker-Whitman Papers, McDonald to the Rev. Elkanah Walker, February 18, 1842, and October 1841.
201	HBCA, D.5/6, McDonald to Simpson, October 21, 1841.
202	Father Pierre-Jean DeSmet, *Life, Letters and Travels*, vol. 2.
202	Walker-Whitman Papers, McDonald to the Rev. Elkanah Walker, November 9, 1841.
202	Archibald McDonald Papers, McDonald to Edward Ermatinger, March 15, 1843.
203	HBCA, D.5/7, McDonald to Simpson, April 23, 1842.
203	Colvile Correspondence, McDonald to McLoughlin, June 16, 1842.
203	HBCA, D.5/6, John Rowand to Simpson, June 12, 1841.
203	Ibid., Peter Skene Ogden to Simpson, August 6, 1841.
203-4	Colvile Correspondence, McDonald to McLoughlin, June 30, 1842.
204	Ibid., McDonald to McLoughlin, August 8, 1842.
204	Colvile Correspondence, August to September 1842.
204	Glazebrook, *James Hargrave Correspondence*, Harriott to Hargrave, December 2, 1842.
205	Archibald McDonald Papers, McDonald to Edward Ermatinger, February 1, 1839.
205	Colvile Correspondence, McDonald to James Douglas, October 27, 1838.
205	See *The Beaver* (September 1942), pp. 19-21.
205-6	Landerholm, *Notices and Voyages*, p. 8.
206	Lamb, *The Letters of John McLoughlin*, Second Series, p. 57.
206	Colvile Correspondence, McDonald to Archibald McKinley, June 8, 1842.
206	Hooker Correspondence, McDonald to Hooker, April 2, 1843.
206	Walker-Whitman Papers, McDonald to the Rev. Elkanah Walker, February 1843.
206-7	Oregon Historical Society, E. E. Dye Papers, Ranald MacDonald to E. E. Dye, September 17, 1892.
207	Lamb, *The Letters of John McLoughlin*, Second Series, Introduction.
207	BCPA, A B 40 Er.62.3, Ermatinger Papers, McLoughlin to Edward Ermatinger, March 4, 1845.
208	HBCA, D.5/8, McDonald to Simpson, April 27, 1843.
209	BCPA, Ermatinger Papers, McLoughlin to Edward Ermatinger, February 1, 1843.
209	Hooker Correspondence, McDonald to Hooker, October 20, 1843.
210	Ibid., October 20, 1843, and April 2, 1843.

Notes

210-11   British Museum of Natural History, Register of Accessions, 1843, 1844, and 1845.
211   Colvile Correspondence, McDonald to James Douglas, January 11, 1841.
211   HBCA, D.5/11, McDonald to Governor and Council, April 20, 1844.
211   George Bryce, *Sir George Simpson*, pp. 287, 289.
211   HBCA, D.5/9, McDonald to Simpson, November 5, 1843.
212   Ibid., McDonald to Simpson, April 20, 1844.
212   Ibid., McDonald to Governor and Council, April 20, 1844.
212   Archibald McDonald Papers, McDonald to Edward Ermatinger, March 22, 1844.
212   HBCA, D.5/7, McDonald to Simpson, April 23, 1842.
212   Glazebrook, *James Hargrave Correspondence*, McDonald to Hargrave, March 21, 1843.
213   Colvile Correspondence, Pelly, Pelly & Simpson to McDonald, March 3, 1841.
213   Glazebrook, *James Hargrave Correspondence*, Finlayson to Hargrave, June 19, 1843.
213   Colvile Correspondence, McDonald to Pelly, April 1, 1844.
214   Archibald McDonald Papers, McDonald to Edward Ermatinger, February 2, 1838.
214   Hooker, *London Journal of Botany*, 1845-46.
214   Hooker Correspondence, McDonald to Hooker, April 20, 1844.
214-15   Drury, *First White Women*, vol. 2.
215   Walker-Whitman Papers, McDonald to the Rev. Elkanah Walker, February 1843.

Chapter 14
His Life Was One of Much Usefulness (1844-1853)

218   HBCA, A.11/70, London Inward from Fort Vancouver, McDonald to James Douglas, September 29, 1844.
218   Ibid., Report of Heathfield and Burgess, Experimental Chemists, Princess Square, April 27, 1846.
218   Ibid., McDonald to Douglas, September 29, 1844.
218   Walker-Whitman Papers, McDonald to the Rev. Elkanah Walker, October 11, 1844.
219   HBCA, D.5/7, McDonald to Simpson, January 18, 1842.
219   Merk, *Fur Trade and Empire*, p. 33.
219   Kane, *Wanderings of an Artist*, p. 240.
220   BCPA, A E R73 R78, Donald Ross Papers, John Rowand to Ross, December 21, 1844.
220   HBCA, Reel C75, Hargrave Papers, John Rowand to Hargrave, December 26, 1844.
221   HBCA, D.5/14, McDonald to Simpson, May 12, 1845.
221   Ibid., McDonald to Simpson, August 2, 1845.
222   Donald Ross Papers, McDonald to Ross, May 1, 1846.

Exile in the Wilderness

222   Archibald Mcdonald Papers, McDonald to Edward Ermatinger,
       March 30, 1842.
223   T. C. Elliott, "Peter Skene Ogden, Fur Trader," *Oregon Historical
       Quarterly*, vol. 11 (1910).
223   Donald Ross Papers, McDonald to Ross, May 1, 1846.
223   Bancroft Library, Berkeley, California, Frank Ermatinger Corre-
       spondence, Reel P-W4, Frank Ermatinger to Edward Ermatinger,
       March 26, 1846.
224   PAC, R.G.4, B.28, vol.134, bonds nos. 360,1217.
225   Archibald McDonald Papers, McDonald to Alex C. Anderson,
       April 12, 1849.
225   HBCA, Reel C76, Hargrave Papers, George Barnston to Hargrave,
       April 7, 1848, April 12, 1848.
225   Carillon Museum, Diary of Julia Antrobus.
226   Lewis and Murakami, *Ranald MacDonald*, p. 83.
226   Public Record Office, England, Last will and testament of Archi-
       bald McDonald, May 19, 1852. Probate, October 29, 1853.
226-7 Montreal *Gazette*, January 21, 1853.

Postscript
228-32 Sources of most of the information in the Postcript are in the pri-
       vate family papers of the McDonald descendants. See also W. S.
       Lewis, "Archibald McDonald: Biography and Genealogy,"
       Washington Historical Quarterly, vol. 9 (April 1918).
228   W. L. Morton, ed., *Alexander Begg's Red River Journal*, p. 286.
228   E. G. May, *A Hundred Years of St. Andrews, P.Q.*
229   Lewis and Murakami, *Ranald MacDonald*.
230   McGill University Archives, Minutes of the Board of Governors,
       June 26, 1855.
230-1 C. Thomas, *History of the Counties of Argenteuil, Que., and Prescott, Ont.,
       from the Earliest Settlement to the Present*, pp. 48, 495-6.

Index

Abbott, J. J. C., 229
Agriculture: at Red River Settlement, 38-43, 50-3, 66; Simpson advocates, 98, 147; at Fort Vancouver, 105-6, 182; fur-trade gardens, 95, 136, 153, 160-3; at Fort Langley, 144-5, 147, 151-3, 156, 160-3; at Fort Nisqually, 171-2; at Fort Colvile, 98, 179-83, 188, 190, 199; McDonald farm, 224-6, 228; Puget's Sound Agricultural Company, 167, 183, 188, 210
Alan Dhu (great-grandfather of Archibald McDonald), 6
Albion, 190
Allan, Dr. John, 70
American Board of Commissioners for Foreign Missions, 183, 185, 189
American fur traders: Treaty of Joint Occupancy, 98, 165, 224; competition to H.B.C. on Pacific coast, 104-5, 146, 151-2, 156-7, 162, 164; competition in Flathead district, 165-6, 173-4
Anderson, A. C., 209
Annance, Francis Noel, 115-16, 118, 126-7, 147, 149, 151-2, 156, 158
Argyllshire, 6, 175
Assiniboia, 36, 45, 58, 87, 101; Selkirk's grant of, 5; Council of, 39, 42
Assiniboine River, 33, 35, 64
Astor, John Jacob, 101
Astoria, *see* Fort George
Athabasca District, 105; McDonald and Simpson to, xiii, 93; contest in, 59-60, 67, 95-7
Athabasca Pass, 100, 108, 129, 134, 174, 179, 218
Athabasca River, 108, 134, 220
Auld, William, 21, 23; opposition to Red River Settlement, 10, 14-21, 23, 30-1, 35

Ball, John, 163-4
Banks, Peter, 205-6
Bannerman, Christian, 19
Bannerman, George, 26
Bannerman, John, I, 19
Bannerman, John, II, 62
Bannerman, William, I, 46
Bannerman, William, II, 62
Barnston, George, 223, 230
Barnston, Dr. James, 230
Barnston, MaryAnne (née McDonald), 174, 176, 217, 221, 223-5, 230-1
Bathurst, Henry, 3rd Earl of (Colonial Secretary), 12, 59, 75
Beaver: trade in, 121, 124, 172, 174; disappearance of, 119, 181-3, 211-12
Bellevue Point, *see* Fort Vancouver
Bernard, Jean Baptiste, 137, 140
Bernard's River, 137
Big Head, Kettle Falls Chief, 185, 191
Bitter Root Valley, 202
Black, Samuel, murder of, 196-7, 202-3
Blackwood's Magazine, 190
Blanchet, Father Francis M., 182, 184-5, 205-6
Blue Mountains, 183
Bluebell Mine, 218n
Boat Encampment, 108, 129, 134, 174, 180, 198, 200, 205, 218-19
Borrox's Falls, 32
Boucher, François, 68
Boundary Creek, Washington, 229
Boundary question, 165, 207, 215, 223-4; U.S. claims, 98, 105, 166, 183-4; Wilkes expedition, 197; 1846 agreement, 224
Bourke, John, 50, 68
Bow River traverse, 198, 200

Brandon House, 36, 46, 68, 85-6
Brasse's Falls, 32
British Columbia, first map of interior, 121
British government: grant of exclusive
  trading rights to Hudson's Bay
  Company, 98; agreement with Russians,
  165; lack of interest in Oregon territory,
  166, 183-4; boundary negotiations, 215,
  224
British Museum, 122, 210-11
Bruce, John, 47-8
Bryce, George, xviii

Cadarotte, Okanagan Chief, 123-4
California, 225
Callander, 6-7, 63, 81-2
Cameron, Duncan: arrives at Red River,
  44; entertains settlers, 45-6; leads
  opposition to settlement, 47-8, 50-3, 58,
  61, 65, 67; arrested by Colin Robertson,
  66; charges against, 85
Cameron, John Dugald, 100, 222
Campbell, George, 40; leader of rebellious
  settlers, 46, 48-9
Campbell, Robert, of Glenlyon, 6
Canoes: Express, 115, 178; portaging, 22,
  136, 149, 156; 1829 journey from
  Hudson Bay to Pacific, 132-43; on
  Athabasca River, 220
Car-cum-cum, aunt cares for Ranald
  MacDonald, 104
Carillon Bay, 224, 230-1
Carlton House, 221
Cathcart, Charles Murray, 2nd Earl
  (Governor-General of British North
  America 1846-47), 223-4
Cathcart, Lady Henrietta, 224
Chalifoux, André, 205-6
Chambly, 223
Character Book (George Simpson's), 93-4
Charles, John, 20
Charles, Pierre, 172
Chehalis River, 170
Chihalucum, Squamish Chief, 171
Christ Church, St. Andrews East, 226, 228-9
Churchill Creek, 15-16, 18, 20, 23-4, 38
Churchill Factory, see Fort Churchill
Churchill River, 16, 21

Clarke, John: in Athabasca District, 60,
  67, 95-7; named chief factor, 98; in
  Montreal, 223
Clearwater River (Methye Lake), 136
Clearwater River (Columbia District), 183
Coal beds, 169
Cobourg, 222
Cockran, Rev. William, 113, 174, 176-7,
  192
Coeur d'Alènes, 173
Colonial Office, 59, 62, 75, 84, 166
Coltman, William, 73-4, 76-7, 81, 83
Coltman Commission, 73-4, 83
Columbia District, xiv, 156, 172, 179, 187,
  215, 222, 225; McDonald sent to, 98-
  100; lack of profits, 101; Simpson 1824-
  25 visit to, 104-5, 107; McLoughlin
  superintendent, 104, 107; American
  competition in, 98, 146, 151-2, 156-7,
  162, 164, 165-6, 173-4; Russian
  competition, 98, 165; Simpson 1841 visit
  to, 198-200; river tragedies, 205-7;
  settlement in, 183-4, 186-7, 200-1, 215;
  Protestant missionaries in, 176, 182-6,
  188-91, 196, 201, 211, 214-15, 218;
  Roman Catholic missionaries in, 182-4,
  202, 205-6
Columbia Maternal Association, 189-91,
  215
Columbia River, 101, 103-4, 106, 108, 127,
  151, 157, 166, 168, 174, 179-80, 197,
  199-200, 205-6, 214, 217, 232
Colvile, Andrew (Wedderburn), 15, 62-3,
  91-2, 99
Comcomly, Chinook Chief, 101-4, 192
Connolly, William, 115, 118, 139, 231
Cook, W. H., 29-31
Country marriages: definition of, 30n;
  H.B.C. policy toward, 131; attitudes
  toward, 102-4, 109, 148, 153, 176-7, 187
Court Apatte, Lower Shuswap Chief, 123-
  6, 139
Coutamine (Nicola) River, 119-20, 126
Covenanters, 6
Cowlitz portage, 149, 156
Cowlitz River, 168-9, 172
Cowlitz Settlement, 183, 200-1, 215
Cowlitz Valley, 166, 170, 182-3, 200, 215
Culloden, 6
Cumberland House, 95, 97, 221

Index

Dalles des Morts, 180, 205
Demers, Father Modeste, 182, 184, 205-6
de Meurons, 67, 70-2, 76-7, 80
deSmet, Father Pierre Jean, 182, 202
Dickson, Col. Robert, 78-80
Diefenbaker, John G., 26n
Disease: ague, 220; Columbia "leprosy," 201; consumption, 19; coughs and colds, 19; intermittent fever, 157, 159, 161-2, 168-9; typhus fever, 13-14, 15-16, 19; scarlet fever, 221; scurvy, 16, 19, 21; snow blindness, 23, 26-8; treatment of, 16, 18, 19, 23-5, 27
d'Orsonnens, Capt. P., 70-1, 74
Douglas, David, 129; friendship with McDonald, xiv, 122, 127-8, 163, 167, 174; at horse fair, 116-17; death of, 175-6
Douglas, Dunbar James (Lord Daer, son of Lord Selkirk), 10, 75, 161
Douglas, Lady Isabella (daughter of Lord Selkirk), 10, 161-2
Douglas, James, 116, 139, 162-3, 178, 204-5, 211, 218, 231
Douglas, Lady Katherine (daughter of Lord Selkirk), 75
Douglas, Lady Katherine (sister of Lord Selkirk), 63
Dram Stone, 32
Drummond, Sir Gordon, 62
Dumfries & Galloway Courier, 84
Dunvegan, 137

Eastward Tent, 25-6
Echimamish Basin, 33
Edmonton House, *see* Fort Edmonton
Education: at Red River Settlement, 47, 163-4, 176; at Fort Vancouver, 164, 174; on H.B.C. posts, 131; of McDonald family, 153, 160, 163-4, 173-4, 176-7, 187, 189-90, 192-3, 223-4; of John McLoughlin junior, 208
Edwards, Dr. Abel, 15-21, 23-4
Eells, Rev. Cushing, 183, 186, 189, 196, 214
Eells, Myra, 186, 190, 196, 214
Elgin, James Bruce, 8th Earl (Governor-General of Canada 1847-54), 225
Ermatinger, Charles, 72-3, 107
Ermatinger, Edward: correspondence with

McDonald, xiv, 94, 137, 156, 161-2, 177-8, 181, 187, 191, 193-5, 202, 214; sent to Columbia, 107,109; at horse fair, 115; and music, 116; in charge of Express, 127-9; McDonald boys apprenticed to, 192-3, 231; at St.Thomas, 192-3, 222, 231; member of legislature, 195, 223
Ermatinger, Francis: sent to Columbia, 107; at Kamloops, 115, 127, 139; and Flathead trade, 173-4; friendship with McDonald, 94, 187, 194, 223; named chief trader, 202
Ermatinger, Lawrence, 107

Farley, A. L., 122
Fauché, Lieut. G. A., 72-3
Ferris, Charlotte, 204, 217
Festive occasions, 33, 47, 124-7, 130, 147, 160, 194-6, 198, 214-15
Fidler, Peter, 39-43, 46, 54, 60
Finlayson, Duncan, 161, 163, 174-5, 178, 213, 223
Flathead District, 165, 173, 179, 182
Flathead primer, 215
Fletcher, John: appointed to Coltman Commission, 73; strange behavior of, 74, 76-81
Flett, Charles, 31
Flett, David, 206-7
Food: of settlers, 16-17, 21, 24-6, 28, 31, 33, 36-7, 43, 45; of fur traders, 123, 126-7, 132, 134, 147, 151-2, 198, 215; grouse, 17, 21, 24-6, 28, 132; maple sugar, 33, 226; pemmican, 36n, 37, 43, 51, 137-8, 220
Fort Alexander, 221-2
Fort Alexandria, 106, 115, 139
Fort Chipewyan, 136
Fort Churchill, 13-16, 19-20, 22, 222
Fort Colvile: descriptions of, 179-82, 188-9, 198-9; Simpson selects site of, 107; McDonald sent to, 173; gateway to Columbia District, 179; supplies Russian posts, 188; missionaries at, 176, 182-6, 188-91, 196, 201-2, 205-6, 211, 214-15, 218; Simpson's 1841 visit to, 196, 198-200; Wilkes party at, 197. *See also all of Chapters 12 and 13.*
Fort Daer, *see* Pembina

Fort des Prairies, *see* Fort Edmonton

Fort Douglas, 50-2, 66-70, 74, 85

Fort Edmonton, 67, 129-30, 134, 178, 198, 220-1

Fort Frances, 222

Fort George, xiv, 100-1, 104-5, 108

Fort Gibraltar, 38-9, 44, 46-7, 49-51, 66-7

Fort Île à la Crosse, 93, 95-6, 134

Fort Kamloops, 134, 145, 161; McDonald in charge at, xiv, 101, 106-7, 109, 113-29; Indians at, 114-15, 118-19, 121-7, 129, 139; murder of Samuel Black at, 196-7

Fort Langley, xiv, 106, 134-5, 144-64, 181; James McMillan founds, 142; McDonald and Simpson arrive at, 142; description of, 144-6; fishery at, 147, 153-8, 161-2; lumbering at, 154-6, 161, 215; gardens at, 145, 147, 151-3, 158, 160-2

Fort McLeod, 136-7

Fort McLoughlin, 168, 172

Fort Nisqually, xiv, 168, 173, 181, 210; establishment of, 164, 166-7; McDonald and Tolmie at, 170-2

Fort Okanagan, 107, 113, 115, 118, 121, 127-9, 182, 204

Fort Qu'Appelle, 67

Fort St. James, 106, 134, 138-9

Fort Simpson, 207

Fort Spokane, 101, 107, 115, 200

Fort Stikine, 208

Fort Superior, 97

Fort Vancouver, 134, 145, 149, 157, 164, 169-70, 197, 200-1, 204-5, 207-8, 218; site chosen at Bellevue Point, 105; first farm in Columbia District, 106, 182; christened by Simpson, 107; Ermatingers arrive at, 107-8; McDonald at, 109, 116, 156, 163, 167-8, 172, 179, 194, 214; furs sent to, 114-15, 127, 144, 148; school at, 164, 174

Fort Walla Walla, 101, 115-16, 127, 151, 173, 182-3, 196-7, 200, 206

Fort Wedderburn, 93, 96

Fort William, 79-80, 222; Selkirk seizes, 70-4

Forty-Nine, The (first steamer on Columbia River), 232

Fraser, Colin, 134, 142

Fraser, Simon, 98, 140

Fraser River, 106, 114, 119, 121-2, 129, 134, 139-40, 143-5

Fraser's Lake, 203

Frog Plain (Métis camp), 50, 53, 67

Gaelic, 6, 11, 19, 45

Gairdner, Dr. Meredith, 167-8

Gale, Samuel: and Fletcher incident, 76-81; J. B. Robinson writes to, 85; advises McDonald on investments, 212

Gate Dalles, 141

Geyer, Charles (Karl), 214

Gladman, George, 222

Glasgow, 175

Glencoe, 1, 6, 8, 63

Glencoe Cottage (St. Andrews East), 225-6, 228

Gold: in California, 225; in Australia, 229; in Cariboo, 229, 232

Goudie (Colvile carpenter), 196

Grafton, 222

Grant, Cuthbert: captain of Métis, 45; son of North West Company partner, 49; rallies Métis at Qu'Appelle, 67, 71; at Seven Oaks, 68-9; Warden of the Plains, 130-1

Graves (captain of *Eagle*), 163

Gray, Dr. J. E. (of British Museum), 210-11

Gulf of Georgia, 144, 156

Gunn, Alexander (Sandy), 24, 32, 39, 49, 66

Gunn, Mary, 25-6

Gunn, Robert, 24-5, 27, 46

Gunn, Widow, 62

Gunn, William, 65-6

Gwillimbury Township, 53

Haldane, John, 100

Halkett, John, 63, 122, 161-2

Hamlyn, Dr. Richard, 133, 139

Hargrave, James, 213

Harrison, Benjamin, 175

Hawaii, 176

Hayes River, 21, 23, 29, 31-2, 132

Heron, Francis, 95, 172-3

Highland clearances, 5, 7, 10-11

Hill River, 32

Index

Historical Cartography of British Columbia, 122

Hood's Canal, 171, 211

Hooker, William Jackson, 174-6, 185, 206, 209

Hopkins, Edward, 198

Horses, care of, 114; trading, 85-7, 115-18; as transport, 108, 129, 139, 169-70, 172, 178, 198, 200, 219-20; pack trains, 114-15, 118, 127; as food, 127; Pierre Pambrun falls from, 197

Hudson Bay, 1, 10, 22, 28, 31, 64, 120, 129

Hudson Strait, 13, 62

Hudson's Bay Company, 11, 53, 76-7, 179, 193; agreement with Lord Selkirk, 5; charter not acknowledged by North West Company, 35; conflict with North West Company, 35-6, 44, 59, 62, 65, 75, 91-3, 96-7; merger with North West Company, xiii, 91-2, 97-8, 130; Northern Council, 129-30, 149, 174, 176, 182, 202, 221; Northern Department, 97, 101, 122, 127, 131; standing rules and regulations, 131; headquarters in London, 62, 175, 210; London committee, 81, 105, 175, 179, 207, 212; and American competition in Columbia District, 105, 165-6, 173-4; and Russian fur traders, 98, 105, 165, 188; and Columbia Express, 107, 113, 115, 127-9, 134, 156, 174, 178-9, 218; Outfits of, 131, 157, 204; Servants of, 7, 30-3, 30n, 132, 182, 203, 205, 221; and religion, 131, 160; and settlement, 183 (*see also* Red River Settlement); and Puget's Sound Agricultural Company, 167, 183, 188, 210; mills of, 155, 157, 171, 215

  ships of: *Beaver* (first steamer on Pacific coast), 194, 207; *Cadboro*, 151-2; *Eagle*, 157, 163; *Eddystone*, 8; *Ganymede*, 167; *Isabella*, 157; *King George*, 8; *Lama*, 163; *Man of War*, 61; *Prince George*, 174; *Prince of Wales*, 12-14, 60, 82, 107; *Robert Taylor*, 8; *Staffa*, 8; *Vancouver*, 157-8, 168, 171-2; *William and Anne*, 151-2

  officers of, 17, 20, 33, 166, 177, 183, 196; description of, xiv, 30n; opposition to Red River Settlement, 10, 15, 35, 42; and country wives, 30, 30n, 187; and merger with North West Company, 92, 97, 130; and Northern Council, 130, 174; unrest in Columbia, 165; food of,

132-4; pay of, 177, 212; investments, 166-7, 212-13; interest in natural science, xiv, 209-10; habit of command, 214; clerks, 30n, 182, 196, 203

  and Indians: at Red River Settlement, 54-7, 66, 68-9; on Columbia River, 101-4; at Fort Kamloops, 124-6; relations with George Simpson, 135, 138, 199-200; at Nisqually, 169-71

Indian tribes and bands: Assiniboines, 86, 220; Blackfoot, 220; Blood, 220; Cayuse, 123, 201; Chamniemuchs, 117; Chawhapton, 117; Chinooks, 101-4, 123, 192; Chipewyan, 136; Clallam, 145-6, 211; Coutamine, 124, 126; Cowichan, 146, 150, 154, 159; Cree, 101, 220; Flathead, 123, 182, 202; Kettle Falls, 180, 185, 191, 199-200; Kootenay, 123; Kwantlen, 146, 149-50, 154, 159; Mandan, 85, 101; Nanaimo, 154, 159; Nez Percés, 115-18, 123, 151, 183, 201; Okanagan, 114, 118-19, 121, 123-6, 139, 145; Piegan, 220; Quiarlpi (*see* Kettle Falls); Saanich (Sandish), 150; Sarcee, 220; Saulteau, 45, 54-7, 69, 85, 101; Scadchads, 150; Schimilicameach, 126; Shuswap, 114, 118-19, 121, 123-6, 139, 145, 196-7; Sioux, 85; Spokane, 185; Squamish (Soquamus), 171; Stone, 85-6; Yukulta (Kwakiutl), 145-7, 149-50, 156, 159

Indians, 33, 72, 122-3, 125, 129, 139, 140-2, 170; and alcohol, 136; dress of, 101, 123; feasting, 124-6; and fever epidemic, 157, 159, 161-2, 168-9; friendly, 45, 54-7, 66, 69, 101-4, 136, 171, 184-6, 217-18; and gambling, 101, 123, 185; guides, 21, 24, 28, 118-19; hunters, 21, 28-9, 37, 95, 123; love of ceremony, 54-7, 102-3, 115-17, 135, 138, 184-5, 199-200, 202; salmon tribes, 122-3; and slaves, 103, 123, 146; and tobacco, 123-6, 135, 202; warlike, 144-7, 149-51, 159, 196-7, 201; attitude to children, 190

Inverrigan, 1, 6

Jack River Post, 33-4, 37, 54, 59-60, 66, 133

Jasper House, 108, 129, 134, 173-4, 178, 218, 220

Jones, Rev. David, 177

Kaministikwia River, 70
Kanaka boatmen (Sandwich Islanders),
    168-70
Kane, Paul, 185, 219. *See also illustrations.*
Kennedy, Alexander, 104, 107
Kennedy, Dr. John, 161
Kettle Falls, 106-7, 172, 180-1, 187
Keveny, Owen, 8, 10
Kew Gardens, xiv, 175, 209
Kippling, Pisk, 85
Kirkcudbright, 10
Klyne, Adam, 228
Klyne, George, 228
Klyne, Jane, *see* McDonald, Jane
Klyne, Joseph, 200
Klyne, Michel: father of Jane McDonald,
    108; postmaster at Jasper House, 109,
    128-9; Jane at Jasper House, 164, 173-4;
    retires to Red River Settlement, 176
Kootenay District, 198
Kootenay Lake, 217, 232
Kootenay Post, 173, 179

Lac la Loche (Methye Lake), 96, 136
Lachine, 76, 223
Lagimonière, Jean Baptiste, 47
LaGrave, 86
Lake Athabasca, 93
Lake of Two Mountains, 225
Lake Ontario, 222
Lake Roosevelt, 181n
Lake Superior, 70
Lake Winnipeg, 31, 33, 37, 54, 221
Lamb, W. Kaye, xiii
Lamont, Samuel, 22, 31
Lapwai Mission, 183, 201
Laserre, Dr. Peter, 12-13
La Souris, 36
Leacantuim, 6
Leblanc, Pierre, 205-6
Lesser Slave Lake, 108
Lewes, John Lee, 100-1
Lewis, W. L., 229
Linklater, William, 15-16
London, 53, 81, 175
London, 222
London Journal of Botany, 175

Lumber trade: at Fort Langley, 154-6,
    161, 215; in Norway, 213-14
Lytton, B.C., 121, 139-40

McBean, John, 223
McBeath, Andrew, 25, 46, 49, 65
McBeath, Charles, 25, 27-8
MacDonald, Alexander (son of Archibald
    and Jane), 176, 190, 223-4, 226, 229
McDonald, Alexander, of Dalilia, 1, 6-10,
    12, 63, 87
MacDonald, Allan (son of Archibald and
    Jane), 162, 164, 176, 223-4, 226, 229-30,
    232
McDonald, Angus (father of Archibald),
    6-7
McDonald, Angus (son of Archibald and
    Jane), 118, 152, 164, 176, 190-1, 201-2,
    211
MacDonald, Angus Michel (son of
    Archibald and Jane), 224, 232
McDonald, Archibald: ancestry, 6; early
    life and education, 6-7, 9-10
    and Lord Selkirk: appointed clerk
    and agent by, 7; meets at Sligo, 8;
    reports to, 41-42, 60, 85-6; hears news of
    Seven Oaks at Sault Ste. Marie, 69-70;
    at Fort William, 70-2; in Montreal, 66;
    charged with "conspiracy to ruin the
    trade of the North West Company," 83-
    4
    and Lady Selkirk: in London, 9-10; in
    Montreal, 72-4, 76, 81; seeks help from,
    82; loyalty to, 96
    and Red River Settlement: recruits
    settlers for, 7, 10, 81; role of, 9; sails from
    Stromness as second in command, 12;
    takes charge on death of Dr. Laserre,
    13; care of settlers at Fort Churchill, 14;
    opposition from William Auld, 14-17,
    19-21, 30; at Churchill Creek, 15-24;
    shares responsibility with Dr. Abel
    Edwards, 19, 23-4; leads walk to York
    Factory, 24-30; first journey to Red
    River Settlement, 31-8; relations with
    Miles Macdonell, 38-9, 41, 53, 61;
    appointed to Council of Assiniboia, 39,
    42; surveys farms with Peter Fidler, 38-
    40; opposition from North West
    Company, 35-8, 44-57, 59-71; returns to
    Britain, 61-3; author of *Narrative
    respecting the destruction of the Earl of*

Index

Selkirk's settlement upon Red River and *Reply to the letter, lately addressed to the Earl of Selkirk, by the Hon. and Rev. John Strachan* . . . , 63; meets Robert Semple at York Factory, 60; brigade harassed by Fletcher en route to Fort William, 76-81; reports to H.B.C. committee in London, 81; returns to settlement in 1818, 82; brings horses from Mandans, 85-7

joins H.B.C., xiii, 87, 91; named chief trader, 129; named chief factor, 202-3

and George Simpson: meets at Norway House, 93; Character Book, 94; to Athabasca District, 93-7; appoints McDonald to Columbia District, 98-9; in the Columbia, 104-7, 142-4, 147, 198-200

in Athabasca District, 93-7

in Columbia District, 98-9; accountant at Fort George, 100-4; at Fort Vancouver, 108-9; at Fort Kamloops, 113-29; at Fort Langley, 142-64; at Fort Nisqually, 166-7, 170-2; at Fort Colvile, 173-4 (*see also Chapters 12 and 13*); 1828 journey from Hudson Bay to the Pacific, 120, 131-43

on furlough, 174-6, 178-216

attends Northern Council, 130-1, 174

wives of: first, Princess Raven (Princess Sunday), daughter of Chief Comcomly, 102-4, 109; second, Jane Klyne, daughter of Michel Klyne, xiv, 108-9, 113, 118, 127-8, 145, 148, 152, 158, 162, 173-4, 176-7, 186-91, 198, 201, 204, 211, 214, 217-21, 223, 225-6; wed, 108-9, 177; education of, 153, 163, 189-90; teaches children, 189

children of: Ranald (only son of Princess Raven), 102, 104, 109, 113, 118, 153, 160, 162-4, 174, 176, 190, 192-3, 206-7, 226, 229-30, 232; Angus, 118, 152, 164, 176, 190-1, 201-2, 211; Archibald junior, 129, 152, 164, 176, 190, 192, 223-4, 226, 229; Alexander, 176, 190, 223-4, 226, 229; Allan, 162, 164, 176, 223-4, 226, 229-30, 232; MaryAnne, 174, 176, 217, 221, 223-5, 230-1; James and Donald (twins), 190-1, 211, 221; John, 190, 211, 230-1; Samuel, 191, 201, 211, 230-1; Joseph, 211, 217, 221; Benjamin, 102, 113n, 220, 224, 228-32; Angus Michel, 224, 232

family life, xvii, xviii, 113, 115, 118, 127, 145, 148, 152-3, 158, 160, 162-4, 173-4, 176-8, 181, 186-7, 189-93, 201, 206, 211, 223-4

develops fishery, agriculture, lumbering at Fort Langley, 147-64

interest in medicine, 9, 12-19, 23-8, 168, 172

interest in natural history, 116-17, 121-2, 127-9, 163, 214, 224; suggests nature preserve, 211; contributes specimens to British Museum, 122, 210; contributes to Kew Gardens, 209; honorary member Royal Horticultural Society, 209; discovers silver on Kootenay Lake, 218; corresponds with William Jackson Hooker, 174-6, 185, 206, 209-10; friendship with William F. Tolmie, 167-72, 209-10

explorations: Thompson River, 119-22; Puget Sound region, 164; Willamette Valley, 167; draws first map of British Columbia interior, 121-2

relations with Indians, 28, 136, 138, 170-1, 186, 191; at Red River Settlement, 45, 54-7, 69, 85-6; with Chinooks, 102-4, 192; at horse fair, 116-18; at Fort Kamloops, 118-19, 121-7; at Fort Langley, 144-7, 149-51, 153-4, 156-61; at Fort Colvile, 180, 184-6, 192, 196-7, 199-200, 212, 217-18

relations with missionaries: at Red River Settlement, 177, 192; at Fort Colvile, 182-6, 188-91, 201-2, 211, 214-15, 218

friendship with Edward Ermatinger, xiv, xv, 91, 107-9, 115-16, 127-9, 156, 161-2, 177-8, 181, 187, 191-5, 202, 214, 222-3, 231

investments, 166-7, 212-14

retirement: reasons for, 211-12; leaves Fort Colvile, 217; at Fort Edmonton, 220-1; visits old friends, 222-3; Oregon boundary question, 223-4; purchases farm at St. Andrews East, 224-6; surveyor of lands, 224; justice of the peace, 224; interest in politics, 195-6, 224-5; will of, 226; death of, 226

MacDonald, Archibald, junior (son of Archibald and Jane), 129, 152, 164, 176, 190, 192, 223-4, 226, 229; schooling, 190,192

MacDonald, Benjamin (son of Archibald

and Jane), 102, 113n, 220, 224, 228-32
McDonald, Donald (twin son of Archibald
    and Jane), 190-1, 211, 221
MacDonald, Elizabeth (née Pyke, wife of
    Benjamin), 231
MacDonald, Emily Elizabeth (née
    Roberts, wife of Samuel), 231
MacDonald, Harriet (née Robertson, wife
    of Allan), 230
McDonald, James (twin son of Archibald
    and Jane), 190-1, 211, 221
McDonald, Jane (née Klyne, second wife
    of Archibald), xiv, 113, 127-8, 145, 148,
    152, 158, 164, 173, 204; wed, 108-9, 177;
    baptised, 176; education of, 153, 160,
    162-3, 189-90; births of children, 118,
    162, 174, 190, 201, 211, 220; teaches
    children, 189-90; travels of, 118, 174,
    178, 191, 214, 217-20, 229; member of
    Columbia Maternal Association, 189-
    90; and American missionaries, 186-91;
    accomplishments, 187, 189-90, 198-9,
    214; deaths of children, 202, 221, 229,
    231-2; life in east, 223, 225-6, 228-9;
    death of, 229
McDonald, Jean (daughter of Dalilia), 82,
    87
McDonald, John (grandfather of
    Archibald), 6
MacDonald, John (son of Archibald and
    Jane), 190, 211, 230-1
McDonald, Joseph (son of Archibald and
    Jane), 211, 217, 221
MacDonald, Kate (née Antrobus, wife of
    Archibald junior), 229
McDonald, Mary (née Rankin, mother of
    Archibald), 6, 63
McDonald, MaryAnne (only daughter of
    Archibald and Jane), 174, 176, 217, 221,
    223-5, 230-1
MacDonald, Ranald (only son of
    Archibald and Princess Raven), 206-7,
    226; describes parents' wedding, 102-3;
    death of mother, 104; goes to
    Comcomly's lodge, 104; returns to
    father, 109, 113, 118; education of, 153,
    160, 162-4, 174, 176-7, 192; at St.
    Thomas, 190-2; runs away, 193; later
    life, 229-30, 232
MacDonald, Samuel (son of Archibald
    and Jane), 191, 201, 211, 230-1

Macdonell, Alexander, 44, 50, 53-4, 64,
    67-8, 72
Macdonell, Duncan, 51
Macdonell, Miles, 29, 38, 40-1, 44, 46-53,
    59, 67, 70; named governor of Red
    River Settlement, 7; background of, 35;
    criticism of, 10, 14, 36, 41-2, 60; seizes
    pemmican, 36-7; and McDonald, 9, 39,
    61
McDougal, Duncan, 102
McGill, Andrew, 64
McGillivray, Joseph, 129, 139
McGillivray, Simon, 7n, 37
McGillivray, William, 37, 62, 64, 70-4, 76,
    79
McGillivray family, 75
McIntyre, John, 52-3
McKay, Angus, 27, 29, 43, 222
McKay, George, 62
McKay, Jean, 26-7, 29, 43, 222
McKay, John, 43, 222
McKay, John Richard, 50
Mackenzie, Alexander (explorer), 98
McKenzie, Alexander (murdered by
    Clallams), 146, 171
McKenzie, Kenneth, 53, 71-2
Mackenzie River, 136
McKinley, Archibald, 200, 206
McKinnon, Donald, 49
McLean, Alexander: granted 10,000 acres
    in Assiniboia, 11; resists North West
    Company, 48-50; wounded, 51;
    buildings burned, 54; taken to Netley
    Creek, 56; meets Colin Robertson, 60;
    dies at Seven Oaks, 69
McLean, Donald, 197
McLeod, Archibald Norman, 44, 69, 71
MacLeod, Hector, 26
McLeod, John, 134, 152, 161-2, 223; at
    Red River Settlement, 66; at Kamloops,
    106, 113-14
MacLeod, Margaret Arnott, xiii
McLeod's Lake, 137
McLoughlin, Dr. John: arrested at Fort
    William, 71; Columbia District
    superintendent, 104, 107, 109, 119, 121,
    127, 149, 151, 161, 163-4, 168, 173, 203;
    farm at Fort Vancouver, 182; sends
    party to avenge murder of McKenzie,

Index

146; and development of Fort Langley,
154-8; fever epidemic at Fort
Vancouver, 157-8; and Oregon Beef and
Tallow Company, 166; and Puget's
Sound Agricultural Company, 167;
favors Roman Catholic missionnaries,
183; remains in west, 187; furlough,
205; and George Simpson, 104, 107,
198, 207-9; death of son John, 208-9
McLoughlin, John, junior, 208-9
McLoughlin, Margaret (née Wadin)
McKay, 208
McMillan, James, 100, 142-5
MacPherson, John, 65
McPherson, John, 197, 202
McTavish, John George, 94, 130, 153, 176,
223, 231
Maniso, 158-9
Manitoba legislature, 228
Map-making, 121-2
Martineau, Pierre, 206-7
Martineau, Mrs. Pierre, 207
Matheson, Alexander, 26, 65
Matheson, Angus (H.B.C. employee), 85
Matheson, Angus (Red River settler), 62
Matheson, John: influences settlers, 40;
acting overseer, 46; schoolmaster, 47;
loyal to settlement, 48 (see Appendix)
Matheson, John, "senior" (see Appendix), 49
Matthey, Capt. Frederick, 70
Methye Lake, see Lac la Loche
Methye portage, 136
Métis: sons of Northwesters, 37; Miles
Macdonell prohibits buffalo hunting,
41; settlement threatens way of life, 45;
attack settlers at Red River, 50, 54, 56,
68-70; camp at Frog Plain, 50, 53, 67;
Colin Robertson influences, 66;
Cuthbert Grant named captain of, 45,
67; jubilation after Seven Oaks
massacre, 69; rewarded by North West
Company, 72; at Qu'Appelle, 67, 71; at
Fort William, 70-1; descendants to
Cowlitz Valley, 183, 200-1, 215
Miles, Robert, 95-6, 174
Millbank Sound, 168, 172
Missionaries: Protestants in Columbia
District, 176, 182-6, 188-91, 196, 201,
211, 214-15, 218; Roman Catholic in
Columbia District, 182-4, 202, 205-6; at

Red River Settlement, 113, 174, 176-7,
192
Missouri, 85, 165, 183
Missouri River, 86
Montreal, 69, 83, 84; McDonald in, 66, 73,
221-5
Montreal *Gazette*, 226-7
Montreal Herald, 65, 190
Montrose, 6
Morton, W. L., xv
Mother's Magazine, 190
Mount Fairweather, 188
Murray, Alexander, 62
Murakami, N., 228

Nass, 161-2
Nass River, 157, 161-2
Nature preserve, 211
Nelson River, 21, 28-9, 33
Netley Creek, 54, 56, 69
New Caledonia District, 98, 106, 114-15,
118, 129, 134, 138-9, 179, 197, 203, 209
Nez Percés Forks, 115-17
Nez Percés River, *see* Snake River
Nicaumchin Creek, 120
Nicola River, *see* Coutamine River
Nicolas, Okanagan Chief, 114, 118-19,
121, 123-4, 139
Nisqually River, 170
North West Company, 109; opposition to
Selkirk settlement, 15, 35, 37-9, 44-62,
64-70; partners imprisoned by Selkirk at
Fort William, 71-3; charges in courts,
81-4; competition with H.B.C. in
Athabasca District, 91-3, 96-7; merger
with H.B.C., xiii, 92, 97
Norway House, 33, 92, 96-7, 100, 129, 133,
174, 178, 221
Nottawasaga River, 74

Ogden, Peter Skene, 161, 203, 223
Oregon Beef and Tallow Company, 166-7
Oregon fever, 184
Oregon territory, xiv; trading rights in, 98;
wagon trains to, 183-4; early settlement
in, 183-4, 186, 200-1, 215; McDonald
attitude to settlement in, 186-7; Wilkes
expedition to, 197; attention in east,
223-4

265

Oregon Treaty, 224
Orkney, 12
Ottawa River, 223, 225
Oxford House, 33
Oxford Lake, 33
Owhyhees, *see* Sandwich Islanders
Owl River, 27

Pacific Ocean, 142, 144
Pambrun, Pierre, 196-7, 202-3
Pas, the, 221
Patriot, 190
Peace River District, 95
Peace River Pass, 134-7
Peguis, Saulteau Chief, 45, 54-7, 69
Pelly, Sir John, 212-14
Pelly, Pelly and Simpson, 212-14
Pembina (Fort Daer), 36, 41, 46-7, 49, 85
Pemmican Proclamation, 36
Pennycuttaway Creek, 31
Pensonnant, Louis, 95
Perry, Matthew, 229
Pigeon River, 37
Playgreen Lake, 37
Point Douglas, 38-9
Point Meurons, 79
Poplar River, 37
Port Stanley, 222
Portland Canal, 165, 188
Powell, Mr. Justice William Dummer, 84
Prince Regent's Proclamation, 78
Princess Raven (first wife of Archibald McDonald), 102-4, 109
Protestant missions, *see* Missionaries
Puget Sound, 145-6, 149-50, 156-7, 164, 166-7, 170-1, 211
Puget Sound Falls, 157
Puget's Sound Agricultural Company, 167, 183, 188, 210
Pyke, Rev. James, 231

Quebec *Gazette*, 190

Rebellion Losses Bill, 225
Red River, 31, 33, 35, 38, 64, 74, 79
Red River Settlement I (to 1820)
    Selkirk colony: grant of Assiniboia to Selkirk, 5; McDonald appointed clerk and agent, 7; Miles Macdonell named governor, 7, 35; first settlers sail from

Sligo, 7; second group sails from Orkney, 12; sickness on board *Prince of Wales*, 13-14; settlers' winter of 1813-14 at Churchill, xiii, 14-24; walk from Churchill to York Factory, xiii, 24-30; at York Factory, 29-31; journey from York Factory to settlement, 31-8; at Jack River Post, 33-5; arrive at Point Douglas, 38; lands allotted, 41; entertained by North West Company, 45; troubles at the settlement, 44-57; births and marriages, 43, 48, 52-3; support of Indians for, 54-7, 69; opposition of H.B.C. officers, 10, 14, 16-21, 23, 30, 31, 35, 36; opposition of North West Company, 35-85 *passim*; "risen from ashes," 66; "paper controversy," 63; attacked by Rev. John Strachan, 63-6; Seven Oaks massacre, 68-70, 72-3, 75, 84, 131; charges in courts, 81-5; Irish settlers, 7-8, 10, 17, 36, 51-2; Scotch settlers, 10-15, 22 on, 36, 43, 47-8, 51, 63; Semple group, 58, 60-2; Council of Assiniboia, 39, 42; government house, 38, 48, 51; military protection for, 12, 60-1, 76
Red River Settlement II (after 1820), 198, 217, 220-2, 228; retired fur traders to, 98, 187; McDonald family at, 174, 176-8; Michel Klyne retires to, 176; Red River Academy, 163-4, 176; settlers move to Cowlitz Valley, 183, 200-1; missionaries at, 113, 174, 176-7, 192; Convention of Forty, 228
Riel, Louis, 228
Roberts, Sir Charles G. D., 231
Robertson, Colin, 14, 67, 81, 87, 92, 97; warns Selkirk of North West Company opposition, 58; takes charge of settlers, 59-60, 66; describes jails in Montreal, 83; attends Northern Council with McDonald, 130-1
Robinson, John Beverley, 85
Rocky Landing portage, 32
Rocky Mountains, 94, 98, 100-1, 114, 129, 134, 177, 179, 183, 189, 212, 218-19
Roman Catholic missions, *see* Missionaries
Ross, Donald, 221-2
Rowand, John, 130, 185, 198, 203, 220-1
Rowand, Dr. John (junior), 199
Royal Horticultural Society, xiv, 116, 128, 167, 175, 209
Royal Humane Society, 231

Index

Rupert's Land, 5, 92, 98, 101
Russian American Company, 188
Russian fur traders, 98, 105, 165, 188
Russian government, 165, 208
Ryan, captain of *Vancouver*, 158, 171

St. Andrews East, 224-6, 228-31
St. John's Anglican Cathedral, Winnipeg, 43
St. Lawrence River, 224
St. Thomas, Ontario, 187, 203, 222, 231
Salmon fishery, xviii, 215; at Fort Kamloops, 115, 121, 123, 126; at Fort Langley, 147-8, 153-8, 161-3
Sam's Creek (Salmis), 28
Sandwich (Windsor), 82
Sandwich Islanders (Owhyhees, Kanaka), 152, 158, 168-70
Saskatchewan District, 203, 220-1
Saskatchewan River, 178, 220-1
Sault Ste. Marie, 70, 72-3, 222
Schultz, Dr. John, 228
Selkirk, Jean (née Wedderburn), Countess of, 10, 15, 72, 73, 75-6, 81-4, 96
Selkirk, Thomas Douglas, 5th Earl of, xiii, xviii, 1, 19, 25, 39, 41, 44, 48, 59, 62, 74-7; appoints McDonald clerk and agent, 7; takes McDonald to London, 7, 9; correspondence with Alexander McDonald of Dalilia, 5-10, 12, 87; on colonization, 5, 10, 39, 63-4; appoints Miles Macdonell governor of Red River Settlement, 7, 35; urges caution in dealing with North West Company, 36; appoints Semple governor of Red River Settlement, 57; hears news of Seven Oaks massacre, 69-70; seizes Fort William, 70-2; attacked by Rev. John Strachan, 63-6; at Red River Settlement, 79; charges in courts, 81-5; death of, 96
Selkirk settlements: Baldoon, Prince Edward Island, 5; Cape Breton, 39; *see also* Red River Settlement I
Semple, Robert, 59-61, 66-7, 84; appointed governor of Red River Settlement, 58; attacked at Seven Oaks, 68-9
Seven Oaks Massacre, 68-70, 72-3, 75, 84, 131
Shaw, William, 49-50

Sherbrooke, Sir John, 73, 75, 80, 83
Shields, Edward, 17
Simpson, Æmelius, 152
Simpson, Lady Frances, 94
Simpson, Sir George: joins H.B.C., 91-2; governor of Northern Department, 97; knighted, 196; Character Book, 93-4; Athabasca campaign, xiii, 92-3, 95-7; and McDonald, 91, 93-101, 103-4, 106-7, 119-21, 129-44, 147, 174, 182, 197-203, 208, 212, 221, 223; death of son, 94; and John McLoughlin, 104, 107, 198, 207-9; and the Columbia District, 98-101, 103-7, 119-21, 131-43, 147, 180, 197-200; 1828 journey from Hudson Bay to the Pacific, 119-21, 131-43, 147, 219; treatment of country wife, 153, 176; investments for H.B.C. officers, 166, 212-14; and Indians, 135, 138, 180, 199-200; 1841 journey around the world, 197-200, 207-8; sons at Fort Edmonton, 220
Simpson's Falls, 142
Sinclair, James, 183, 200-1
Sitka, 208
Sligo, 7, 10
Smith, Donald A., xiv
Smith, Edward, 136
Smith, John, 40
Smith, William, 175
Snake River (Nez Percés River), 115-17, 173-4
Snowshoes, 21-6, 129, 219
Spalding, Eliza, 189, 201
Spalding, Rev. Henry Harmon, 183, 201
Spencer, John, 36, 43-4, 51
Spokane House, *see* Fort Spokane
Stave River, 154
Sterling, Captain, 13
Stewart, Alexander, 161
Stewart, Donald, of Appin, 11, 14
Stewart, Widow (Mrs. Donald), 40
Strachan, Rev. John, 36, 45, 65; attacks Selkirk, 63-6
Stromness, 1, 12
Stuart, James, 76
Stuart Lake, 138-9
Sugar Loaf Mountain, 142
Sutherland, Alex, 48
Sutherland, Betty, 19
Sutherland, Catherine (Kitty), 52-3
Sutherland, Christy, 43

Sutherland, Duchess of, 7
Sutherland, George (age 17), 25, 27-8
Sutherland, George, "senior" (age 18), 48
Sutherland, James, I, 54
Sutherland, James, II, 62
Sutherland, Jannet, 25-8
Sutherland, Mary, 43
Sutherland, William, 43
Sutherlandshire, 10
Swampy Lake, 32

Therien, Pierre, 158
Thew, William, 203-4
Thomas, Thomas, 59-60
Thompson, David, 98
Thompson River, 120-1, 134, 139
Thompson's River District, 114, 119, 122, 179; see also Fort Kamloops
Thompson's River Post, see Fort Kamloops
Tobermory, 7, 8
Tod, John, 137, 174, 187, 197, 205
Tolmie, Dr. William Fraser: arrives in Columbia District, 167; journey with McDonald, 168-9; at Fort Nisqually, 170-2; friend of William Jackson Hooker, 175, 209; in charge of Puget's Sound Agricultural Company, 210
Trade goods, 77-8, 85, 126, 172-3; at Fort Langley, 149-51, 154, 157, 162
Tranquille, Shuswap Chief, 114, 118, 196
Treaty of Joint Occupancy, 98, 165-6, 224
Trois Butes, 173
Tshimakain mission, 183, 185-6, 189-91, 196, 201, 214
Turner, John, captain of Prince of Wales, 13-14
Turtle Mountain, 86

Umphreville, Canote, 206-7
Umphreville, Canote, junior, 206-7
United States government, 186-7, 197; claims in Columbia District, 98, 105, 166, 183-4, 208; boundary negotiations, 215, 223; agreement with Russians, 165
Upper Burnt Wood portage, 32
Upper Shuswap Lake, 124

Vancouver Island, 144, 146, 150, 171, 207
VanKirk, Sylvia, 30n

Voyageurs, life of, 104, 131-42, 149, 152, 219
Voyageurs Corps, 44

Wagon trains, 183-4
Waiilatpu mission, 183, 186, 189, 201, 211
Walker, Cyrus, 186
Walker, Rev. Elkanah, 183-4, 186, 196, 201, 214-15, 218
Walker, Mary, 185-6, 188-91, 196, 214
Wallace, Robert, 205-6
Wallace, W. S., 63
Warren, John, 51-2, 56, 59
Washington (capital), 183
Wedderburn, Andrew, see Andrew Colvile (after 1814)
Wedderburn, Jean, see Selkirk, Jean, Countess of
White, Dr. Elijah, 183, 191
White, Dr. James, 48-9, 54, 60-1, 69
White Mud portage, 32
Whitman, Marcus, 183, 186, 201, 211
Whitman, Narcissa, 189, 201
Whitman massacre, 201
Wilkes, Capt. Charles, 197
Willamette River, 104-5, 167, 194
Willamette Valley, 163, 166-7, 182-4, 207, 209, 215
Williams, William, 87, 91-2, 96-7
Windsor, Ontario, 82, 222
Wishart, Jonathan, 31
Wolseley, Col. Garnet, 230
Women in fur trade, 32-4, 152, 178, 183, 190, 198, 204; hardships, 197, 205-7, 217-18; country wives, xiv, 30, 102-4, 109, 131, 148, 153, 176-7, 187; family life, 114-15, 118, 127, 131, 139, 145, 148, 152-3, 156, 158, 162-4, 173-4, 176-8, 181, 186-93, 197, 214
Work, John, 115-16, 129
Wyeth, Nathaniel, 163

Yale, James Murray, 139, 140, 145n, 147, 149-50, 156-7
York boats, 31-3, 94, 132, 220
York Factory: and Selkirk settlers, xiii, 13-14, 16, 18, 20-1, 23, 27-32, 42, 60-1, 222; and McDonald, 83, 87, 128-9, 132, 135; Express, 107, 178; and Northern Council, 130, 173-4

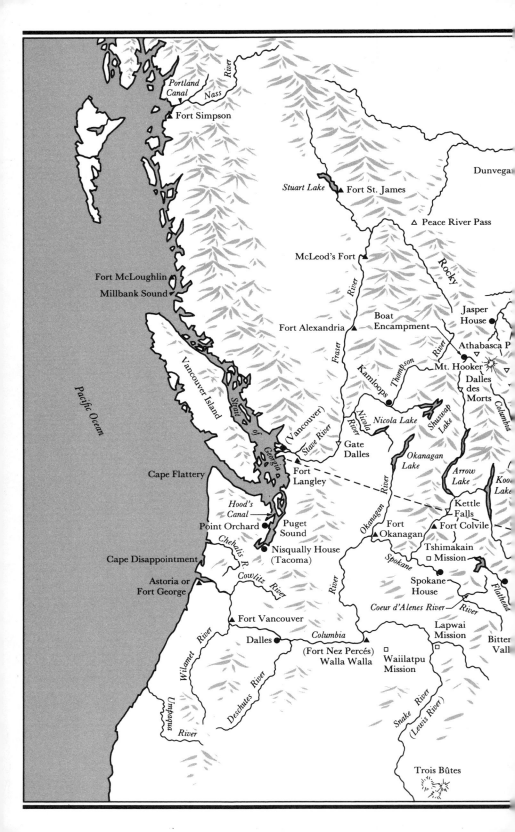